Dream Homes
HOMES FROM 1,278 TO 4,826 SQ. FT.

Home Plans - Dream Homes - This book is a collection of best-selling plans from some of the nation's leading designers and architects. Only quality plans with sound design, functional layout, energy efficiency and affordability have been selected.

These plans cover a wide range of architectural styles in a popular range of sizes. A broad assortment is presented to match a wide variety of lifestyles and budgets. Each design page features floor plans, a front view of the house, and a list of special features. All floor plans show room dimensions, exterior dimensions and the interior square footage of the home.

Technical Specifications - At the time the construction drawings were prepared, every effort was made to ensure that these plans and specifications meet nationally recognized building codes (BOCA, Southern Building Code Congress and others). Because national building codes change or vary from area to area some drawing modifications and/or the assistance of a professional designer or architect may be necessary to comply with your local codes or to accommodate specific building site conditions. We advise you to consult with your local building official for information regarding codes governing your area.

Blueprint Ordering - Fast and Easy - Your ordering is made simple by following the instructions on page 290. See page 289 for more information on which types of blueprint packages are available and how many plan sets to order.

Your Home, Your Way - The blueprints you receive are a master plan for building your new home. They start you on your way to what may well be the most rewarding experience of your life.

House shown on front cover is Plan #529-NDG-322 and is featured on page 169.
Photo courtesy of Nelson Design Group

Lowe's Home Plans Dream Homes is published by Home Design Alternatives, Inc. (HDA, Inc.) 4390 Green Ash Drive, St. Louis, MO 63045. All rights reserved. Reproduction in whole or in part without written permission of the publisher is prohibited. Printed in U.S.A © 2001. Artist drawings and photos shown in this publication may vary slightly from the actual working drawings. Some photos are shown in mirror reverse. Please refer to the floor plan for accurate layout.

CONTENTS

LOWE'S *Signature* SERIES

Home Design Alternatives is proud to bring you this unprecedented offer of our Lowe's Signature Series featuring our most popular residential plans. Never before has there been a compilation of home plans offering such unique services as you will find in this publication.

Home Plans included in the Lowe's Signature Series are indicated by the Lowe's Signature Series logo shown above, and are found on pages 6 through 130.

One of the main reasons for purchasing home plans from a publication such as this is to save you time and money. And, you will discover the extra benefits of the unique services offered through our Lowe's Signature Series of Home Plans.

Besides providing the expected beauty and functional efficiency of all our home plans, the Lowe's Signature Series offers you detailed Material Lists, free Estimated Material Pricing and a free Fax-a-Plan Service. This combination of services are not to be found in any other home plan book or magazine on the market today.

Plan Number   0108
Dry-In Price $28,800
Total Price $47,500

Free Estimated Material Pricing

When selecting the home plan that's right for you, the cost of materials can play a major roll. Staying within your budget is easier when choosing a plan from the Lowe's Signature Series. We provide free estimated material pricing on home plans you've selected. Call us at 1-314-770-2228. This unique service is provided "around-the-clock" to enable us to better serve you.

Fax-a-Plan™ Service

Our free Fax-a-Plan service offers the ideal option for those who have interest in several home designs and want more information to help narrow down the selection. Rear and side views for designs in the Signature Series are available via fax, along with a list of key construction features (i.e. roof slopes, ceiling heights, insulation values, type of roof and wall construction) and more.   Just call our automated FAX-A-PLAN service at 1-314-770-2228 available 24 hours a day - 7 days a week and the cost is FREE.

Material Lists

To enhance the quality of our blueprint packages, we offer one of the most precise and thorough material lists in the industry. An accurate and detailed material list can save you a considerable amount of time and money. Our material lists give you the quantity, dimensions, and descriptions of the major building materials necessary to construct your home. You'll get faster and more accurate bids from your contractors and material suppliers and you'll save money by paying for only the materials you need.

QUICK AND EASY CUSTOMIZING
MAKE CHANGES TO YOUR HOME PLAN IN 4 STEPS

HERE'S AN **AFFORDABLE** AND **EFFICIENT** WAY TO MAKE CHANGES TO YOUR PLAN.

1 **Select the house plan that most closely meets your needs.** Purchase of a reproducible master is necessary in order to make changes to a plan.

2 **Call 1-800-373-2646 to place your order.** Tell the sales representative you're interested in customizing a plan. A $50 refundable consultation fee will be charged. You will then be instructed to complete a customization checklist indicating all the changes you wish to make to your plan. You may attach sketches if necessary. If you proceed with the custom changes the $50 will be credited to the total amount charged.

3 **FAX the completed customization checklist** to our design consultant at 1-866-477-5173 or e-mail **blarochelle@drummonddesigns.com**. Within *24-48 business hours you will be provided with a written cost estimate to modify your plan. Our design consultant will contact you by phone if you wish to discuss any of your changes in greater detail.

4 **Once you approve the estimate,** a 75% retainer fee is collected and customization work gets underway. Preliminary drawings can usually be completed within *5-10 business days. Following approval of the preliminary drawings your design changes are completed within *5-10 business days. Your remaining 25% balance due is collected prior to shipment of your completed drawings. You will be shipped five sets of revised blueprints or a reproductible master, plus a customized materials list if required.

*Terms are subject to change without notice.

BEFORE
Plan 2829

Customized Version of Plan 2829

AFTER

MODIFICATION PRICING GUIDE

CATEGORIES	Average Cost from...	to
Adding or removing living space (square footage)	Quote required	
Adding or removing a garage	$400	$680
Garage: Front entry to side load or vice versa	Starting at $300	
Adding a screened porch	$280	$600
Adding a bonus room in the attic	$450	$780
Changing full basement to crawl space or vice versa	Starting at $220	
Changing full basement to slab or vice versa	Starting at $260	
Changing exterior building material	Starting at $200	
Changing roof lines	$360	$630
Adjusting ceiling height	$280	$500
Adding, moving or removing an exterior opening	$55 per opening	
Adding or removing a fireplace	$90	$200
Modifying a non-bearing wall or room	$55 per rooom	
Changing exterior walls from 2"x4" to 2"x6"	Starting at $200	
Redesigning a bathroom or a kitchen	$120	$280
Reverse plan right reading	Quote required	
Adapting plans for local building code requirements	Quote required	
Engineering stamping only	$450 / any state	
Any other engineering services	Quote required	
Adjust plan for handicapped accessibility	Quote required	
Interactive illustrations (choices of exterior materials)	Quote required	
Metric conversion of home plan	$400	

Note: Any home plan can be customized to accommodate your desired changes. The average prices specified above are provided only as examples for the most commonly requested changes, and are subject to change without notice. Prices for changes will vary according to the number of modifications requested, plan size, style, and metod of design used by the original designer. To obtain a detailed cost estimate, please contact us.

5

Plan #529-0339
Price Code E

Total Living Area: 2,287 Sq. Ft.

Home has 4 bedrooms, 2 1/2 baths, 2-car side entry garage and slab foundation.

Special features

■ Double-doors lead into an impressive master suite which accesses covered porch and features deluxe bath with double closets and step-up tub

■ Kitchen easily serves formal and informal areas of home

■ The spacious foyer opens into formal dining and living rooms

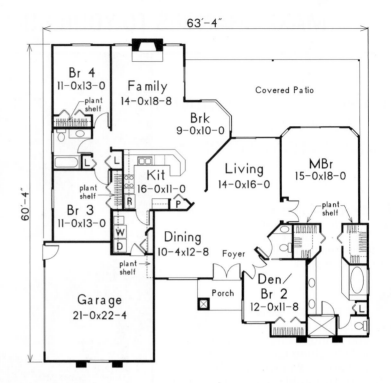

63'-4"

60'-4"

Br 4
11-0x13-0
plant shelf

Family
14-0x18-8

Covered Patio

Brk
9-0x10-0

plant shelf

Kit
16-0x11-0

Living
14-0x16-0

MBr
15-0x18-0

Br 3
11-0x13-0

R

P

plant shelf

W
D

Dining
10-4x12-8

Foyer

plant shelf

Den/
Br 2
12-0x11-8

Garage
21-0x22-4

Porch

Second Floor
1,874 sq. ft.

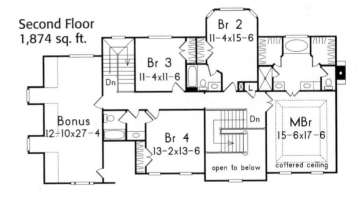

Br 2
11-4x15-6

Br 3
11-4x11-6

Bonus
12-10x27-4

Br 4
13-2x13-6

MBr
15-6x17-6
coffered ceiling

Dn

Dn

open to below

Plan #529-0445
Price Code F

Total Living Area: 3,427 Sq. Ft.

Home has 4 bedrooms, 3 1/2 baths, 2-car side entry garage and basement foundation.

Special features

- 10' ceilings on first floor
- Elaborate master suite features coffered ceiling and luxurious private bath
- Two-story showplace foyer flanked by dining and living rooms

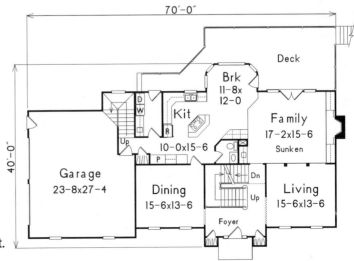

70'-0"

40'-0"

Deck

Brk
11-8x
12-0

Kit
10-0x15-6

Family
17-2x15-6
Sunken

Garage
23-8x27-4

Dining
15-6x13-6

Living
15-6x13-6

Foyer

Up

P

Dn

Up

D W

First Floor
1,553 sq. ft.

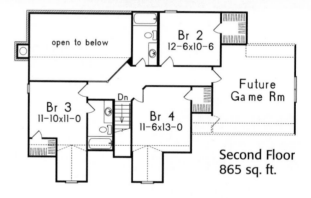

Br 2
12-6x10-6

open to below

Future
Game Rm

Br 3
11-10x11-0

Dn

Br 4
11-6x13-0

Second Floor
865 sq. ft.

Plan #529-0434
Price Code D

Total Living Area:	2,357 Sq. Ft.

Home has 4 bedrooms, 3 1/2 baths, 2-car side entry garage and slab foundation, drawings also include crawl space foundation.

Special features

- 9' ceilings on first floor
- Balcony overlooks living room with large fireplace
- Second floor has three bedrooms and expansive game room

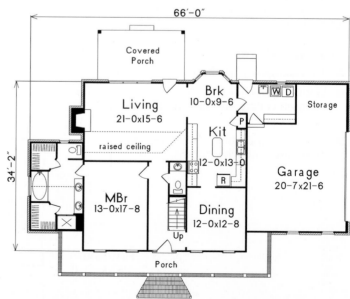

66'-0"

Covered
Porch

Living
21-0x15-6

Brk
10-0x9-6

W D

Storage

raised ceiling

Kit
12-0x13-0

Garage
20-7x21-6

34-2"

MBr
13-0x17-8

R

Dining
12-0x12-8

First Floor
1,492 sq. ft.

Up

Porch

Second Floor
1,544 sq. ft.

Br 5
12-1x14-3

Sunken
Solarium
Below

Br 2
13-11x15-9

Loft

Dn

Br 4
12-1x12-0

Library
15-8x9-8

Br 3
15-5x12-0

open to below

Plan #529-0418
Price Code F
Total Living Area: 3,850 Sq. Ft.

Home has 5 bedrooms, 3 1/2 baths, 3-car garage and basement foundation.

Special features

- Entry, with balcony above, leads into a splendid great room with sunken solarium
- Kitchen layout boasts a half-circle bar and cooktop island with banquet-sized dining nearby
- Solarium features U-shaped stairs with balcony and arched window
- Master suite includes luxurious bath and large study with bay window

80'-8"

Patio

Brk

Kit
3-10x
18-0
vaulted

Hearth Rm
12-1x18-3

Sunken
Solarium

Up   Dn

MBr
16-8x13-0

Dining
12-1x16-0

Great Rm
18-0x21-8

Study
16-8x12-3

Garage
30-4x21-4

51-8"

Entry

First Floor
2,306 sq. ft.

Interior View

LOWE'S

Signature SERIES

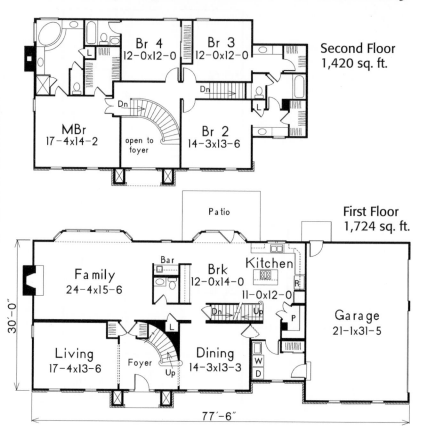

Second Floor
1,420 sq. ft.

Br 4
12-0x12-0

Br 3
12-0x12-0

MBr
17-4x14-2

Dn

open to foyer

Br 2
14-3x13-6

First Floor
1,724 sq. ft.

Patio

Family
24-4x15-6

Bar

Brk
12-0x14-0

Kitchen

Garage
21-1x31-5

Living
17-4x13-6

Foyer

Dining
14-3x13-3

W D

30'-0"

77'-6"

Plan #529-0352

Price Code E

Total Living Area: 3,144 Sq. Ft.

Home has 4 bedrooms, 4 1/2 baths, 3-car side entry garage and basement foundation.

Special features

- 9' ceilings on first floor
- Kitchen offers large pantry, island cooktop and close proximity to laundry and dining room
- Expansive family room includes wet bar, fireplace and attractive bay window

LOWE'S

Signature SERIES

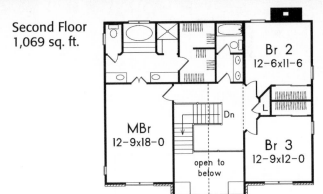

Second Floor
1,069 sq. ft.

Plan #529-0449
Price Code D

Total Living Area: 2,505 Sq. Ft.

Home has 3 bedrooms, 2 1/2 baths, 2-car side entry garage and basement foundation, drawings also include crawl space foundation.

Special features

- The garage features extra storage area and ample work space
- Laundry room accessible from the garage and the outdoors
- Deluxe raised tub and immense walk-in closet grace master bath

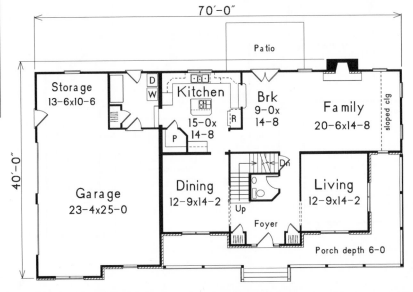

First Floor
1,436 sq. ft.

Signature SERIES

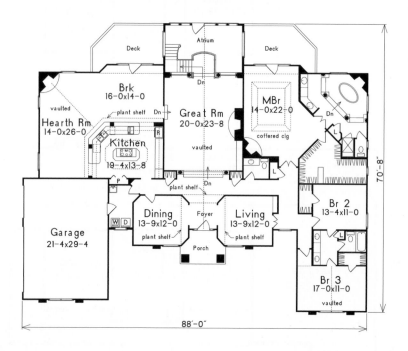

Rear View

Plan #529-0355
Price Code F

Total Living Area: 3,814 Sq. Ft.

Home has 3 bedrooms, 2 1/2 baths, 3-car side entry garage and walk-out basement foundation.

Special features

- Massive sunken great room with vaulted ceiling includes exciting balcony overlook of towering atrium window wall
- Breakfast bar adjoins open "California" kitchen
- Master bath complemented by colonnade and fireplace surrounding sunken tub and deck
- 3,566 square feet on the first floor and 248 square feet on the lower level atrium

Prestige Abounds In A Classic Ranch

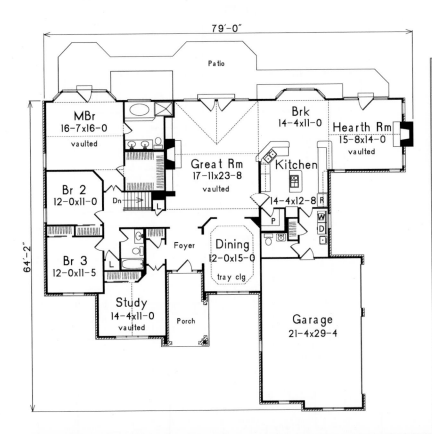

Plan #529-0707
Price Code E
Total Living Area: 2,723 Sq. Ft.

Home has 3 bedrooms, 2 1/2 baths, 3-car side entry garage and basement foundation.

Special features

■ Large porch invites you into an elegant foyer which accesses a vaulted study with private hall and coat closet

■ Great room is second to none, comprised of fireplace, built-in shelves, vaulted ceiling and a 1 1/2 story window wall

■ A spectacular hearth room with vaulted ceiling and masonry fire-place opens to an elaborate kitchen featuring two snack bars, cooking island and walk-in pantry

LOWE'S

Signature SERIES

Second Floor
1,218 sq. ft.

Br 2
13-6x14-9

open to below

L

Br 4
14-9x11-8

Furn Room

storage

Dn

open to below

Br 3
13-2x14-6

L

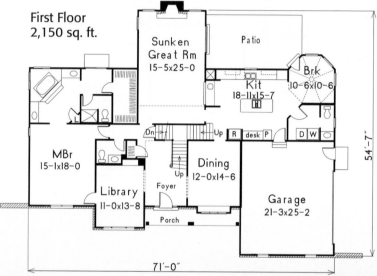

First Floor
2,150 sq. ft.

Sunken Great Rm
15-5x25-0

Patio

Brk
10-6x10-6

Kit
18-11x15-7

MBr
15-1x18-0

Dn

Up

R desk P

D W

Dining
12-0x14-6

Library
11-0x13-8

Foyer

Up

Garage
21-3x25-2

Porch

54'-7"

71'-0"

Plan #529-0159
Price Code F

Total Living Area:	3,368 Sq. Ft.

Home has 4 bedrooms, 3 full baths, 2 half baths, 2-car side entry garage and basement foundation.

Special features

- Sunken great room with cathedral ceiling, wooden beams, skylights and a masonry fireplace

- Octagon-shaped breakfast room has domed ceiling with beams, large windows and door to patio

- Master bedroom in a private wing with deluxe bath and dressing area

- Oversized walk-in closets and storage areas in each bedroom

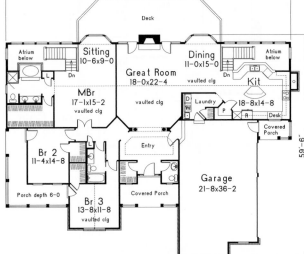

Rear View

Plan #529-0713

Price Code E

Total Living Area: 3,199 Sq. Ft.

Home has 3 bedrooms, 2 1/2 baths, 3-car side entry garage and walk-out basement foundation.

Special features

■ Grand scale kitchen features bay-shaped cabinetry built over atrium that overlooks two-story window wall

■ A second atrium dominates the master suite which boasts a sitting area with bay window and luxurious bath, which has whirlpool tub open to the garden atrium and lower level study

First Floor
2,349 sq. ft.

Lower Level
850 sq. ft.

Lowe's Signature SERIES

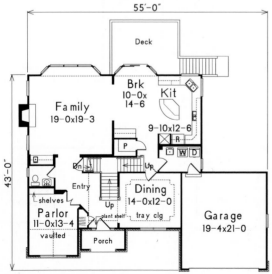

Br 2
11-0x11-4

MBr
17-0x13-9
vaulted

plant shelf

Br 3
11-0x11-0

open to below

Br 4
11-10x12-0

plant shelf

Second Floor
1,203 sq. ft.

55'-0"

Deck

Family
19-0x19-3

Brk
10-0x
14-6

Kit
9-10x12-6

43'-0"

Dn

Up

Entry

Up

Dining
14-0x12-0
tray clg

Garage
19-4x21-0

shelves

Parlor
11-0x13-4
vaulted

plant shelf

Porch

First Floor
1,412 sq. ft.

Plan #529-0708
Price Code E
Total Living Area: 2,615 Sq. Ft.

Home has 4 bedrooms, 2 1/2 baths, 2-car garage and basement foundation.

Special features
- Grand two-story entry features majestic palladian window, double French doors to parlor and access to powder room
- State-of-the-art kitchen has corner sink with two large arch-top windows, island snack bar, menu desk and walk-in pantry
- Master bedroom is vaulted and offers a luxurious step-up tub, palladian window, built-in shelves and columns with plant shelf

Arched Elegance

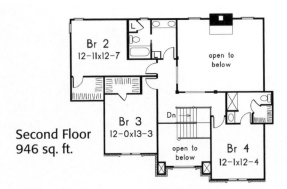

Second Floor
946 sq. ft.

Br 2
12-11x12-7

open to
below

Br 3
12-0x13-3

Dn

open to
below

Br 4
12-1x12-4

87'-8"

46'-10"

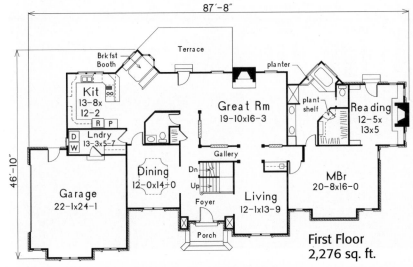

Brk fst
Booth

Terrace

planter

Kit
13-8x
12-2

Great Rm
19-10x16-3

plant
shelf

Reading
12-5x
13x5

Lndry
13-3x5-7

D R P
W

Gallery

Dining
12-0x14-0

Dn
Up

MBr
20-8x16-0

Garage
22-1x24-1

Foyer

Living
12-1x13-9

Porch

First Floor
2,276 sq. ft.

Plan #529-0219
Price Code F

Total Living Area: 3,222 Sq. Ft.

Home has 4 bedrooms, 3 1/2 baths, 2-car side entry garage and basement foundation, drawings also include crawl space and slab foundations.

Special features

- Two-story foyer features central staircase and views to second floor, dining and living rooms
- Built-in breakfast booth surrounded by windows
- Gourmet kitchen with view to the great room
- Two-story great room features large fireplace and arched openings to the second floor
- Elegant master suite has separate reading room with bookshelves and fireplace

Plan #529-0367
Price Code D
Total Living Area: 2,523 Sq. Ft.

Home has 3 bedrooms, 2 baths, 3-car garage and basement foundation.

Special features

- Entry with high ceiling leads to massive vaulted great room with wet bar, plant shelves, pillars and fireplace with a harmonious window trio
- Elaborate kitchen with bay and breakfast bar adjoins morning room with fireplace-in-a-bay
- Vaulted master suite features fireplace, book and plant shelves, large walk-in closet and his and her baths

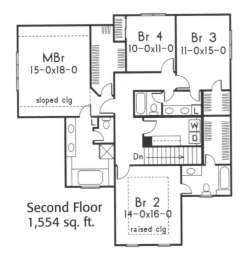

MBr
15-0x18-0

sloped clg

Br 4
10-0x11-0

Br 3
11-0x15-0

Dn

W
D

L

Second Floor
1,554 sq. ft.

Br 2
14-0x16-0

raised clg

59'-4"

47'-4"

Garage
22-0x23-0

P

Brk
20-0x12-0

Covered
Deck

Kit
18-0x14-0

Family
18-0x18-0

Dining
12-0x14-0

Dn R Up

Living
14-0x16-0

Porch

First Floor
1,459 sq. ft.

Plan #529-0299
Price Code E

Total Living Area: 3,013 Sq. Ft.

Home has 4 bedrooms, 3 1/2 baths, 2-car side entry garage and basement foundation.

Special features

- Oversized rooms throughout
- Kitchen features island sink, large pantry and opens into sunny breakfast room
- Master bedroom includes large walk-in closet and private deluxe bath
- Large family room with fireplace accesses rear deck and front porch

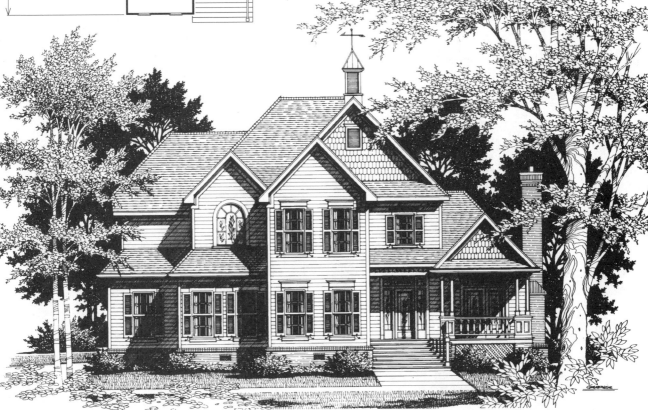

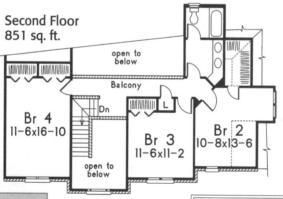

Second Floor
851 sq. ft.

open to below

Balcony

Br 4
11-6x16-10

Dn

L

Br 3
11-6x11-2

Br 2
10-8x13-6

open to below

Plan #529-0137

Price Code E

<u>Total Living Area:</u>   2,282 Sq. Ft.

Home has 4 bedrooms, 2 1/2 baths, 2-car drive under garage and basement foundation.

Special features

- Balcony and two-story foyer add spaciousness to this compact plan
- First floor master suite has corner tub in large master bath
- Out-of-the-way kitchen is open to the full-windowed breakfast room

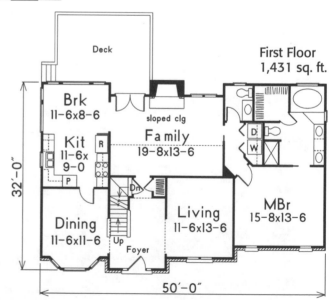

Deck

First Floor
1,431 sq. ft.

Brk
11-6x8-6

sloped clg

Family
19-8x13-6

Kit
11-6x
9-0

R

P

D

W

32'-0"

Dining
11-6x11-6

Up

Dn

Living
11-6x13-6

MBr
15-8x13-6

Foyer

50'-0"

Dramatic Entry With Soaring Staircase

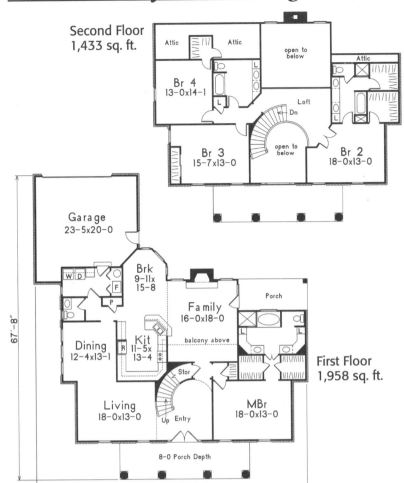

Second Floor
1,433 sq. ft.

Attic | Attic

open to below

Attic

Br 4
13-0x14-1

Loft
Dn

Br 3
15-7x13-0

open to below

Br 2
18-0x13-0

Garage
23-5x20-0

W D

Brk
9-11x
15-8

Family
16-0x18-0

Porch

balcony above

67'-8"

Dining
12-4x13-1

Kit
11-5x
13-4

Stor

Living
18-0x13-0

Up Entry

MBr
18-0x13-0

First Floor
1,958 sq. ft.

8-0 Porch Depth

62'-8"

Plan #529-0220
Price Code F

Total Living Area: 3,391 Sq. Ft.

Home has 4 bedrooms, 3 1/2 baths, 2-car rear entry garage and crawl space foundation, drawings also include slab foundation.

Special features

- Magnificent first floor master suite has two walk-in closets and double vanities
- Generous secondary bedrooms
- Bedroom #2 has private bath and plenty of closet space
- Two-story family room with fire-place and balcony above

Plan #529-0755

Price Code B

Total Living Area: 1,787 Sq. Ft.

Home has 3 bedrooms, 2 baths, 2-car rear entry garage and walk-out basement foundation.

Special features

- Large great room with fireplace and vaulted ceiling features three large skylights and windows galore

- Cooking is sure to be a pleasure in this L-shaped well-appointed kitchen which includes bayed breakfast area with access to rear deck

- Every bedroom offers a spacious walk-in closet with a convenientlaundry room just steps away

- 415 square feet of optional living area on the lower level

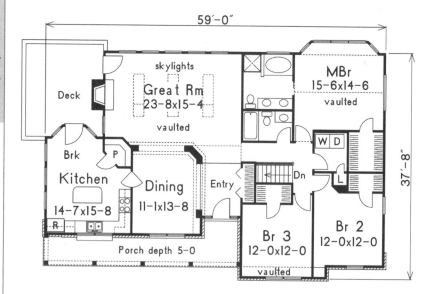

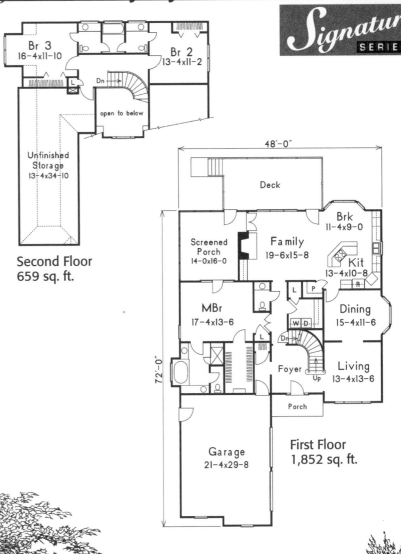

Second Floor
659 sq. ft.

Plan #529-0599
Price Code D
Total Living Area: 2,511 Sq. Ft.

Home has 3 bedrooms, 2 1/2 baths, 2-car side entry garage and basement foundation, drawings also include crawl space and slab foundations.

Special features

- Unfinished storage area above garage provides room for future expansion
- Screened porch is accessible from three different living areas
- Feeling of spaciousness created by vaulted kitchen and family area

First Floor
1,852 sq. ft.

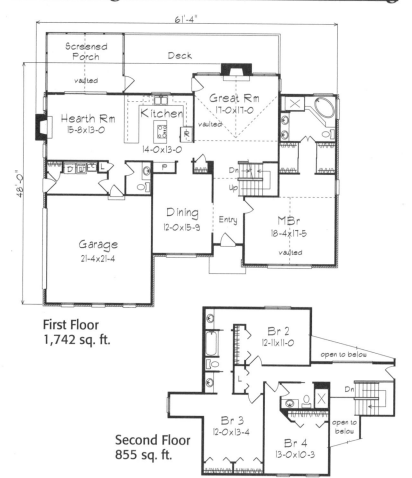

First Floor
1,742 sq. ft.

Second Floor
855 sq. ft.

Plan #529-0354
Price Code D

Total Living Area: 2,597 Sq. Ft.

Home has 4 bedrooms, 3 1/2 baths, 2-car side entry garage and walk-out basement foundation, drawings also include crawl space and slab foundations.

Special features

- Large U-shaped kitchen features island cooktop and breakfast bar
- Entry and great room enhanced by sweeping balcony
- Bedrooms #2 and #3 share a bath; the 4th has a private bath
- Vaulted great room with transomed arch windows

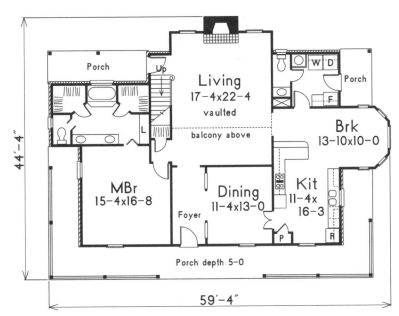

Second Floor
780 sq. ft.

open to below

Dn

Br 2
11-8x14-8

sloped clg

desk

Game Rm
12-10x14-8

L

seat

Br 3
11-4x14-8

seat

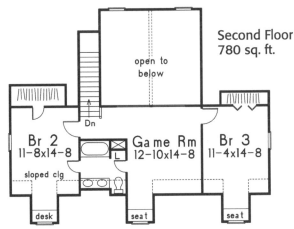

Porch

Up

Living
17-4x22-4
vaulted

W D

Porch

F

balcony above

Brk
13-10x10-0

44'-4"

MBr
15-4x16-8

L

Foyer

Dining
11-4x13-0

Kit
11-4x
16-3

P

R

Porch depth 5-0

59'-4"

First Floor
1,669 sq. ft.

Plan #529-0143
Price Code E

Total Living Area: 2,449 Sq. Ft.

Home has 3 bedrooms, 2 1/2 baths, 2-car detached garage and slab foundation, drawings also include crawl space foundation.

Special features
- Striking living area features fireplace flanked with windows, cathedral ceiling and balcony
- First floor master bedroom with twin walk-in closets and large linen storage
- Dormers add space for desks or seats

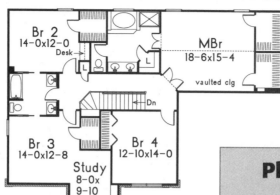

Second Floor
1,490 sq. ft.

Br 2
14-0x12-0
Desk

MBr
18-6x15-4
vaulted clg

Br 3
14-0x12-8

Br 4
12-10x14-0

Study
8-0x
9-10

Dn

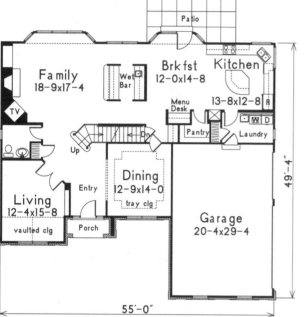

Patio

Family
18-9x17-4

Wet Bar

Brkfst
12-0x14-8

Kitchen
13-8x12-8

TV

Menu Desk

Pantry

Laundry

W D

Up

Dining
12-9x14-0
tray clg

Living
12-4x15-8
vaulted clg

Entry

Porch

Garage
20-4x29-4

49'-4"

55'-0"

First Floor
1,679 sq. ft.

Plan #529-0716
Price Code F

Total Living Area: 3,169 Sq. Ft.

Home has 4 bedrooms, 2 1/2 baths, 3-car side entry garage and basement foundation.

Special features

- Formal areas include enormous entry with handcrafted stairway and powder room, French doors to living room and open dining area with tray ceiling

- Informal areas consist of a large family room with bay window, fireplace, walk-in wet bar and kitchen open to breakfast room

- Stylish master suite is located on second floor for privacy

- Front secondary bedroom includes a private study

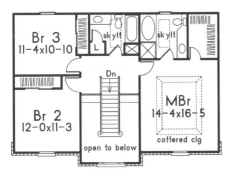

Br 3
11-4x10-10

skylt   skylt

Dn

Br 2
12-0x11-3

MBr
14-4x16-5

coffered clg

open to below

Second Floor
859 sq. ft.

Plan #529-0228
Price Code C

Total Living Area: 1,996 Sq. Ft.

Home has 3 bedrooms, 2 1/2 baths, 2-car side entry garage and basement foundation, drawings also include crawl space and slab foundations.

Special features

- Dining area features octagon-shaped coffered ceiling and built-in china cabinet

- Second floor baths both feature cheerful skylights

- Family room includes wet bar and fireplace flanked by attractive quarter round windows

- 9' ceilings throughout first floor with plant shelving in foyer and dining area

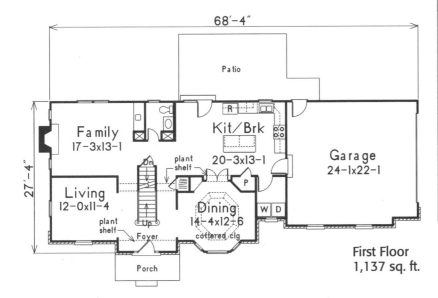

68'-4"

Patio

Family
17-3x13-1

Kit/Brk
20-3x13-1

Garage
24-1x22-1

27'-4"

R

plant shelf

Dn

P

Living
12-0x11-4

plant shelf

Up

Dining
14-4x12-6
coffered clg

W D

Foyer

Porch

First Floor
1,137 sq. ft.

Plan #529-0366
Price Code E

Total Living Area: 2,624 Sq. Ft.

Home has 4 bedrooms, 2 1/2 baths, 2-car side entry garage and basement foundation.

Special features

- Dramatic two-story entry opens to bayed dining room through classic colonnade
- Magnificent great room with 18' ceiling brightly lit with three palladian windows
- Master suite includes bay window, walk-in closets, plant shelves and sunken bath

69'-8"

46'-0"

MBr
17-0x17-8
vaulted
plant shelf

Great Rm
20-6x15-10

Brk
14-10x10-0

Kitchen
14-10x10-6

Garage
21-4x20-4

Dining
14-10x12-4

Foyer

Dn   Up

First Floor
1,774 sq. ft.

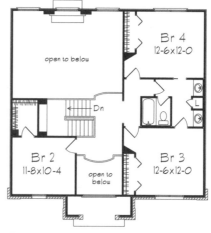

open to below

Br 4
12-6x12-0

Dn

Br 2
11-8x10-4

open to below

Br 3
12-6x12-0

Second Floor
850 sq. ft.

Interior View - Master Bath

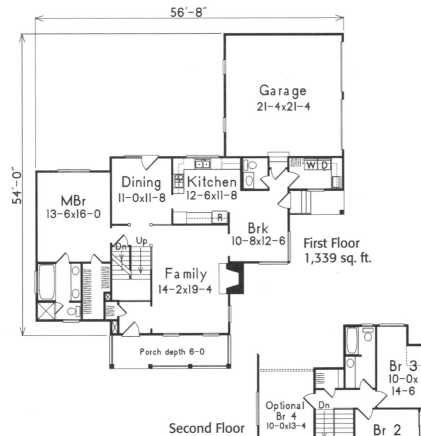

56'-8"

54'-0"

Garage
21-4x21-4

MBr
13-6x16-0

Dining
11-0x11-8

Kitchen
12-6x11-8

W D

Brk
10-8x12-6

First Floor
1,339 sq. ft.

Dn   Up

Family
14-2x19-4

Porch depth 6-0

Second Floor
490 sq. ft.

Optional
Br 4
10-0x13-4

Dn

Br 3
10-0x
14-6

Br 2
12-8x11-0

Plan #529-0492
Price Code C
Total Living Area: 1,829 Sq. Ft.

Home has 3 bedrooms, 2 1/2 baths, 2-car side entry garage and partial basement/crawl space foundation.

Special features

- Entry foyer with coat closet opens to large family room with fireplace
- Two second floor bedrooms share a full bath
- Optional bedroom #4 can be finished as your family grows
- Cozy porch provides convenient side entrance into home

LOWE'S

Signature SERIES

Plan #529-0184
Price Code D

Total Living Area: 2,411 Sq. Ft.

Home has 3 bedrooms, 2 1/2 baths, 2-car garage and basement foundation, drawings also include slab and crawl space foundations.

Special features

- Elegant entrance features a two-story vaulted foyer
- Large family room enhanced by masonry fireplace and wet bar
- Master bedroom suite includes walk-in closet, oversized tub and separate shower
- Second floor study could easily convert to a fourth bedroom

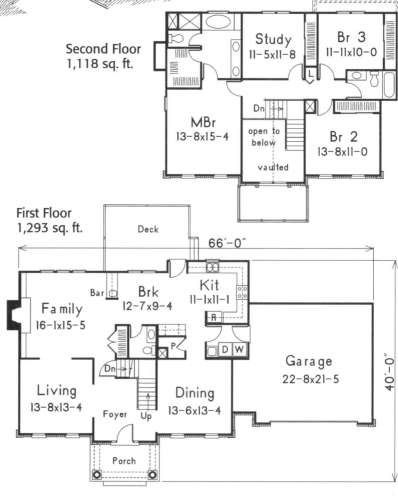

Second Floor
1,118 sq. ft.

Study
11-5x11-8

Br 3
11-11x10-0

MBr
13-8x15-4

Dn

open to below

vaulted

Br 2
13-8x11-0

First Floor
1,293 sq. ft.

Deck

66'-0"

Bar

Brk
12-7x9-4

Kit
11-1x11-1

Family
16-1x15-5

R

Dn

P

D W

Garage
22-8x21-5

40'-0"

Living
13-8x13-4

Foyer   Up

Dining
13-6x13-4

Porch

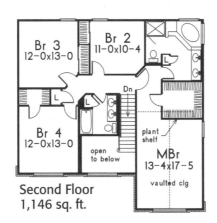

Second Floor
1,146 sq. ft.

Br 3
12-0x13-0

Br 2
11-0x10-4

Dn

Br 4
12-0x13-0

plant
shelf

open
to below

MBr
13-4x17-5

vaulted clg

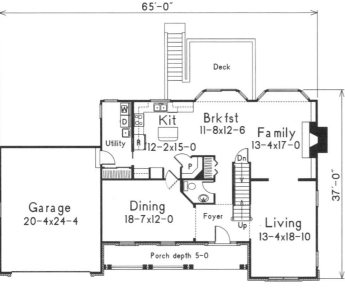

65'-0"

Deck

Kit
12-2x15-0

Brkfst
11-8x12-6

Family
13-4x17-0

Utility

W
D

Dn

Garage
20-4x24-4

Dining
18-7x12-0

Foyer

Up

Living
13-4x18-10

P

37'-0"

Porch depth 5-0

First Floor
1,375 sq. ft.

Plan #529-0709
Price Code D

<u>Total Living Area:</u>   2,521 Sq. Ft.

Home has 4 bedrooms, 2 1/2 baths,
2-car garage and basement foundation.

Special features

- ■ Spacious living and dining rooms
  are a plus for formal entertaining or
  large family gatherings

- ■ Informal kitchen, breakfast and
  family rooms feature a 37' vista and
  double bay windows

- ■ Generous-sized master bedroom
  suite and three secondary bedrooms grace the second floor

LOWE'S

Signature SERIES

Plan #529-0386
Price Code C

Total Living Area: 2,186 Sq. Ft.

Home has 3 bedrooms, 2 1/2 baths, 2-car garage and basement foundation.

Special features

- See-through fireplace is a focal point in family and living areas
- Attractive columns enhance entrance into living room
- Large laundry room with adjoining half bath
- Ideal second floor bath includes separate vanity with double sinks

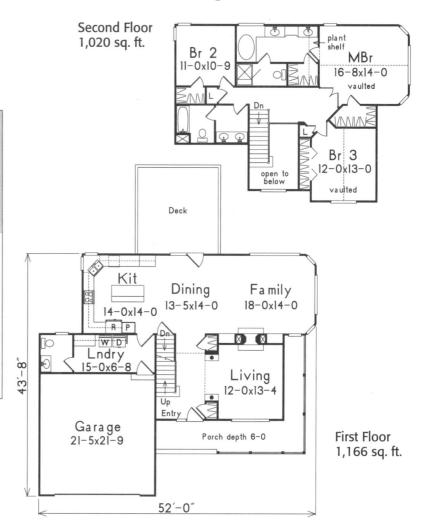

Second Floor
1,020 sq. ft.

Br 2
11-0x10-9

plant shelf

MBr
16-8x14-0
vaulted

Dn

L

L

Br 3
12-0x13-0
vaulted

open to below

Deck

Kit
14-0x14-0

Dining
13-5x14-0

Family
18-0x14-0

R P

W D

Lndry
15-0x6-8

Dn

Up Entry

Living
12-0x13-4

43'-8"

Garage
21-5x21-9

Porch depth 6-0

52'-0"

First Floor
1,166 sq. ft.

Plan #529-0316
Price Code C
Total Living Area: 1,824 Sq. Ft.

Home has 3 bedrooms, 2 baths, 2-car detached garage and slab foundation.

Special features

- Living room features 10' ceiling, fireplace and media center

- Dining room includes bay window and convenient kitchen access

- Master bedroom features large walk-in closet and double-doors leading into master bath

- Modified U-shaped kitchen features pantry and bar

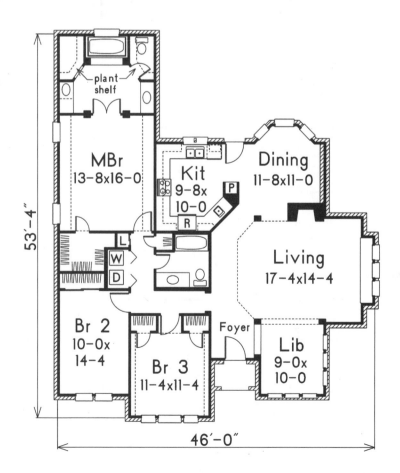

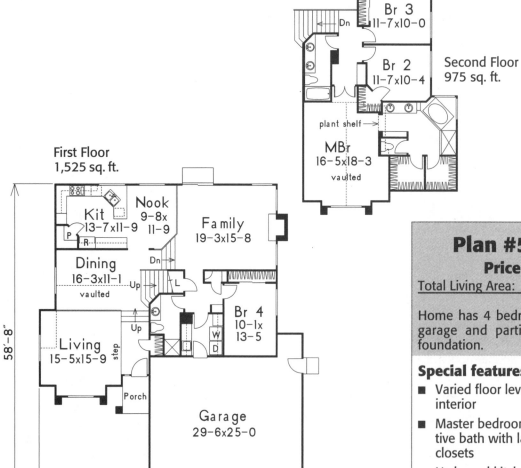

Second Floor
975 sq. ft.

Br 3
11-7x10-0

Dn

Br 2
11-7x10-4

plant shelf →

MBr
16-5x18-3
vaulted

First Floor
1,525 sq. ft.

Kit
13-7x11-9

Nook
9-8x
11-9

Family
19-3x15-8

Dining
16-3x11-1
vaulted

Dn

Up

L

Up

Br 4
10-1x
13-5

Living
15-5x15-9

step

Porch

Garage
29-6x25-0

58'-8"

51'-0"

Plan #529-0444
Price Code D
Total Living Area: 2,500 Sq. Ft.

Home has 4 bedrooms, 3 baths, 3-car garage and partial slab/crawl space foundation.

Special features
- Varied floor levels create dramatic interior
- Master bedroom includes a distinctive bath with large double walk-in closets
- U-shaped kitchen features walk-in pantry and corner sink

Timeless Country Facade

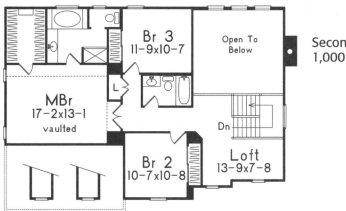

Second Floor
1,000 sq. ft.

Br 3
11-9x10-7

Open To
Below

MBr
17-2x13-1
vaulted

Br 2
10-7x10-8

Loft
13-9x7-8

First Floor
977 sq. ft.

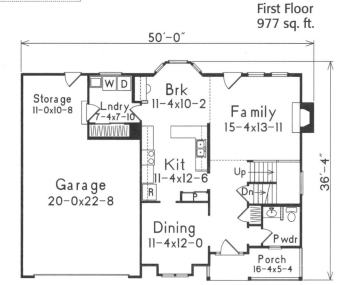

50'-0"

36'-4"

Storage
11-0x10-8

Lndry
7-4x7-10

W D

Brk
11-4x10-2

Family
15-4x13-11

Garage
20-0x22-8

Kit
11-4x12-6

Up

Dn

Dining
11-4x12-0

Pwdr

Porch
16-4x5-4

Plan #529-0725
Price Code C

Total Living Area: 1,977 Sq. Ft.

Home has 3 bedrooms, 2 1/2 baths,
2-car garage and basement foundation.

Special features

- An enormous entry with adjacent dining area and powder room leads to a splendid two-story family room with fireplace

- Kitchen features an abundance of cabinets, built-in pantry and breakfast room with menu desk and bay window

- A spacious vaulted master suite, two secondary bedrooms with bath and loft area adorn the second floor

- Extra storage area in garage

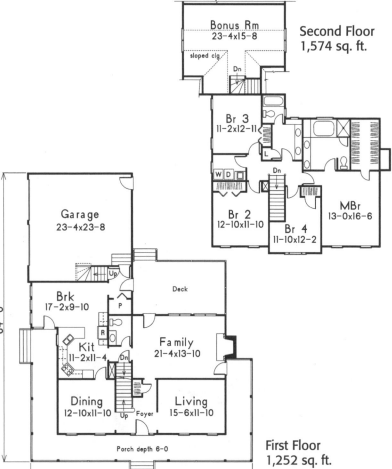

Bonus Rm
23-4x15-8

Second Floor
1,574 sq. ft.

sloped clg.

Dn

Br 3
11-2x12-11

W D

Dn

Br 2
12-10x11-10

Br 4
11-10x12-2

MBr
13-0x16-6

Garage
23-4x23-8

Up

Deck

Brk
17-2x9-10

P

R

Kit
11-2x11-4

Family
21-4x13-10

Dn

Dining
12-10x11-10

Up   Foyer

Living
15-6x11-10

64'-0"

Porch depth 6-0

51'-0"

First Floor
1,252 sq. ft.

Plan #529-0141
Price Code E
Total Living Area: 2,826 Sq. Ft.

Home has 4 bedrooms, 2 1/2 baths, 2-car side entry garage and basement foundation.

Special features
- Wrap-around covered porch is accessible from family and breakfast rooms in addition to front entrance
- Bonus room with separate entrance suitable for an office or private accommodations
- Large, full-windowed breakfast room

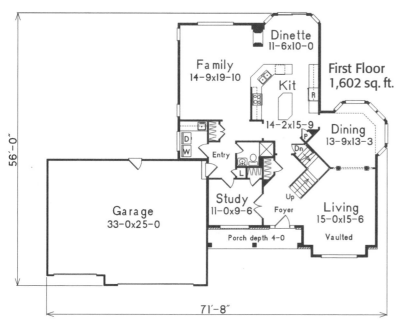

Dinette
11-6x10-0

Family
14-9x19-10

Kit

First Floor
1,602 sq. ft.

14-2x15-9

Dining
13-9x13-3

R

P

D
W

Entry

Dn

L

Up

Garage
33-0x25-0

Study
11-0x9-6

Foyer

Living
15-0x15-6

Porch depth 4-0

Vaulted

56'-0"

71'-8"

MBr
13-6x17-0

Second Floor
1,236 sq. ft.

Br 3
13-10x11-6

L

Br 4
12-0x10-0

Dn

Br 2
11-0x9-6

open to
below

Plan #529-0373
Price Code E

Total Living Area: 2,838 Sq. Ft.

Home has 4 bedrooms, 2 1/2 baths, 3-car garage and basement foundation.

Special features

- 10' ceilings throughout first floor
- Dining room enhanced with large corner bay windows
- Master bath boasts double sink and oversized tub
- Kitchen features an island and double sink which overlooks dinette and family room

Plan #529-0302

Price Code D

Total Living Area: 1,854 Sq. Ft.

Home has 3 bedrooms, 2 1/2 baths, 2-car side entry garage and basement foundation.

Special features

- Front entrance enhanced by arched transom windows and rustic stone
- Isolated master bedroom with dressing area and walk-in closet
- Family room features high, sloped ceilings and large fireplace
- Breakfast area accesses covered rear porch

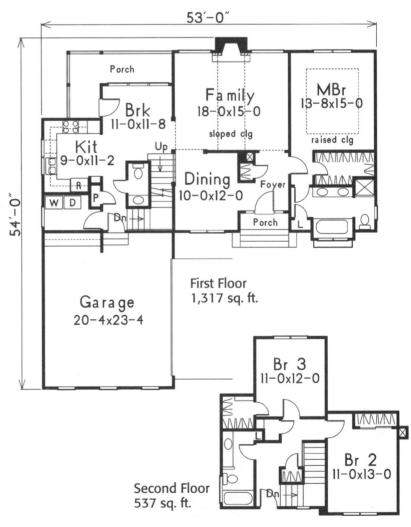

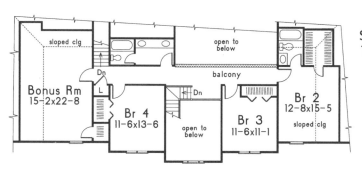

Second Floor
1,375 sq. ft.

Bonus Rm
15-2x22-8

Br 4
11-6x13-6

Br 3
11-6x11-1

Br 2
12-8x15-5
sloped clg

sloped clg

open to below

balcony

open to below

Dn

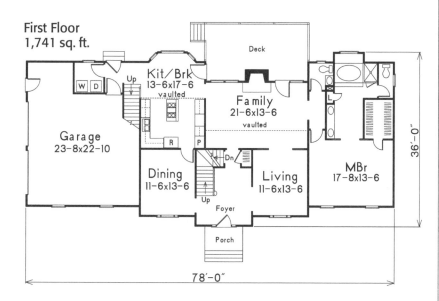

First Floor
1,741 sq. ft.

Deck

Kit/Brk
13-6x17-6
vaulted

Family
21-6x13-6
vaulted

Garage
23-8x22-10

Dining
11-6x13-6

Living
11-6x13-6

MBr
17-8x13-6

Foyer

Porch

W D

Up

Up

Dn

R P

36'-0"

78'-0"

Plan #529-0146
Price Code F

Total Living Area: 3,116 Sq. Ft.

Home has 4 bedrooms, 3 1/2 baths, 2-car side entry garage and basement foundation.

Special features

- Arched mullioned windows provide balance across the impressive facade

- First floor master bedroom and bedroom #2 on second floor have private baths and walk-in closets

- Large area above the garage available for future use

- Vaulted ceiling and balcony add to spaciousness

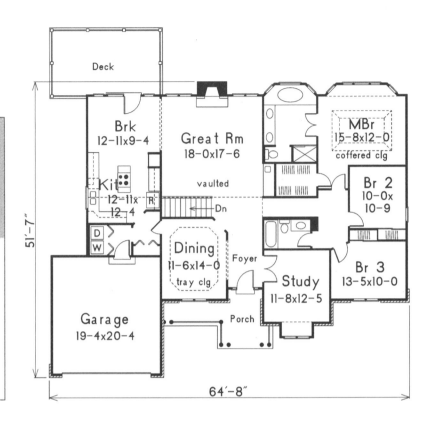

Plan #529-0320
Price Code D

__Total Living Area:__   2,228 Sq. Ft.

Home has 3 bedrooms, 2 baths, 2-car garage and basement foundation.

Special features

- Convenient entrance from garage into home through laundry room
- Master bedroom features walk-in closet and double-door entrance into master bath with oversized tub
- Formal dining room with tray ceiling
- Kitchen features island cooktop and adjacent breakfast room

LOWE'S

Signature SERIES

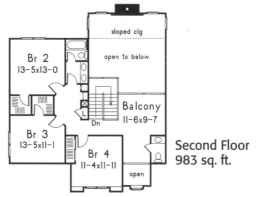

sloped clg

open to below

Br 2
13-5x13-0

Balcony
11-6x9-7

L
Dn

Br 3
13-5x11-1

Br 4
11-4x11-11

open

Second Floor
983 sq. ft.

Plan #529-0236
Price Code F
Total Living Area: 3,357 Sq. Ft.

Home has 4 bedrooms, 2 full baths, 2 half baths, 2-car side entry garage and basement foundation, drawings also include crawl space and slab foundations.

Special features

- Attractive balcony overlooks entry foyer and living area

- Balcony area could easily convert to a fifth bedroom

- Spacious kitchen also opens into sunken family room with a fireplace

- First floor master suite boasts large walk-in closet and dressing area

- Central laundry room with laundry chute from second floor

69'-0"

Patio

Brk
11-5x9-3

Dn

Living
18-9x25-0

MBr
15-8x16-7

Family
14-0x22-5

Kit
11-1x14-9

W
D

P

Dn Up

55'-8"

Dining
12-4x12-11

Foyer

L

Garage
22-9x22-10

Porch

Study
11-5x13-0

sloped clg

First Floor
2,374 sq. ft.

Signature SERIES

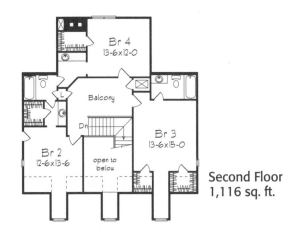

Second Floor
1,116 sq. ft.

Br 4
13-6x12-0

Balcony

Dn

Br 3
13-6x15-0

Br 2
12-6x13-6

open to below

Plan #529-0429
Price Code E
Total Living Area: 3,149 Sq. Ft.

Home has 4 bedrooms, 3 1/2 baths, 2-car detached garage and slab foundation, drawings also include crawl space foundation.

Special features

- 10' ceilings on first floor and 9' ceilings on second floor
- All bedrooms include walk-in closets
- Formal living and dining rooms flank two-story foyer

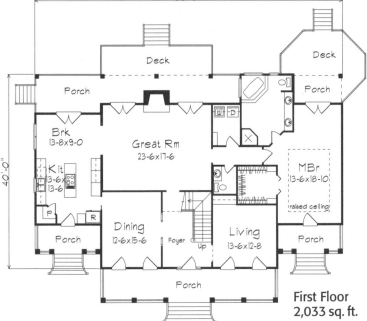

66'-0"

40'-0"

Deck

Deck

Porch

Porch

Brk
13-8x9-0

Great Rm
23-6x17-6

MBr
13-6x18-10

raised ceiling

Kit
13-6x
13-6

Dining
12-6x15-6

Foyer

Up

Living
13-6x12-8

Porch

Porch

Porch

First Floor
2,033 sq. ft.

Signature **SERIES**

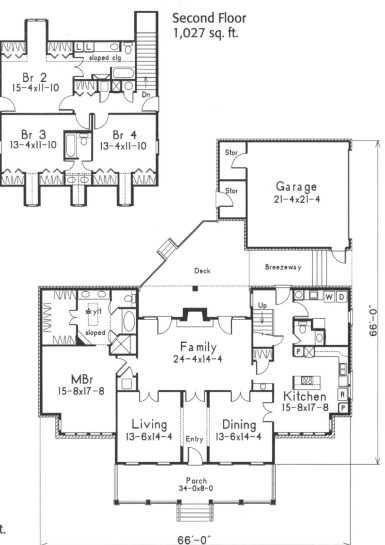

Second Floor
1,027 sq. ft.

sloped clg

Br 2
15-4x11-10

Dn

Br 3
13-4x11-10

Br 4
13-4x11-10

Plan #529-0187
Price Code E

Total Living Area:	3,035 Sq. Ft.

Home has 4 bedrooms, 3 1/2 baths, 2-car side entry garage and crawl space foundation, drawings also include slab and basement foundations.

Special features

- Front facade includes large porch
- Private master bedroom with windowed sitting area, walk-in closet, sloped ceiling and skylight
- Formal living and dining rooms adjoin the family room through attractive French doors
- Energy efficient home with 2" x 6" exterior walls

Stor

Stor

Garage
21-4x21-4

Breezeway

Deck

Up

W D

P

skylt

sloped

Family
24-4x14-4

P

Kitchen
15-8x17-8

MBr
15-8x17-8

R

P

Living
13-6x14-4

Entry

Dining
13-6x14-4

Porch
34-0x8-0

First Floor
2,008 sq. ft.

66'-0"

66'-0"

Plan #529-0372

Price Code C

Total Living Area: 1,859 Sq. Ft.

Home has 3 bedrooms, 2 1/2 baths, 2-car garage and basement foundation.

Special features

- Fireplace highlights vaulted great room
- Master suite includes large closet and private bath
- Kitchen adjoins breakfast room providing easy access outdoors

Br 2
10-8x11-3

MBr
11-10x17-2

Dn

open to below

Br 3
11-8x10-2

Second Floor
789 sq. ft.

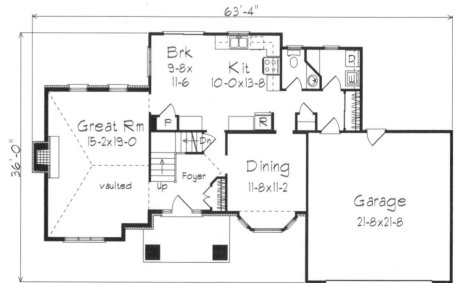

63'-4"

36'-0"

Brk
9-8x
11-6

Kit
10-0x13-8

Great Rm
15-2x19-0

P

Dn

R

vaulted

Up

Foyer

Dining
11-8x11-2

Garage
21-8x21-8

First Floor
1,070 sq. ft.

Elegant Two-Story Exterior And Entry

 *Signature* SERIES

Second Floor
1,569 sq. ft.

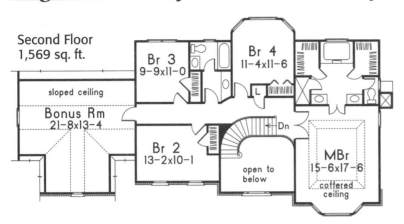

Br 3
9-9x11-0

Br 4
11-4x11-6

sloped ceiling

L

Bonus Rm
21-8x13-4

Br 2
13-2x10-1

Dn

open to
below

MBr
15-6x17-6

coffered
ceiling

First Floor
1,277 sq. ft.

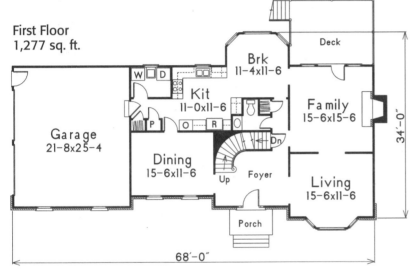

W D

Brk
11-4x11-6

Deck

Kit
11-0x11-6

Family
15-6x15-6

Garage
21-8x25-4

P

O R

Dn

Dining
15-6x11-6

Up

Foyer

Living
15-6x11-6

Porch

34'-0"

68'-0"

Plan #529-0178
Price Code E

Total Living Area: 2,846 Sq. Ft.

Home has 4 bedrooms, 2 1/2 baths, 2-car side entry garage and basement foundation, drawings also include slab and crawl space foundations.

Special features

- 9' ceilings on first floor and 8' ceilings on second floor
- Bonus room over garage
- Prominent double-bay windows add brightness and space to both floors
- Master suite with double-door entry and coffered ceiling includes an elaborate bath with large tub, separate shower and individual walk-in closets

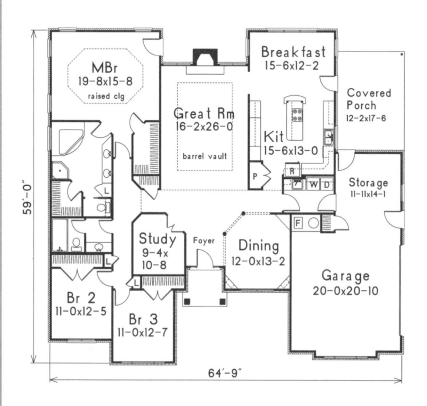

Plan #529-0721
Price Code D

Total Living Area: 2,437 Sq. Ft.

Home has 3 bedrooms, 2 baths, 2-car side entry garage and slab foundation, drawings also include crawl space foundation.

Special features

- Spacious breakfast area with access to the covered porch is adjacent to kitchen and great room

- Elegant dining area has columned entrance and built-in corner cabinets

- Cozy study has handsome double-door entrance off a large foyer

- Raised ceiling and lots of windows in master suite create a spacious, open feel

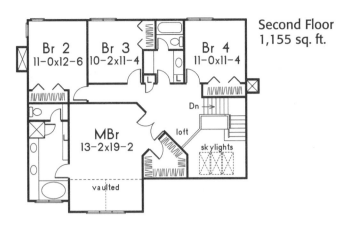

Second Floor
1,155 sq. ft.

Br 2
11-0x12-6

Br 3
10-2x11-4

Br 4
11-0x11-4

MBr
13-2x19-2

Dn

loft

skylights

vaulted

Plan #529-0208
Price Code E

Total Living Area: 2,445 Sq. Ft.

Home has 4 bedrooms, 2 1/2 baths, 3-car garage and basement foundation.

Special features

■ Sunken living room has a corner fireplace, vaulted ceiling and is adjacent to the dining room for entertaining large groups

■ Large vaulted open foyer with triple skylights provides an especially bright entry

■ Loft area overlooks foyer and features a decorative display area

■ Bedrooms located on second floor for privacy and convenience, with a vaulted ceiling in the master suite

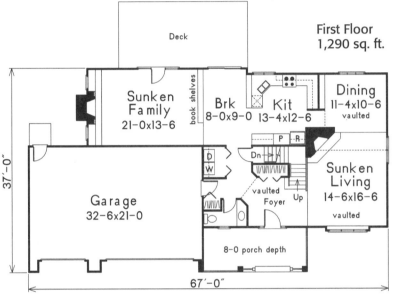

Deck

First Floor
1,290 sq. ft.

Sunken Family
21-0x13-6

book shelves

Brk
8-0x9-0

Kit
13-4x12-6

Dining
11-4x10-6
vaulted

Dn

vaulted Foyer

Up

Sunken Living
14-6x16-6
vaulted

Garage
32-6x21-0

8-0 porch depth

37'-0"

67'-0"

Second Floor
814 sq. ft.

open to below

Br 4
14-8x11-1

Br 3
17-0x11-0

skylt

Dn

L

Br 2
12-3x12-8

Plan #529-0170
Price Code E
Total Living Area: 2,618 Sq. Ft.

Home has 4 bedrooms, 2 1/2 baths, 2-car garage and basement foundation.

Special features

- Stylish front facade with covered porch and distinctive window treatment

- Great room features vaulted ceiling, skylights and large fireplace

- Master bedroom and bath with two large walk-in closets, separate oversized tub and shower, first floor convenience and privacy

- Kitchen overlooks the deck and features circle-top windows and corner window view from the sink

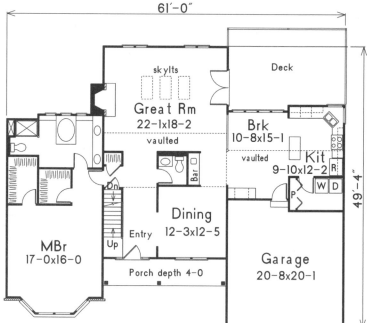

61'-0"

skylts

Great Rm
22-1x18-2
vaulted

Deck

Brk
10-8x15-1
vaulted

Kit
9-10x12-2

W D
P

Bar

Dn

MBr
17-0x16-0

Entry

Up

Dining
12-3x12-5

Porch depth 4-0

Garage
20-8x20-1

49'-4"

First Floor
1,804 sq. ft.

LOWE'S

Signature SERIES

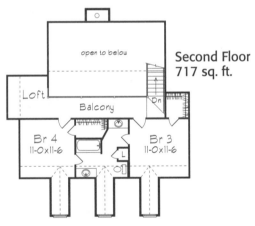

open to below

Second Floor
717 sq. ft.

Loft

Balcony   Dn

Br 4
11-0x11-6

Br 3
11-0x11-6

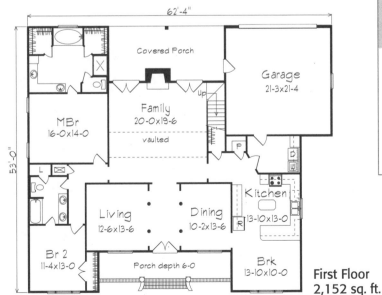

62'-4"

53'-0"

Covered Porch

Garage
21-3x21-4

Family
20-0x19-6
vaulted

up

MBr
16-0x14-0

P

D W

Kitchen
13-10x13-0

Living
12-6x13-6

Dining
10-2x13-6

R

Br 2
11-4x13-0

Porch depth 6-0

Brk
13-10x10-0

First Floor
2,152 sq. ft.

Plan #529-0430
Price Code E
<u>Total Living Area:</u>   2,869 Sq. Ft.

Home has 4 bedrooms, 3 baths, 2-car rear entry garage and slab foundation, drawings also include crawl space foundation.

Special features
- Foyer, flanked by columned living and dining rooms, leads to vaulted family room with fireplace and twin sets of French doors
- 10' ceilings on first floor and 9' ceilings on second floor

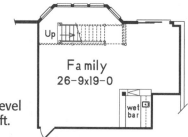

Lower Level
557 sq. ft.

Family
26-9x19-0

Up

wet
bar

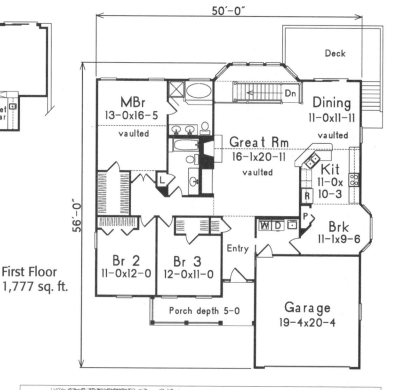

50'-0"

Deck

56'-0"

MBr
13-0x16-5
vaulted

Dining
11-0x11-11
vaulted

Dn

Great Rm
16-1x20-11
vaulted

Kit
11-0x
10-3

R

L

Br 2
11-0x12-0

Br 3
12-0x11-0

Entry

WD

P

Brk
11-1x9-6

First Floor
1,777 sq. ft.

Porch depth 5-0

Garage
19-4x20-4

Plan #529-0710
Price Code D
Total Living Area: 2,334 Sq. Ft.

Home has 3 bedrooms, 2 baths, 2-car garage and walk-out basement foundation.

Special features

- Roomy front porch gives home a country flavor

- Vaulted great room boasts a fireplace, TV alcove, pass-through snack bar to kitchen and atrium featuring bayed window wall and ascending stair to family room

- Oversized master bedroom and bath features a vaulted ceiling, double entry doors and large walk-in closet

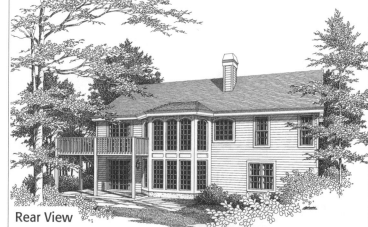

Rear View

Signature SERIES

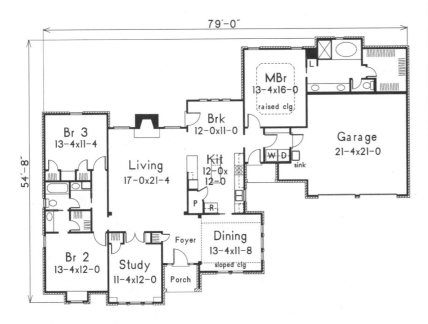

79'-0"

54'-8"

Br 3
13-4x11-4

Living
17-0x21-4

MBr
13-4x16-0
raised clg

Brk
12-0x11-0

Garage
21-4x21-0

W D
sink

Kit
12-0x
12-0

P R

Br 2
13-4x12-0

Study
11-4x12-0

Foyer

Porch

Dining
13-4x11-8
sloped clg

L

Plan #529-0245
Price Code D

Total Living Area: 2,260 Sq. Ft.

Home has 3 bedrooms, 2 baths, 2-car garage and slab foundation.

Special features

- Luxurious master suite includes raised ceiling, bath with oversized tub, separate shower and large walk-in closet
- Convenient kitchen and breakfast area with ample pantry storage
- Formal foyer leads into large living room with warming fireplace
- Convenient secondary entrance for everyday traffic

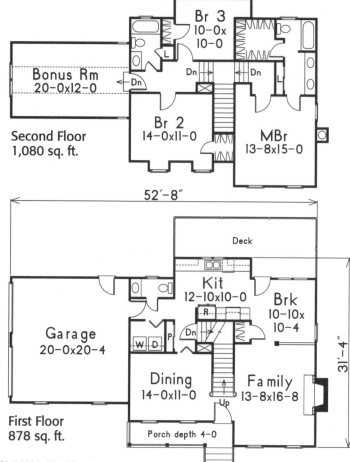

Second Floor
1,080 sq. ft.

Br 3
10-0x
10-0

Bonus Rm
20-0x12-0

Dn

Br 2
14-0x11-0

MBr
13-8x15-0

52'-8"

Deck

Kit
12-10x10-0

Brk
10-10x
10-4

Garage
20-0x20-4

31'-4"

W D P

Dn R

Dining
14-0x11-0

Family
13-8x16-8

Up

First Floor
878 sq. ft.

Porch depth 4-0

Plan #529-0202
Price Code D

Total Living Area: 1,958 Sq. Ft.

Home has 3 bedrooms, 2 1/2 baths, 2-car side entry garage and basement foundation, drawings also include crawl space and slab foundations.

Special features

- Spacious kitchen and breakfast area opens to rear deck
- Open floor plan with rail separating family room from breakfast area
- Dormers add interest and spaciousness in bedroom #2

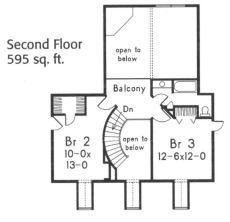

Second Floor
595 sq. ft.

open to below

Balcony

Dn

Br 2
10-0x
13-0

open to below

Br 3
12-6x12-0

First Floor
1,765 sq. ft.

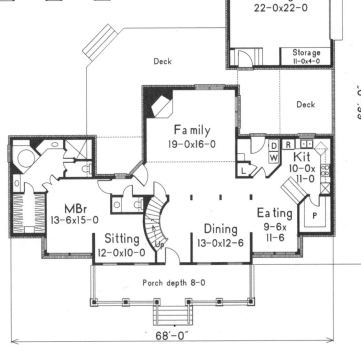

Garage
22-0x22-0

Storage
11-0x4-0

Deck

Deck

Family
19-0x16-0

Kit
10-0x
11-0

D R J
DW
L

MBr
13-6x15-0

Eating
9-6x
11-6

P

Sitting
12-0x10-0

Up

Dining
13-0x12-6

Porch depth 8-0

68'-0"

66'-0"

Plan #529-0306
Price Code D

Total Living Area: 2,360 Sq. Ft.

Home has 3 bedrooms, 2 1/2 baths, 2-car side entry garage and crawl space foundation, drawings also include slab and basement foundations.

Special features

- Master suite includes sitting area and large bath
- Sloped family room ceiling provides view from second floor balcony
- Kitchen features island bar and walk-in butler's pantry

Second Floor
749 sq. ft.

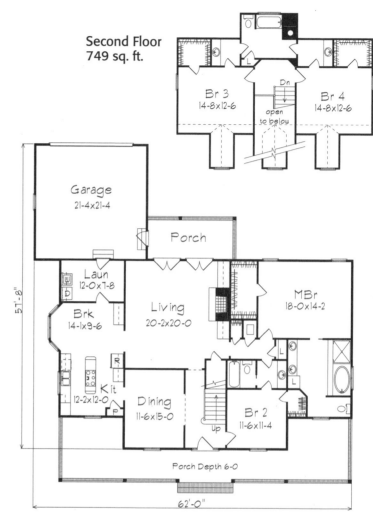

Br 3
14-8x12-6

Dn
open
to below

Br 4
14-8x12-6

Plan #529-0439

Price Code E

Total Living Area: 2,665 Sq. Ft.

Home has 4 bedrooms, 3 baths, 2-car rear entry garage and slab foundation, drawings also include crawl space foundation.

Special features

- 9' ceilings on first floor
- Spacious kitchen features many cabinets, center island cooktop and breakfast room with bay, adjacent to laundry room
- Second floor bedrooms boast walk-in closets, dressing areas and share a bath
- Twin patio doors and fireplace grace living room

Garage
21-4x21-4

Porch

51'-8"

Laun
12-0x7-8

Living
20-2x20-0

MBr
18-0x14-2

Brk
14-1x9-6

Kit
12-2x12-0

Dining
11-6x15-0

Br 2
11-6x11-4

Up

Porch Depth 6-0

62'-0"

First Floor
1,916 sq. ft.

Signature SERIES

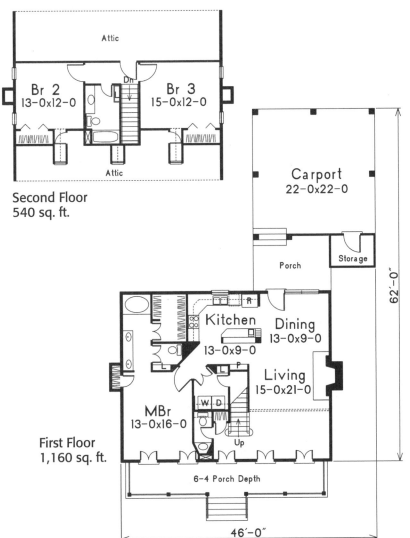

Second Floor
540 sq. ft.

First Floor
1,160 sq. ft.

6-4 Porch Depth

46'-0"

62'-0"

Plan #529-0290
Price Code B

Total Living Area: 1,700 Sq. Ft.

Home has 3 bedrooms, 2 1/2 baths, 2-car attached carport and crawl space foundation, drawings also include basement and slab foundations.

Special features

- Fully appointed kitchen with wet bar
- Energy efficient home with 2" x 6" exterior walls
- Linen drop from second floor bath to utility room
- Master bath includes raised marble tub and sloped ceilings

Plan #529-0232

Price Code F

Total Living Area: 2,932 Sq. Ft.

Home has 4 bedrooms, 3 1/2 baths, 2-car side entry garage and slab foundation.

Special features

- 9' ceilings throughout home
- Rear stairs create convenient access to second floor from living area
- Spacious kitchen has pass-through to the family room, a convenient island and pantry
- Cozy built-in table in breakfast area
- Secluded master suite with luxurious bath and patio access

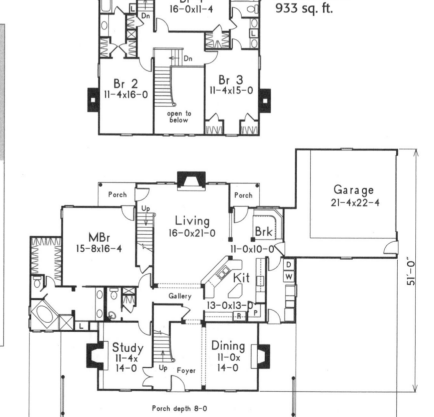

Second Floor
933 sq. ft.

Br 4
16-0x11-4

Br 2
11-4x16-0

Br 3
11-4x15-0

open to below

Porch

Up

Living
16-0x21-0

Porch

Brk
11-0x10-0

Garage
21-4x22-4

MBr
15-8x16-4

Kit
13-0x13-0

Gallery

Study
11-4x
14-0

Up   Foyer

Dining
11-0x
14-0

Porch depth 8-0

First Floor
1,999 sq. ft.

51'-0"

79'-4"

Traditional Exterior Boasts Exciting Interior

77'-0"

Deck

Covered Deck

Dining
17-0x12-2
vaulted

plant shelf

Atrium
open to below

plant shelf

36'-8"

Garage
21-4x21-4

P

Kit
10-6x
13-0

W
D

R

Great Rm
18-7x17-0
vaulted

plant shelf
Dn

MBr
13-0x16-8
vaulted

Porch
32-8x5-0

**First Floor
1,297 sq. ft.**

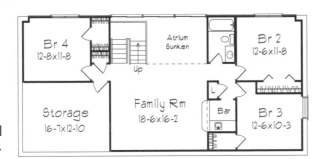

Br 4
12-8x11-8

Up

Atrium
Sunken

Br 2
12-6x11-8

Storage
16-7x12-10

Family Rm
18-6x16-2

Bar

L

Br 3
12-6x10-3

**Lower Level
1,234 sq. ft.**

Plan #529-0364
Price Code D

Total Living Area: 2,531 Sq. Ft.

Home has 4 bedrooms, 2 1/2 baths, 2-car side entry garage and walk-out basement foundation.

Special features

- Charming porch with dormers leads into vaulted great room with atrium
- Well-designed kitchen and breakfast bar adjoins extra large laundry/mud room
- Double sinks, tub with window above and plant shelf complete vaulted master suite

Rear View

Striking Double Arched Entry

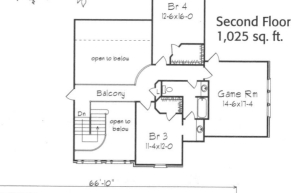

Br 4
12-6x16-0

**Second Floor
1,025 sq. ft.**

open to below

Balcony

Game Rm
14-6x17-4

Dn

open to below

Br 3
11-4x12-0

Plan #529-0405

Price Code F

Total Living Area: 3,494 Sq. Ft.

Home has 4 bedrooms, 3 1/2 baths, 3-car side entry garage and slab foundation, drawings also include crawl space foundation.

Special features

- Majestic two-story foyer opens into living and dining rooms, both framed by arched columns
- Balcony overlooks large living area featuring French doors to covered porch
- Luxurious master suite
- Convenient game room supports lots of activities

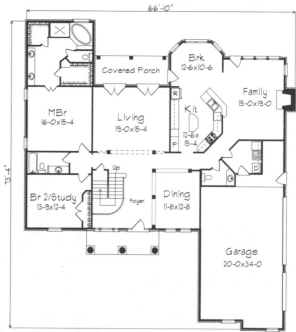

66'-10"

Covered Porch

Brk
12-6x10-6

Family
15-0x19-0

MBr
16-0x15-4

Living
19-0x15-4

Kit
12-6x
15-4

73'-4"

Br 2/Study
13-9x12-4

Up

Foyer

Dining
11-8x12-8

Garage
20-0x34-0

**First Floor
2,469 sq. ft.**

Two-Story Provides Room For Large Family

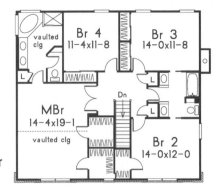

Second Floor
1,310 sq. ft.

Br 4
11-4x11-8
vaulted clg

Br 3
14-0x11-8

MBr
14-4x19-1
vaulted clg

Dn

Br 2
14-0x12-0

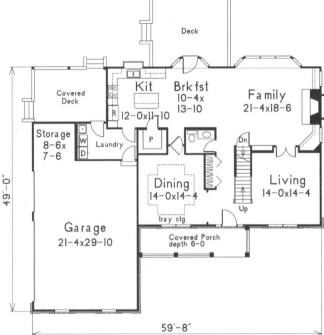

Deck

Covered Deck

Kit
12-0x11-10

Brkfst
10-4x
13-10

Family
21-4x18-6

Storage
8-6x
7-6

Laundry

W
D

R

P

Dn

Dining
14-0x14-4
tray clg

Living
14-0x14-4

Up

Garage
21-4x29-10

Covered Porch
depth 6-0

49'-0"

59'-8"

First Floor
1,420 sq. ft.

Plan #529-0691
Price Code E

Total Living Area: 2,730 Sq. Ft.

Home has 4 bedrooms, 2 1/2 baths, 3-car side entry garage and basement foundation.

Special features

- Spacious kitchen features island and generous walk-in pantry
- Covered deck offers private retreat to the outdoors
- Large master bedroom and bath with whirlpool corner tub, separate shower and his and her walk-in closets
- Oversized utility room conveniently located off kitchen
- Extra storage area in garage

J.N. HANSEN S.D.G.

SERIES

First Floor
3,050 sq. ft.

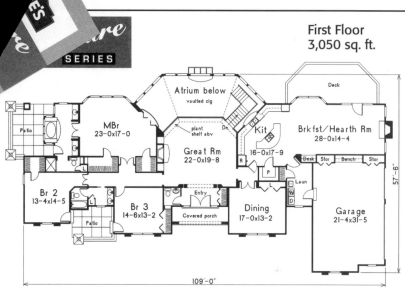

Atrium below
vaulted clg

Deck

MBr
23-0x17-0

Patio

plant
shelf abv

Dn

Kit
16-0x17-9

Brkfst/Hearth Rm
28-0x14-4

Great Rm
22-0x19-8

R

Desk | Stor | Bench | Stor

P

57'-6"

Laun

Br 2
13-4x14-5

L

Br 3
14-6x13-2

Entry

Covered porch

Patio

Dining
17-0x13-2

W
D

L

Garage
21-4x31-5

109'-0"

Lower Level
1,776 sq. ft.

Patio

Atrium
39-0x12-0

Up

Patio

Game Rm
23-0x14-4

Home Theater
22-0x24-0

Guest Rm
25-2x14-4

Lawn &
Garden
18-3x13-8

Mech & Storage

screen

L

Mech & Storage

Unexcavated

Great Room/Atrium
Interior View

Plan #529-0715
Price Code G

Total Living Area: 4,826 Sq. Ft.

Home has 4 bedrooms, 3 1/2 baths,
3-car side entry garage and walk-out
basement foundation.

Special features

- Brightly lit entry connects to great
  room with balcony and massive
  bay-shaped atrium

- Kitchen has island/snack bar, walk-
  in pantry, computer area and atrium
  overlook

- Master suite has sitting area, walk-in
  closets, atrium overlook and luxury
  bath with private courtyard

- Family room/atrium, home theater
  area with wet bar, game room and
  guest bedroom comprise the lower
  level

- Unique lawn and garden workroom
  located on lower level leads to the
  outdoors through double-doors

Massive Ranch With Luxurious Features

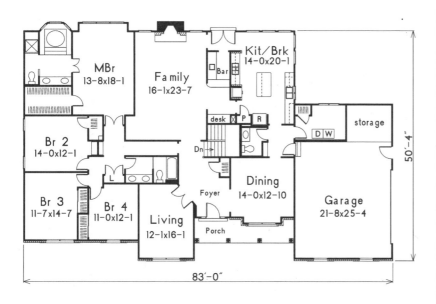

Plan #529-0151
Price Code E
Total Living Area: 2,874 Sq. Ft.

Home has 4 bedrooms, 2 1/2 baths, 2-car side entry garage and basement foundation.

Special features

- Large family room with sloped ceiling and wood beams adjoins the kitchen and breakfast area with windows on two walls

- Large foyer opens to family room with massive stone fireplace and open stairs to the basement

- Private master bedroom suite with raised tub under the bay window, dramatic dressing area and a huge walk-in closet

Plan #529-0703
Price Code D
Total Living Area: 2,412 Sq. Ft.

Home has 4 bedrooms, 2 baths, 3-car side entry garage and walk-out basement foundation.

Special features

- Coffered ceiling in dining room adds character and spaciousness
- Great room enhanced by vaulted ceiling and atrium window wall
- Spacious well-planned kitchen includes breakfast bar and overlooks breakfast room and beyond to deck
- Luxurious master suite features enormous walk-in closet, private bath and easy access to laundry area

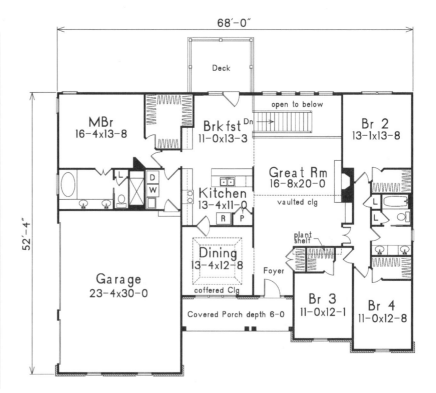

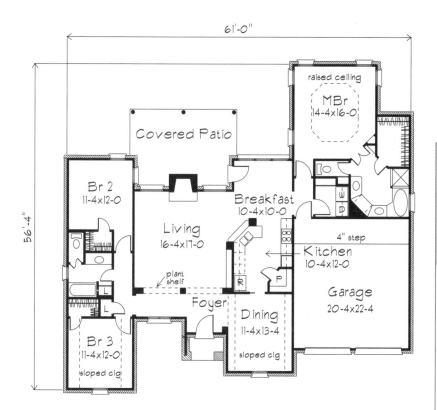

61'-0"

56'-4"

raised ceiling

MBr
14-4x16-0

Covered Patio

Br 2
11-4x12-0

Breakfast
10-4x10-0

Living
16-4x17-0

4" step

Kitchen
10-4x12-0

plant
shelf

Garage
20-4x22-4

Foyer

Dining
11-4x13-4

Br 3
11-4x12-0

sloped clg

sloped clg

Plan #529-0400
Price Code C
Total Living Area: 1,923 Sq. Ft.

Home has 3 bedrooms, 2 baths, 2-car garage and slab foundation.

Special features
- Foyer opens into spacious living room with fireplace and splendid view of covered porch
- Kitchen with walk-in pantry adjacent to laundry area and breakfast room
- All bedrooms feature walk-in closets
- Secluded master bedroom includes unique angled bath with spacious walk-in closet

Rear View

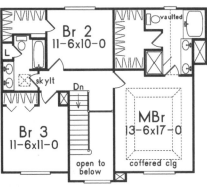

Second Floor
899 sq. ft.

Br 2
11-6x10-0

vaulted

skylt

Dn

Br 3
11-6x11-0

open to below

MBr
13-6x17-0

coffered clg

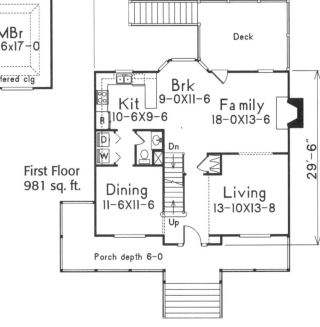

34'-0"

Deck

First Floor
981 sq. ft.

29'-6"

Brk
9-0X11-6

Kit
10-6X9-6

Family
18-0X13-6

Dn

Dining
11-6X11-6

Living
13-10X13-8

Up

Porch depth 6-0

Plan #529-0396
Price Code C

Total Living Area: 1,880 Sq. Ft.

Home has 3 bedrooms, 2 1/2 baths, 2-car drive under garage and basement foundation.

Special features

- Master suite enhanced with coffered ceiling
- Generous family and breakfast areas are modern and functional
- Front porch complements front facade

Plan #529-0705

Price Code E

Total Living Area: 2,758 Sq. Ft.

Home has 4 bedrooms, 2 1/2 baths, 3-car side entry garage and basement foundation.

Special features

- Vaulted great room excels with fireplace, wet bar, plant shelves and skylights
- Fabulous master suite enjoys a fireplace, large bath, walk-in closet and vaulted ceiling
- Trendsetting kitchen/breakfast room adjoins spacious screened porch
- Convenient office near kitchen is perfect for computer room, hobby enthusiast or fifth bedroom

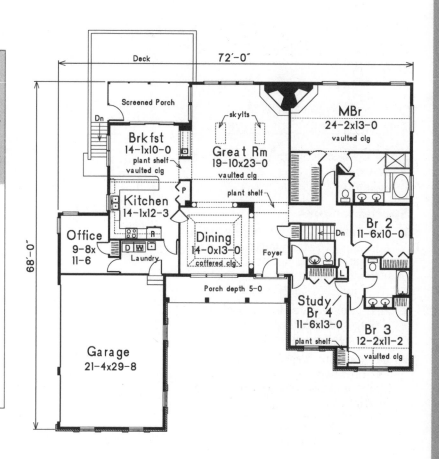

Timeless Elegance In A Five Bedroom Home

Plan #529-0738
Price Code G

Total Living Area: 4,281 Sq. Ft.

Home has 5 bedrooms, 4 1/2 baths, 3-car side entry garage and basement foundation.

Special features

- The classic foyer with marble tile enjoys a two-story vaulted ceiling, a dramatic second floor balcony and views through a 6' x 9' elliptical window
- First floor features large-sized living, dining and family rooms plus a convenient guest bedroom
- Second floor master bedroom suite includes two huge walk-in closets, sitting room with bay window and luxury bath

Second Floor
2,139 sq. ft.

Br 2
13-0x15-0

MBr
22-0x15-0
vaulted clg

Sitting

plant shelf

Br 5
13-7x12-0

open to below

Dn

Br 3
15-8x15-0

open to below
vaulted clg

Br 4
13-0x15-0

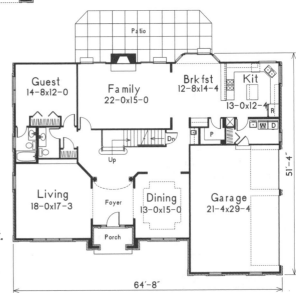

Patio

Guest
14-8x12-0

Family
22-0x15-0

Brk fst
12-8x14-4

Kit
13-0x12-4

Up

Dn

Living
18-0x17-3

Foyer

Dining
13-0x15-0

Garage
21-4x29-4

Porch

First Floor
2,142 sq. ft.

51'-4"

64'-8"

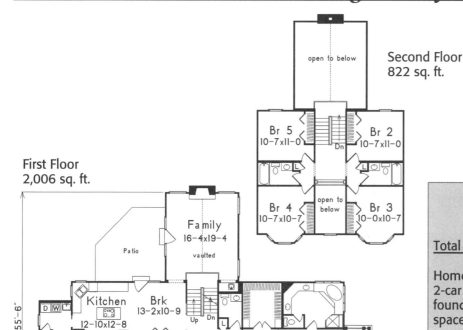

Second Floor
822 sq. ft.

open to below

Br 5
10-7x11-0

Br 2
10-7x11-0

Dn

Br 4
10-7x10-7

open to below

Br 3
10-0x10-7

First Floor
2,006 sq. ft.

Family
16-4x19-4
vaulted

Patio

Kitchen
12-10x12-8

D W

Brk
13-2x10-9

Up   Dn

R

P

Garage
20-4x21-10

Dining
12-2x13-0

Foyer

Study
13-5x13-0

MBr
15-0x16-11
vaulted

Porch depth 6-0

55'-6"

70'-6"

Plan #529-0417
Price Code E
Total Living Area: 2,828 Sq. Ft.

Home has 5 bedrooms, 3 1/2 baths, 2-car side entry garage and basement foundation, drawings also include crawl space and slab foundations.

Special features
- Popular wrap-around porch gives home country charm
- Secluded, oversized family room with vaulted ceiling and wet bar features many windows
- Any chef would be delighted to cook in this smartly designed kitchen with island and corner windows
- Spectacular master suite

Plan #529-0701

Price Code D

Total Living Area: 2,308 Sq. Ft.

Home has 3 bedrooms, 2 baths, 2-car side entry garage and walk-out basement foundation.

Special features

- Efficient kitchen designed with many cabinets and large walk-in pantry adjoins family/breakfast area featuring a beautiful fireplace

- Dining area has architectural colonnades that separate it from living area while maintaining spaciousness

- Enter master suite through double-doors and find double walk-in closets and beautiful luxurious bath

- Living room includes vaulted ceiling, fireplace and a sunny atrium window wall creating a dramatic atmosphere

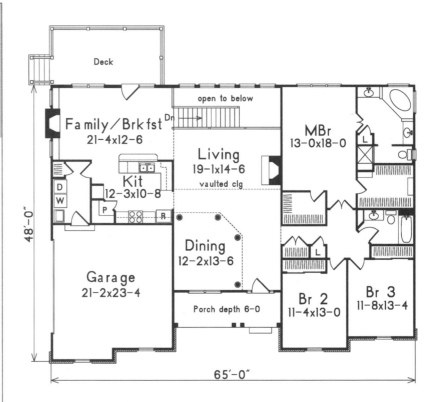

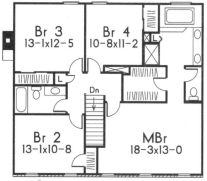

Br 3
13-1x12-5

Br 4
10-8x11-2

Dn

Br 2
13-1x10-8

MBr
18-3x13-0

Second Floor
1,140 sq. ft.

First Floor
1,188 sq. ft.

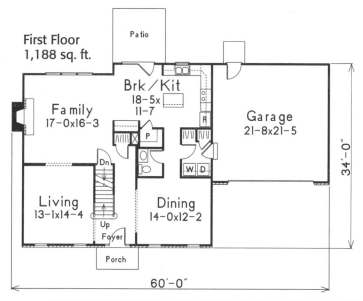

Patio

Family
17-0x16-3

Brk/Kit
18-5x
11-7

R

Garage
21-8x21-5

Dn
P

W D

34'-0"

Living
13-1x14-4

Dining
14-0x12-2

Up
Foyer

Porch

60'-0"

Plan #529-0223
Price Code D

Total Living Area: 2,328 Sq. Ft.

Home has 4 bedrooms, 2 1/2 baths, 2-car garage and basement foundation, drawings also include slab and crawl space foundations.

Special features

- Formal living and dining rooms feature floor-to-ceiling windows
- Kitchen with island counter and pantry makes cooking a delight
- Expansive master suite has luxury bath with double vanity and walk-in closet

Plan #529-0377

Price Code D

Total Living Area:	2,459 Sq. Ft.

Home has 4 bedrooms, 2 1/2 baths, 2-car garage and basement foundation.

Special features

- Open feeling kitchen with angled counter to enjoy views through family and breakfast rooms
- Secluded master suite includes dressing area, access to outdoors and private bath with tub and shower
- Stylish, open stairway overlooks two-story foyer
- Energy efficient home with 2" x 6" exterior walls

Second Floor
598 sq. ft.

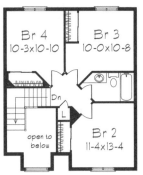

Br 4
10-3x10-10

Br 3
10-0x10-8

Dn

Br 2
11-4x13-4

open to below

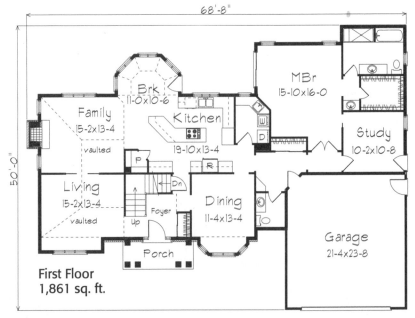

68'-8"

50'-0"

Brk
11-0x10-6

Family
15-2x13-4
vaulted

Kitchen
19-10x13-4

MBr
15-10x16-0

Study
10-2x10-8

Living
15-2x13-4
vaulted

Foyer
Up
Dn

Dining
11-4x13-4

Garage
21-4x23-8

Porch

First Floor
1,861 sq. ft.

Plan #529-0714
Price Code E

Total Living Area: 2,808 Sq. Ft.

Home has 3 bedrooms, 2 1/2 baths, 3-car side entry garage and basement foundation.

Special features

- An impressive front exterior show-cases three porches for quiet times
- Large living and dining rooms flank an elegant entry
- Bedroom #3 shares a porch with the living room and a spacious bath and dressing area with bedroom #2
- Vaulted master suite enjoys a secluded screened porch and sumptuous bath with corner tub, double vanities and huge walk-in closet
- Living room can easily convert to an optional fourth bedroom

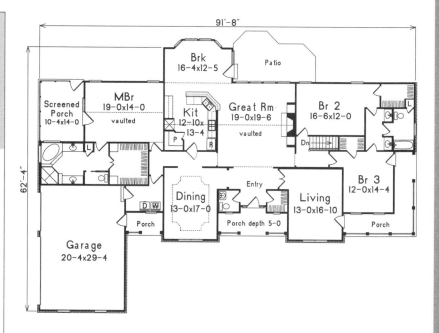

Plan #529-0342
Price Code C

Total Living Area: 2,089 Sq. Ft.

Home has 4 bedrooms, 3 baths, 2-car garage and slab foundation.

Special features

- Family room features fireplace, built-in bookshelves and triple sliders opening to covered patio
- Kitchen overlooks family room and features pantry and desk
- Separated from the three secondary bedrooms, the master bedroom becomes a quiet retreat with patio access
- Master suite features oversized bath with walk-in closet and corner tub

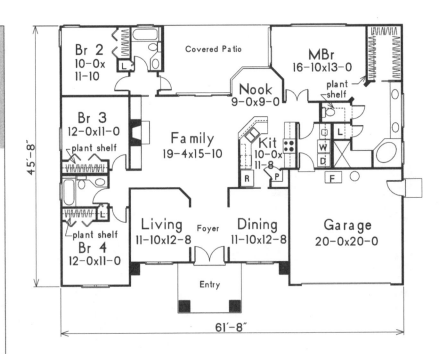

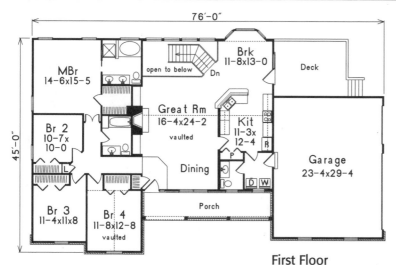

76'-0"

45'-0"

MBr
14-6x15-5

open to below

Brk
11-8x13-0

Dn

Deck

Great Rm
16-4x24-2
vaulted

Br 2
10-7x
10-0

Kit
11-3x
12-4

Dining

Garage
23-4x29-4

Br 3
11-4x11x8

Br 4
11-8x12-8
vaulted

Porch

D W

P

First Floor

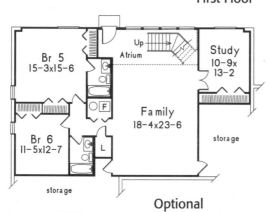

Br 5
15-3x15-6

Up
Atrium

Study
10-9x
13-2

F

Family
18-4x23-6

storage

Br 6
11-5x12-7

L

storage

Optional
Lower Level

Plan #529-0747
Price Code C

Total Living Area: 1,977 Sq. Ft.

Home has 4 bedrooms, 2 1/2 baths, 3-car side entry garage and walk-out basement foundation.

Special features

- Classic traditional exterior always in style
- Spacious great room boasts a vaulted ceiling, dining area, atrium with elegant staircase and feature windows
- Atrium open to 1,416 square feet of optional living area below which consists of an optional family room, two bedrooms, two baths and a study

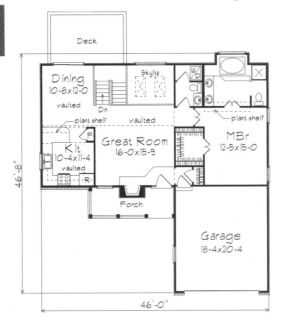

Deck

Dining
10-8x12-0
vaulted

Dn

Skylts

W/D

plant shelf   vaulted

P

Kit.
10-4x11-4
vaulted

Great Room
16-0x15-9

plant shelf

MBr
12-5x15-0

R

Porch

Garage
18-4x20-4

46'-8"

46'-0"

First Floor
996 sq. ft.

46'-0"

Br 3
9-9x10-4

Up

Atrium
9-6x1-1

Br 2
12-3x11-6

24'-4"

Family
16-0x15-5

Bar

L

Br 4
9-9x10-1

Storage
18-0x9-3

D W

Lower Level
945 sq. ft.

Plan #529-0420
Price Code C

<u>Total Living Area:</u>   1,941 Sq. Ft.

Home has 4 bedrooms, 2 1/2 baths, 2-car garage and walk-out basement foundation.

Special features

- Dramatic, exciting and spacious interior
- Vaulted great room brightened by sunken atrium window wall and skylights
- Vaulted U-shaped gourmet kitchen with plant shelf opens to dining room
- First floor half bath features space for stackable washer and dryer

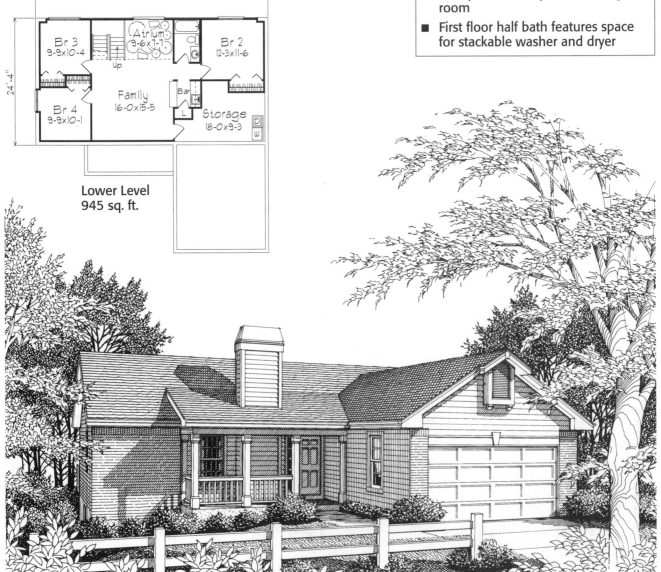

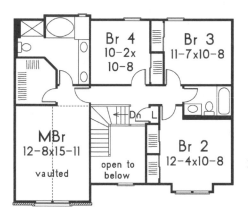

Br 4
10-2x
10-8

Br 3
11-7x10-8

MBr
12-8x15-11
vaulted

Dn
L

open to
below

Br 2
12-4x10-8

Second Floor
1,003 sq. ft.

Plan #529-0138
Price Code E

Total Living Area: 2,286 Sq. Ft.

Home has 4 bedrooms, 2 1/2 baths,
2-car garage and basement foundation,
drawings also include crawl space and
slab foundations.

Special features

- Fine architectural detail makes this
  home a showplace with its large
  windows, intricate brickwork and
  fine woodwork and trim

- Stunning two-story entry with
  attractive wood railing and balus-
  trades in foyer

- Convenient wrap-around kitchen
  with window view, planning center
  and pantry

- Oversized master suite with walk-in
  closet and master bath

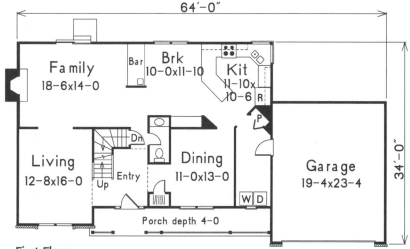

64'-0"

Family
18-6x14-0

Bar

Brk
10-0x11-10

Kit
11-10x
10-6
R

P

Living
12-8x16-0

Dn

Up   Entry

Dining
11-0x13-0

Garage
19-4x23-4

34'-0"

W D

Porch depth 4-0

First Floor
1,283 sq. ft.

Plan #529-0310
Price Code D
Total Living Area: 2,363 Sq. Ft.

Home has 3 bedrooms, 2 1/2 baths, 2-car garage and partial basement/crawl space foundation.

Special features
- Covered porches provide outdoor seating areas
- Corner fireplace becomes focal point of family room
- Kitchen features include island cooktop and adjoining nook
- Energy efficient home with 2" x 6" exterior walls

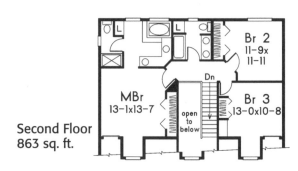

Second Floor
863 sq. ft.

Br 2
11-9x 11-11

MBr
13-1x13-7

open to below

Br 3
13-0x10-8

Dn

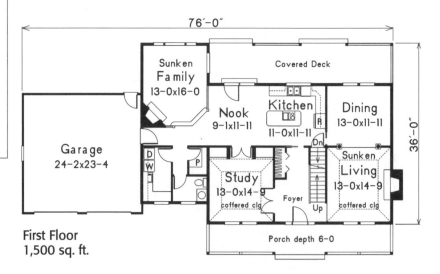

First Floor
1,500 sq. ft.

76'-0"

Sunken Family
13-0x16-0

Covered Deck

Kitchen

Nook
9-1x11-11

Dining
13-0x11-11

Garage
24-2x23-4

Study
13-0x14-9
coffered clg

Foyer

Sunken Living
13-0x14-9
coffered clg

36'-0"

Porch depth 6-0

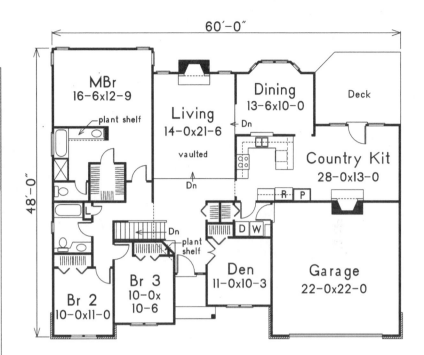

Plan #529-0279
Price Code D

Total Living Area: 1,993 Sq. Ft.

Home has 3 bedrooms, 2 baths, 2-car garage and basement foundation.

Special features

- Spacious country kitchen with fireplace and plenty of natural light from windows
- Formal dining room features large bay window and steps down to sunken living room
- Master suite features corner windows, plant shelves and deluxe private bath
- Entry opens into vaulted living room with windows flanking the fireplace

Signature SERIES

Fully Columned Front Entrance

Plan #529-0440

Price Code D

Total Living Area: 2,365 Sq. Ft.

Home has 4 bedrooms, 2 baths, 2-car carport and slab foundation.

Special features

- 9' ceilings on first floor
- Expansive central living room complemented by corner fireplace
- Breakfast bay overlooks rear porch
- Master bedroom features bath with double walk-in closets and vanities, separate tub and shower and handy linen closet
- Peninsula keeps kitchen private

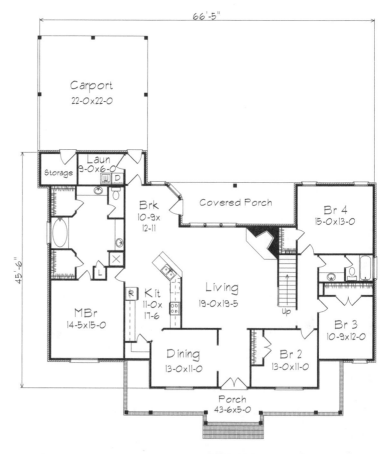

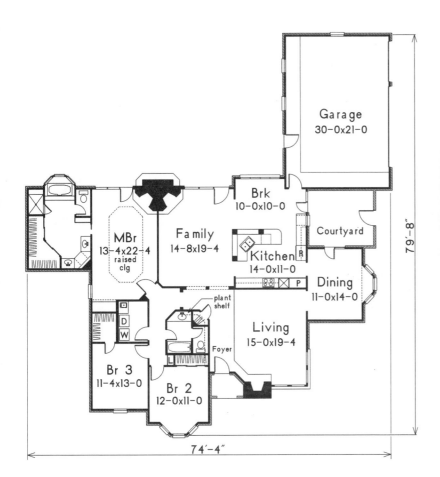

Garage
30-0x21-0

79'-8"

Brk
10-0x10-0

Courtyard

MBr
13-4x22-4
raised
clg

Family
14-8x19-4

Kitchen
14-0x11-0

Dining
11-0x14-0

plant
shelf

Living
15-0x19-4

Foyer

Br 3
11-4x13-0

Br 2
12-0x11-0

74'-4"

Plan #529-0315
Price Code D

Total Living Area: 2,481 Sq. Ft.

Home has 3 bedrooms, 2 baths, 3-car side entry garage and slab foundation.

Special features

- Varied ceiling heights throughout this home
- Master bedroom features built-in desk and pocket door entrance into large master bath
- Master bath includes corner vanity and garden tub
- Breakfast area accesses courtyard

Plan #529-0286

Price Code C

Total Living Area:	1,856 Sq. Ft.

Home has 3 bedrooms, 2 baths, 2-car side entry garage and slab foundation, drawings also include crawl space foundation.

Special features

- Living room features include fireplace, 12' ceiling and skylights
- Energy efficient home with 2" x 6" exterior walls
- Common vaulted ceiling creates open atmosphere in kitchen and eating areas
- Garage with storage areas conveniently accesses home through handy utility room
- Private hall separates secondary bedrooms from living areas

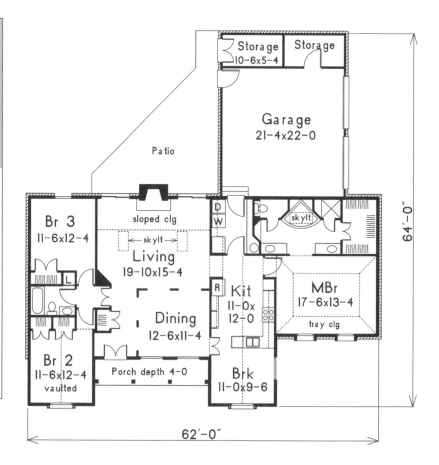

LOWE'S
Signature SERIES

44'-4"

Garage
21-4x25-4

65'-0"

Patio   skylt

Attic   Study   Attic

Br 2
10-0x
13-2

Dn

Br 3
10-8x
13-2

Second Floor
537 sq. ft.

Attic

Attic

open to
below

L D W

MBr
14-0x16-0

Dining
12-0x12-0

Kit
10-0x
12-0

R

Dn

Up

Family
14-0x18-0

First Floor
1,271 sq. ft.

Porch depth 8-0

Plan #529-0491
Price Code C

Total Living Area: 1,808 Sq. Ft.

Home has 3 bedrooms, 2 1/2 baths, 2-car side entry garage and basement foundation.

Special features

- Master bedroom has a walk-in closet, double vanities and separate tub and shower
- Two second floor bedrooms share a study area and full bath
- Partially covered patio is complete with a skylight
- Side entrance opens to utility room with convenient counterspace and laundry sink

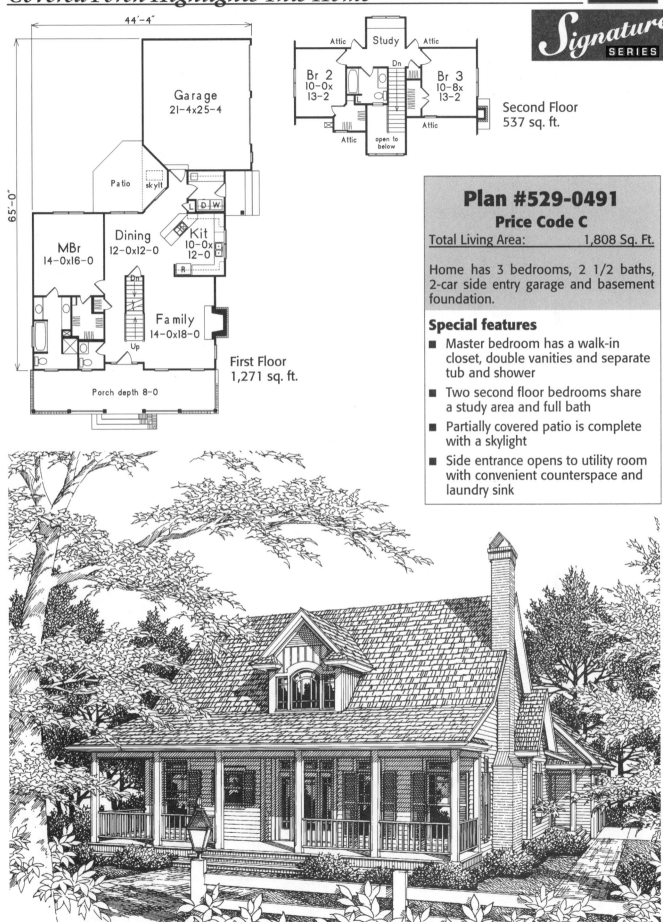

Signature SERIES

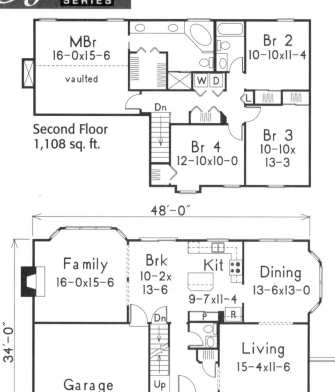

MBr
16-0x15-6
vaulted

Br 2
10-10x11-4

W D

L

Dn

Br 4
12-10x10-0

Br 3
10-10x 13-3

Second Floor
1,108 sq. ft.

48'-0"

34'-0"

Family
16-0x15-6

Brk
10-2x 13-6

Kit
9-7x11-4

Dining
13-6x13-0

Dn

P R

Living
15-4x11-6

Up

Garage
19-4x19-6

Porch depth 6-0

First Floor
1,027 sq. ft.

Plan #529-0322
Price Code D

Total Living Area: 2,135 Sq. Ft.

Home has 4 bedrooms, 2 1/2 baths, 2-car garage and basement foundation.

Special features

- Family room features extra space, impressive fireplace and full wall of windows that joins breakfast room creating spacious entertainment area

- Washer and dryer conveniently located on the second floor

- Kitchen features island counter and pantry

Plan #529-0185
Price Code D

Total Living Area: 2,396 Sq. Ft.

Home has 4 bedrooms, 2 baths, 2-car garage and slab foundation, drawings also include basement and crawl space foundations.

Special features

- Generously sized and wide open entry welcomes guests
- Central living area with a 12' ceiling and large fireplace serves as a convenient traffic hub
- Kitchen is secluded, yet has easy access to the living, dining and eating areas
- Deluxe master bedroom suite with walk-in closet, oversized tub, shower and other amenities
- Energy efficient home with 2" x 6" exterior walls

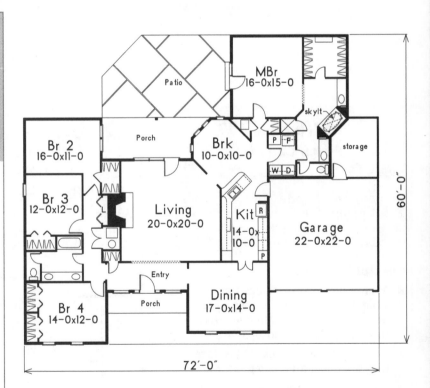

Plan #529-0257
Price Code C
Total Living Area: 1,862 Sq. Ft.

Home has 3 bedrooms, 2 baths, 2-car garage and slab foundation, drawings also include crawl space foundation.

Special features

- Master bedroom includes tray ceiling, bay window, access to patio and a private bath with oversized tub and generous closet space
- Corner sink and breakfast bar faces into breakfast area and great room
- Spacious great room features vaulted ceiling, fireplace and access to rear patio

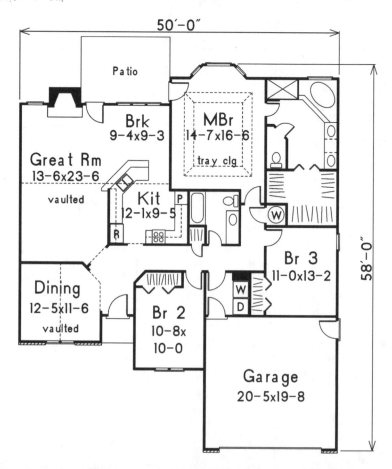

50'-0"

58'-0"

Patio

Brk
9-4x9-3

MBr
14-7x16-6
tray clg

Great Rm
13-6x23-6
vaulted

Kit
12-1x9-5

Dining
12-5x11-6
vaulted

Br 2
10-8x
10-0

Br 3
11-0x13-2

Garage
20-5x19-8

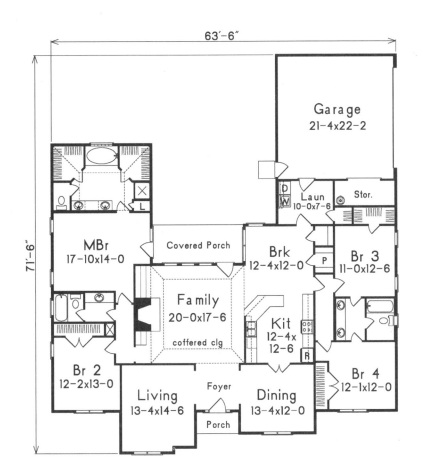

63'-6"

71'-6"

Garage
21-4x22-2

Laun
10-0x7-6

Stor.

D
W

MBr
17-10x14-0

Covered Porch

Brk
12-4x12-0

Br 3
11-0x12-6

P

Family
20-0x17-6

coffered clg

Kit
12-4x
12-6

R

Br 2
12-2x13-0

Living
13-4x14-6

Foyer

Dining
13-4x12-0

Br 4
12-1x12-0

Porch

Plan #529-0438
Price Code D
Total Living Area: 2,558 Sq. Ft.

Home has 4 bedrooms, 3 baths, 2-car side entry garage and slab foundation, drawings also include crawl space foundation.

Special features
- 9' ceilings throughout home
- Angled counter in kitchen serves breakfast and family rooms
- Entry foyer flanked by formal living and dining rooms
- Extra storage space in garage

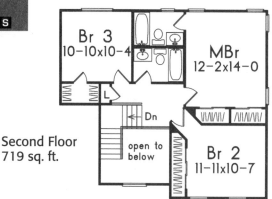

Br 3
10-10x10-4

MBr
12-2x14-0

Second Floor
719 sq. ft.

Dn

open to below

Br 2
11-11x10-7

L

Plan #529-0383
Price Code C
Total Living Area: 1,813 Sq. Ft.

Home has 3 bedrooms, 2 1/2 baths, 2-car garage and basement foundation.

Special features
- Bedrooms located on second floor for privacy
- Living room with large bay window joins dining room for expansive formal entertaining
- Great family area created by family room, dinette and kitchen
- Two-story foyer and L-shaped stairs create an impressive entry
- Inviting covered porch

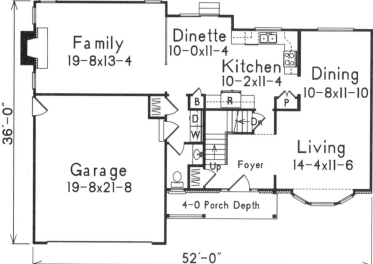

Family
19-8x13-4

Dinette
10-0x11-4

Kitchen
10-2x11-4

Dining
10-8x11-10

Living
14-4x11-6

Garage
19-8x21-8

Foyer

Up

B
D
W
R
P
Dn

36'-0"

52'-0"

4-0 Porch Depth

First Floor
1,094 sq. ft.

Charming Design Features Home Office

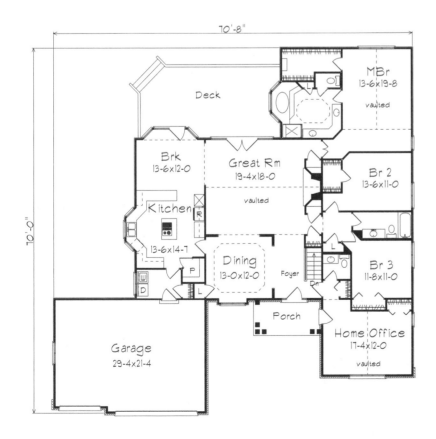

70'-8"

70'-0"

Deck

MBr
13-6x19-8
vaulted

Brk
13-6x12-0

Great Rm
19-4x18-0
vaulted

Br 2
13-6x11-0

Kitchen

13-6x14-7

Dining
13-0x12-0

Foyer

Br 3
11-8x11-0

Garage
29-4x21-4

Porch

Home Office
17-4x12-0
vaulted

Plan #529-0368
Price Code D

__Total Living Area:__ 2,452 Sq. Ft.

Home has 4 bedrooms, 2 1/2 baths, 3-car garage and basement foundation.

Special features

- Cheery and spacious home office room has private entrance and bath, two closets, vaulted ceiling and transomed window perfect shown as a home office or a fourth bedroom

- Delightful great room with vaulted ceiling, fireplace, extra storage closets and patio doors to sundeck

- Extra-large kitchen features walk-in pantry, cooktop island and bay window

- Vaulted master suite includes transomed windows, walk-in closet and luxurious bath

MBr
19-4x13-0
Vaulted

Br 2
14-0x11-0

Second Floor
1,070 sq. ft.

Br 3
12-9x12-0
Vaulted

First Floor
1,112 sq. ft.

Great Rm
19-4x15-0

Breakfast
11-8x13-0

Kit
12-0x14-6

Entry

Up   Dn

Porch Depth 7-8

Dining
15-0x12-0

Garage
21-4x21-10

48'-8"

57'-0"

Plan #529-0413
Price Code C

Total Living Area: 2,182 Sq. Ft.

Home has 3 bedrooms, 3 1/2 baths, 2-car side entry garage and basement foundation.

Special features

- Meandering porch creates inviting look
- Generous great room has four double-hung windows and gliding doors to exterior
- Highly functional kitchen features island/breakfast bar, menu-desk and convenient pantry
- Each secondary bedroom includes generous closet and private bath

Spacious Room Around A Central Foyer

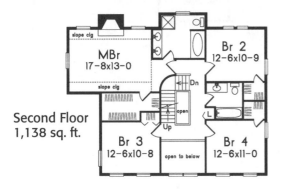

Second Floor 1,138 sq. ft.

MBr
17-8x13-0

Br 2
12-6x10-9

Br 3
12-6x10-8

Br 4
12-6x11-0

open to below

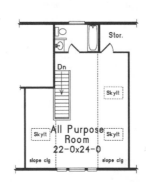

Third Floor 575 sq. ft.

Stor.

Dn

Skylt

Skylt

Skylt

All Purpose Room
22-0x24-0

slope clg

slope clg

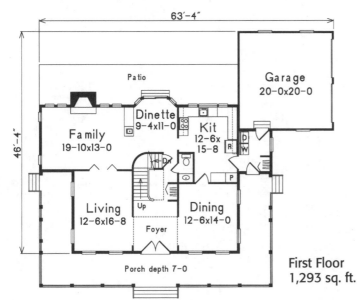

63'-4"

46'-4"

Patio

Garage
20-0x20-0

Dinette
9-4x11-0

Kit
12-6x
15-8

Family
19-10x13-0

Living
12-6x16-8

Dining
12-6x14-0

Foyer

Up

Porch depth 7-0

First Floor 1,293 sq. ft.

Plan #529-0677
Price Code E

Total Living Area: 3,006 Sq. Ft.

Home has 4 bedrooms, 3 1/2 baths, 2-car side entry garage and basement foundation, drawings also include slab foundation.

Special features

- Energy efficient home with 2" x 6" exterior walls
- Large all purpose room and bath on third floor
- Efficient U-shaped kitchen includes a pantry and adjacent planning desk

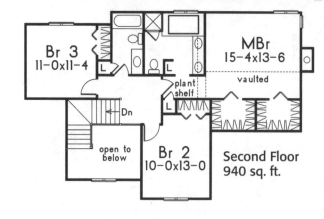

Br 3
11-0x11-4

MBr
15-4x13-6
vaulted

plant shelf

Dn

open to below

Br 2
10-0x13-0

Second Floor
940 sq. ft.

Plan #529-0349
Price Code D

Total Living Area: 2,204 Sq. Ft.

Home has 3 bedrooms, 2 1/2 baths,
2-car garage and basement foundation.

Special features

■ First floor den offers the flexibility of
an office, study or fourth bedroom

■ Large island kitchen with breakfast
bar next to family room provides
open living space

■ Second floor balcony overlooks
entry below

■ Master bedroom features his and
her walk-in closets, private bath
with step-up tub and double-bowl
vanity

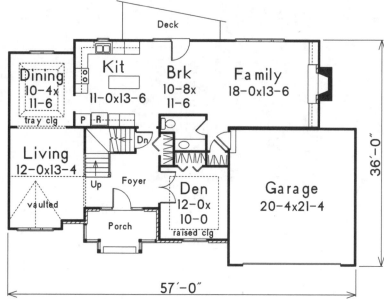

Deck

Dining
10-4x
11-6
tray clg

Kit
11-0x13-6

Brk
10-8x
11-6

Family
18-0x13-6

Living
12-0x13-4
vaulted

Up

Foyer

Dn

Den
12-0x
10-0
raised clg

Garage
20-4x21-4

Porch

36'-0"

57'-0"

First Floor
1,264 sq. ft.

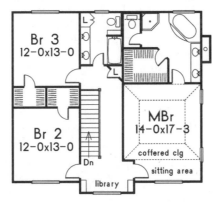

Br 3
12-0x13-0

Br 2
12-0x13-0

MBr
14-0x17-3

coffered clg

sitting area

library

Dn

Second Floor
1,050 sq. ft.

Plan #529-0722
Price Code D

Total Living Area: 2,266 Sq. Ft.

Home has 3 bedrooms, 3 baths, 2-car side entry garage and basement foundation, drawings also include crawl space foundation.

Special features

- Great room includes fireplace flanked by built-in bookshelves and dining nook with bay window

- Unique media room includes double-door entrance, walk-in closet and access to full bath

- Master suite has lovely sitting area, walk-in closets and a private bath with step-up tub and double vanity

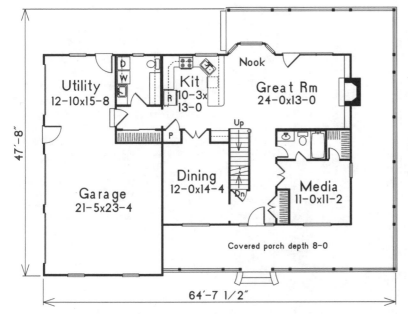

Utility
12-10x15-8

Kit
10-3x
13-0

Nook

Great Rm
24-0x13-0

Up

Dining
12-0x14-4

Dn

Media
11-0x11-2

Garage
21-5x23-4

Covered porch depth 8-0

47'-8"

64'-7 1/2"

First Floor
1,216 sq. ft.

LOWE'S

Signature SERIES

Second Floor
1,204 sq. ft.

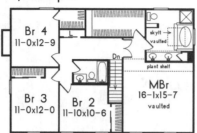

Br 4
11-0x12-9

skylt
vaulted

plant shelf

MBr
16-1x15-7
vaulted

Br 3
11-0x12-0

Br 2
11-10x10-6

Dn

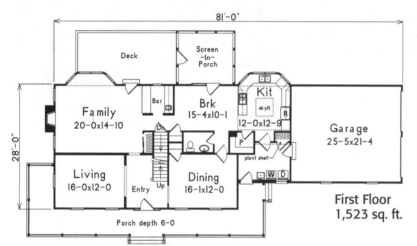

81'-0"

Deck

Screen
-In-
Porch

28'-0"

Family
20-0x14-10

Bar

Brk
15-4x10-1

Kit
skylt
12-0x12-9

Garage
25-5x21-4

Living
16-0x12-0

Entry   Up

Dining
16-1x12-0

plant shelf

W D

Porch depth 6-0

First Floor
1,523 sq. ft.

Plan #529-0749
Price Code E

Total Living Area: 2,727 Sq. Ft.

Home has 4 bedrooms, 2 1/2 baths, 2-car garage and walk-out basement foundation.

Special features

- Wrap-around porch and large foyer create impressive entranceL

- A state-of-the-art vaulted kitchen has walk-in pantry and is open to the breakfast room and adjoining screened porch

- A walk-in wet bar, fireplace bay window and deck access are features of the family room

- Vaulted master bedroom suite enjoys a luxurious bath with skylight and an enormous 13' deep walk-in closet

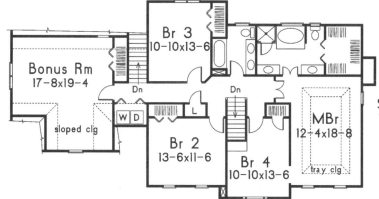

Br 3
10-10x13-6

Bonus Rm
17-8x19-4

Dn

Dn

sloped clg

W D   L

Br 2
13-6x11-6

Br 4
10-10x13-6

MBr
12-4x18-8

tray clg

Second Floor
1,565 sq. ft.

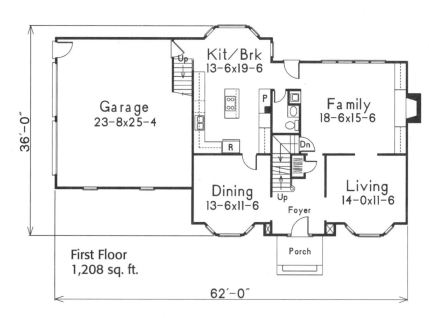

Up

Kit/Brk
13-6x19-6

Garage
23-8x25-4

P

Family
18-6x15-6

R

Dn

36'-0"

Dining
13-6x11-6

Up

Foyer

Living
14-0x11-6

Porch

First Floor
1,208 sq. ft.

62'-0"

Plan #529-0139
Price Code F

<u>Total Living Area:</u>   2,773 Sq. Ft.

Home has 4 bedrooms, 2 1/2 baths, 2-car side entry garage and basement foundation.

Special features

■ Extensive use of bay and other large windows front and rear adds brightness and space

■ Master bedroom suite features double-door entrance, oversized walk-in closet and coffered ceiling

■ Rear stairway leads to bonus room, laundry and the second floor

Signature SERIES

Plan #529-0728

Price Code E

Total Living Area: 2,967 Sq. Ft.

Home has 4 bedrooms, 3 1/2 baths, 3-car side entry garage and basement foundation.

Special features

- An exterior with charm graced with country porch and multiple arched projected box windows

- Dining area is oversized and adjoins a fully equipped kitchen with walk-in pantry

- Two bay windows light up the enormous informal living area to the rear

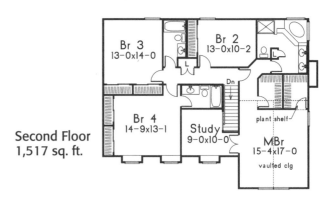

Second Floor
1,517 sq. ft.

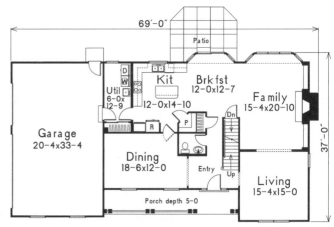

First Floor
1,450 sq. ft.

LOWE'S

Signature SERIES

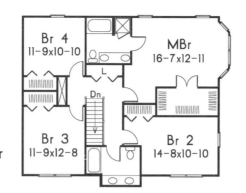

Second Floor
1,174 sq. ft.

Br 4
11-9x10-10

MBr
16-7x12-11

Dn

L

Br 3
11-9x12-8

Br 2
14-8x10-10

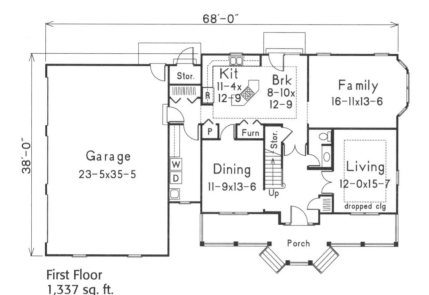

68'-0"

38'-0"

Garage
23-5x35-5

Stor.

R

Kit
11-4x
12-9

Brk
8-10x
12-9

Family
16-11x13-6

P

Furn

Stor.

W
D

Dining
11-9x13-6

Up

Living
12-0x15-7

dropped clg

Porch

First Floor
1,337 sq. ft.

Plan #529-0528
Price Code D
Total Living Area: 2,511 Sq. Ft.

Home has 4 bedrooms, 2 1/2 baths, 3-car side entry garage and basement foundation, drawings also include crawl space and slab foundations.

Special features

- Both kitchen/breakfast area and living room feature tray ceilings
- Various architectural elements combine to create impressive exterior
- Master bedroom includes large walk-in closet, oversized bay window and private bath with shower and tub
- Large utility room with convenient workspace

Handsome Traditional With Gabled Entrance

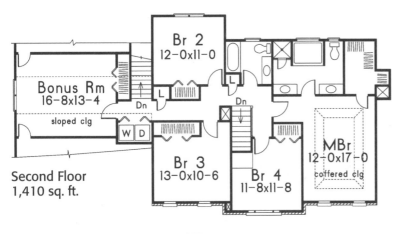

Bonus Rm
16–8x13–4

sloped clg

Br 2
12–0x11–0

Dn

W D

Br 3
13–0x10–6

Br 4
11–8x11–8

Dn

MBr
12–0x17–0
coffered clg

Second Floor
1,410 sq. ft.

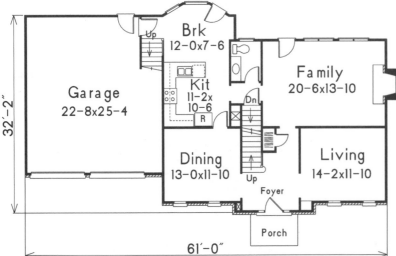

Garage
22–8x25–4

Brk
12–0x7–6

Up

Kit
11–2x
10–6

R

Family
20–6x13–10

Dn

Dining
13–0x11–10

Living
14–2x11–10

Up

Foyer

Porch

32'–2"

61'–0"

First Floor
1,119 sq. ft.

Plan #529-0135
Price Code E

Total Living Area: 2,529 Sq. Ft.

Home has 4 bedrooms, 2 1/2 baths,
2-car garage and basement foundation.

Special features

- Distinguished appearance enhances this home's classic interior arrangement
- Bonus room over the garage has convenient attic access
- Garden tub, walk-in closet and coffered ceiling enhance the master bedroom suite

Casual Exterior, Filled With Great Features

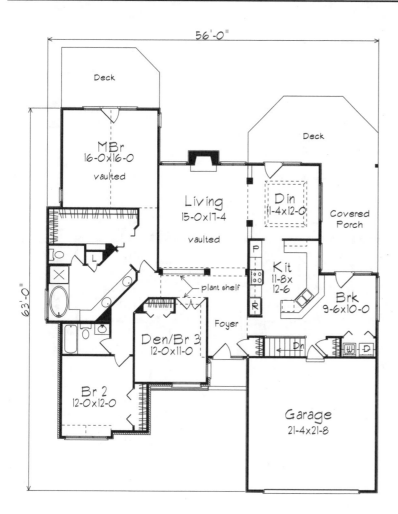

Plan #529-0387
Price Code C
Total Living Area: 1,958 Sq. Ft.

Home has 3 bedrooms, 2 baths, 2-car garage and basement foundation.

Special features

■ Large wrap-around kitchen opens to a bright cheerful breakfast area with access to large covered deck and open stairway to basement

■ Kitchen nestled between the dining and breakfast rooms

■ Master suite includes large walk-in closet, double-bowl vanity, garden tub and separate shower

■ Foyer features attractive plant shelves and opens into living room that includes attractive central fireplace

LOWE'S

Signature SERIES

Plan #529-0338
Price Code E

Total Living Area: 2,397 Sq. Ft.

Home has 3 bedrooms, 2 1/2 baths, 2-car garage and slab foundation.

Special features

- Porch entrance into foyer leads to an impressive dining area with full window and a half-circle window above

- Kitchen/breakfast room features a center island and cathedral ceiling

- Great room with cathedral ceiling and exposed beams accessible from foyer

- Master bedroom includes full bath and walk-in closet

- Two additional bedrooms share a full bath

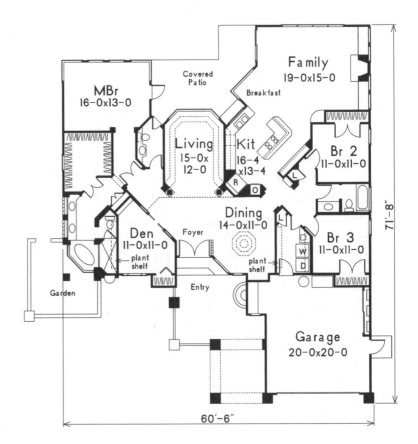

Stylish Features Enhance Open Living

Plan #529-0215
Price Code C

Total Living Area: 1,846 Sq. Ft.

Home has 3 bedrooms, 2 baths, 2-car garage and slab foundation.

Special features

- Enormous living area combines with dining and breakfast rooms complemented by extensive windows and high ceilings
- Master bedroom has walk-in closet, display niche and deluxe bath
- Secondary bedrooms share a bath and feature large closet space and a corner window
- Oversized two-car garage has plenty of storage and work space with handy access to the kitchen through the utility area
- Breakfast nook has wrap-around windows adding to eating enjoyment

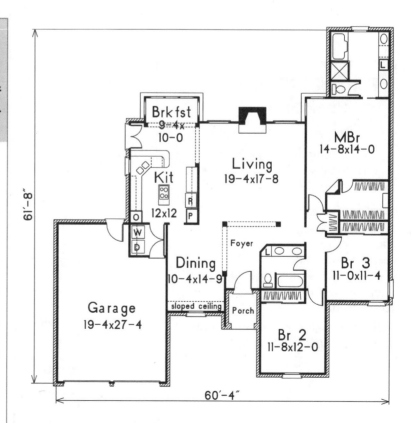

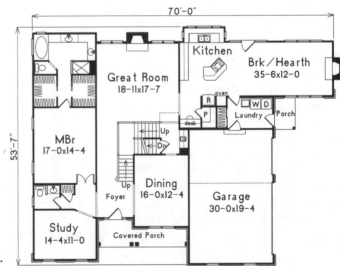

Second Floor
947 sq. ft.

open to below

Br 2
15-9x11-0

L

Br 3
15-3x11-1

Dn

Br 4
16-0x12-4

open to below

Plan #529-0772
Price Code F

Total Living Area: 3,223 Sq. Ft.

Home has 4 bedrooms, 3 1/2 baths, 3-car side entry garage and basement foundation.

Special features

- Traditionally designed home features covered front entry and covered side entry

- Master suite boasts two large walk-in closets and luxury bath with easy access to study

- Kitchen, breakfast and hearth rooms combine for main gathering area

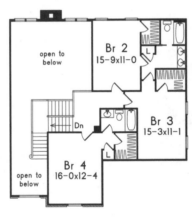

70'-0"

Kitchen

Brk/Hearth
35-6x12-0

Great Room
18-11x17-7

oven

R

P

W D

Laundry

Porch

desk

53'-7"

MBr
17-0x14-4

Up

Dn

Up

Foyer

Dining
16-0x12-4

Garage
30-0x19-4

Study
14-4x11-0

Covered Porch

First Floor
2,276 sq. ft.

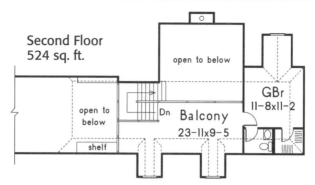

Second Floor
524 sq. ft.

open to below

GBr
11-8x11-2

open to below

Dn

Balcony
23-11x9-5

shelf

Plan #529-0235
Price Code D

Total Living Area: 2,501 Sq. Ft.

Home has 4 bedrooms, 2 1/2 baths, 2-car side entry garage and basement foundation, drawings also include crawl space and slab foundations.

Special features

- Oversized kitchen with work island, vaulted ceiling and plant shelves
- Open staircase overlooks kitchen
- Secluded second floor guest bedroom features private half bath
- Covered deck accessible from dining room and kitchen
- Kitchen complete with pantry, angled bar and adjacent eating area

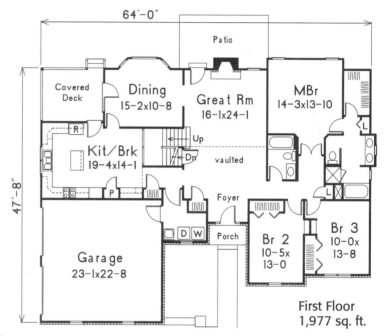

64'-0"

Patio

Covered Deck

Dining
15-2x10-8

Great Rm
16-1x24-1

MBr
14-3x13-10

Kit/Brk
19-4x14-1

Up

Dn

vaulted

P

Foyer

47'-8"

Garage
23-1x22-8

D W

Porch

Br 2
10-5x13-0

Br 3
10-0x13-8

First Floor
1,977 sq. ft.

LOWE'S
Signature SERIES

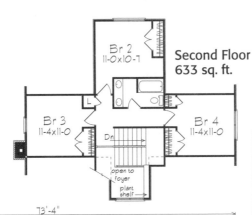

Second Floor
633 sq. ft.

Br 2
11-0x10-7

Br 3
11-4x11-0

Dn

open to foyer

plant shelf

Br 4
11-4x11-0

Plan #529-0362
Price Code C

Total Living Area: 1,874 Sq. Ft.

Home has 4 bedrooms, 2 1/2 baths, 2-car garage and basement foundation, drawings also include slab foundation.

Special features

- 9' ceilings throughout first floor
- Two-story foyer opens into large family room with fireplace
- First floor master suite includes private bath with tub and shower

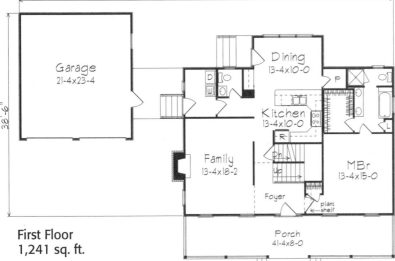

73'-4"

38'-6"

Garage
21-4x23-4

Dining
13-4x10-0

Kitchen
13-4x10-0

Family
13-4x18-2

Dn
Up

MBr
13-4x15-0

Foyer

plant shelf

Porch
41-4x8-0

First Floor
1,241 sq. ft.

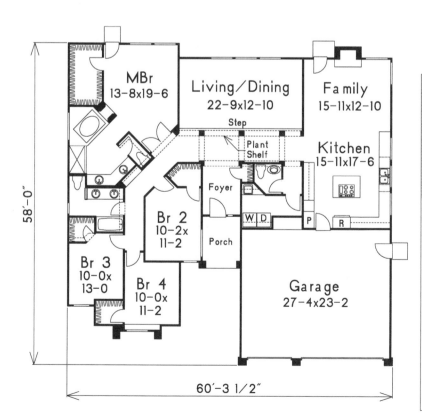

Plan #529-0443
Price Code D
Total Living Area: 2,255 Sq. Ft.

Home has 4 bedrooms, 2 1/2 baths, 3-car garage and slab foundation.

Special features
- Walk-in closets in all bedrooms
- Plant shelf graces hallway
- Large functional kitchen adjoins family room with fireplace and access outdoors
- Master bath comes complete with double vanity, enclosed toilet, separate tub and shower and a cozy fireplace
- Living/dining rooms combine for large formal gathering room

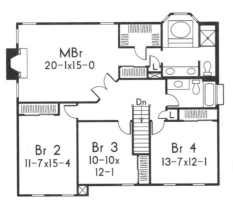

MBr
20-1x15-0

Br 2
11-7x15-4

Br 3
10-10x
12-1

Br 4
13-7x12-1

Dn

Second Floor
1,320 sq. ft.

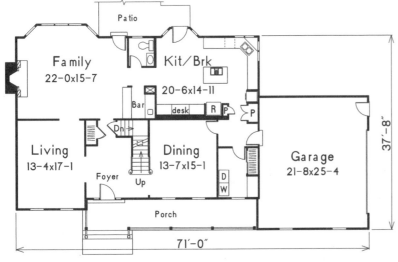

Patio

Family
22-0x15-7

Kit/Brk
20-6x14-11

Bar

desk

Living
13-4x17-1

Dn

Dining
13-7x15-1

Garage
21-8x25-4

Foyer

Up

D
W

Porch

37'-8"

71'-0"

First Floor
1,615 sq. ft.

Plan #529-0152
Price Code E

Total Living Area: 2,935 Sq. Ft.

Home has 4 bedrooms, 2 1/2 baths, 2-car side entry garage and basement foundation.

Special features

■ Gracious entry foyer with handsome stairway opens to separate living and dining rooms

■ Kitchen with vaulted ceiling and skylight, island worktop, breakfast area with bay window and two separate pantries

■ Large second floor master bedroom suite with fireplace, raised tub, dressing area with vaulted ceiling and skylight

Country Comfort

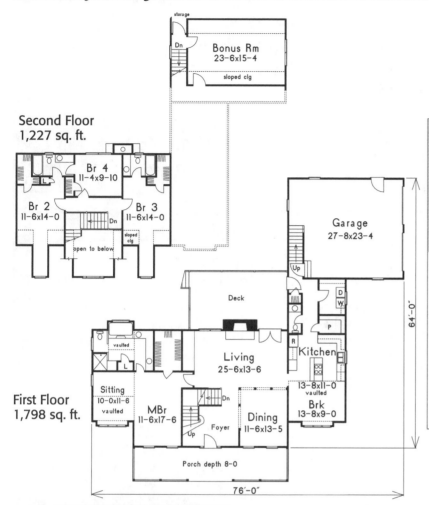

Second Floor
1,227 sq. ft.

storage

Dn

Bonus Rm
23-6x15-4

sloped clg

Br 4
11-4x9-10

Br 2
11-6x14-0

Br 3
11-6x14-0

Dn

sloped clg

open to below

First Floor
1,798 sq. ft.

Garage
27-8x23-4

Up

Deck

D W

P

R

vaulted

L

Living
25-6x13-6

Kitchen

Sitting
10-0x11-6
vaulted

MBr
11-6x17-6

Dn

Up

Foyer

Dining
11-6x13-5

13-8x11-0
vaulted

Brk
13-8x9-0

Porch depth 8-0

64'-0"

76'-0"

Plan #529-0600
Price Code E

Total Living Area: 3,025 Sq. Ft.

Home has 4 bedrooms, 3 1/2 baths, 2-car side entry garage, 1-car drive under garage and basement foundation.

Special features

- Bonus room above garage has its own private entrance - great for home office, hobby or exercise room

- Master suite has generous walk-in closet, luxurious bath and a vaulted sitting area

- Spacious kitchen has an island cooktop and vaulted breakfast nook

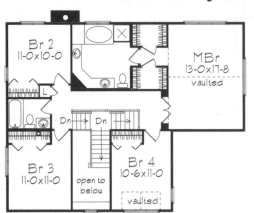

Second Floor
1,045 sq. ft.

Br 2
11-0x10-0

MBr
13-0x17-8
vaulted

Dn   Dn

Br 3
11-0x11-0

open to
below

Br 4
10-6x11-0

vaulted

First Floor
1,291 sq. ft.

Family
20-2x16-8

Brk
10-0x16-8

Kitchen
10-8x11-6

R

W D

P

42'-0"

Dn

Up

Living
11-0x14-8
Sunken

Entry

Dining
10-6x13-3

Garage
19-4x21-4

Up

vaulted

Porch
17-4x5-0

49'-0"

Plan #529-0365
Price Code D
__Total Living Area:__ 2,336 Sq. Ft.

Home has 4 bedrooms, 2 1/2 baths,
2-car garage and basement foundation.

Special features
- Stately sunken living room with partially vaulted ceiling and classic arched transom windows
- Family room features plenty of windows and fireplace with flanking bookshelves

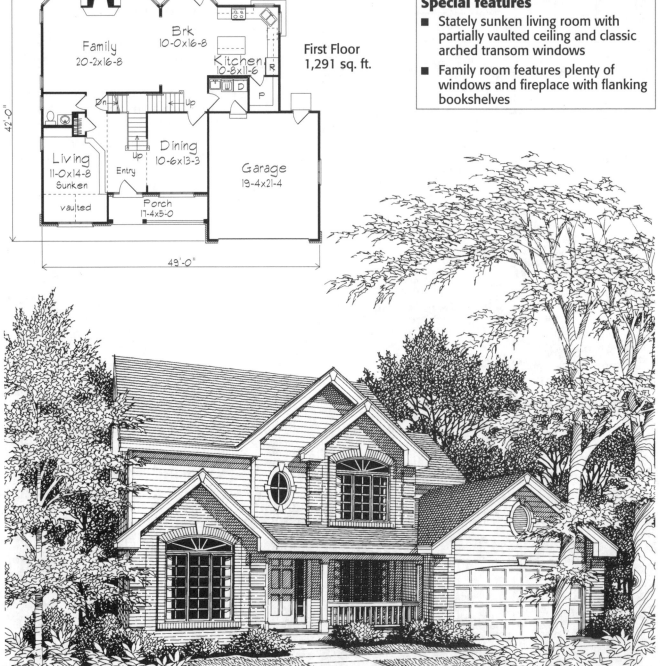

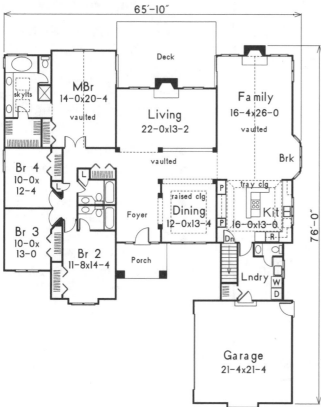

Plan #529-0278

Price Code E

Total Living Area: 2,847 Sq. Ft.

Home has 4 bedrooms, 3 1/2 baths, 2-car side entry garage and basement foundation.

Special features

- Master suite includes skylighted bath, deck access and double closets
- Bedroom #2 converts to guest room with private bath
- Impressive foyer and gallery opens into large living room with fireplace
- Formal dining and living rooms, casual family and breakfast rooms
- Kitchen features desk area, center island, adjacent bayed breakfast area and access to laundry room with half bath

Double Bay Enhances Front Entry

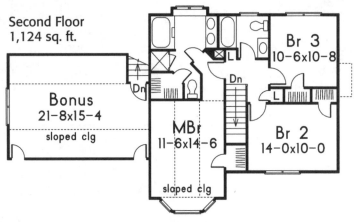

Second Floor
1,124 sq. ft.

Bonus
21-8x15-4
sloped clg

Br 3
10-6x10-8

Dn

L

Dn

MBr
11-6x14-6

Br 2
14-0x10-0

L

sloped clg

Plan #529-0113
Price Code C
Total Living Area: 1,992 Sq. Ft.

Home has 3 bedrooms, 2 1/2 baths, 2-car garage and crawl space foundation, drawings also include basement foundation.

Special features

- Distinct living, dining and breakfast areas
- Master bedroom boasts full end bay window and a cathedral ceiling
- Storage and laundry area located adjacent to the garage
- Bonus room over the garage for future office or playroom

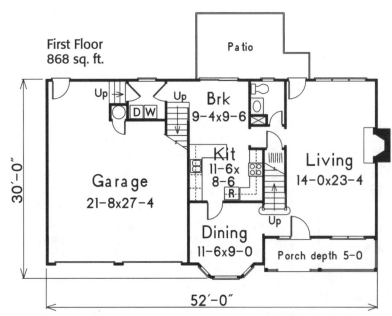

First Floor
868 sq. ft.

Patio

Up

Up

D W

Brk
9-4x9-6

Garage
21-8x27-4

Kit
11-6x
8-6

R

Living
14-0x23-4

Up

30'-0"

Dining
11-6x9-0

Porch depth 5-0

52'-0"

Second Floor
621 sq. ft.

Br 3
12–8x12–6

Br 4
13–6x12–6

tray clg

Dn

First Floor
2,669 sq. ft.

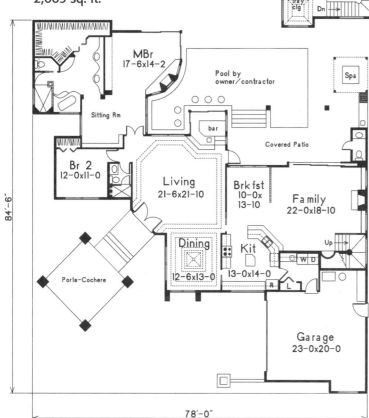

MBr
17–6x14–2

Pool by
owner/contractor

Spa

Sitting Rm

bar

Covered Patio

Br 2
12–0x11–0

Living
21–6x21–10

Brk fst
10–0x
13–10

Family
22–0x18–10

Dining
12–6x13–0

Kit
13–0x14–0

W D

R L

Up

Porte-Cochere

Garage
23–0x20–0

84'–6"

78'–0"

Plan #529-0341
Price Code F

Total Living Area: 3,290 Sq. Ft.

Home has 4 bedrooms, 3 1/2 baths, 2-car side entry garage and slab foundation.

Special features

- Patio area surrounds pool with swim-up bar and spa

- Formal dining room features dramatic drop down ceiling and easy access to kitchen

- Fireplace provides focal point in master suite which includes sitting room and elegant master bath

- Observation room and two bed-rooms with adjoining bath on second floor

- Varied ceiling heights throughout

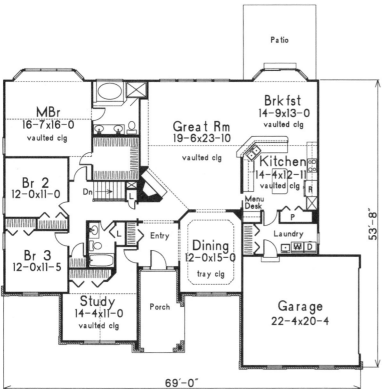

MBr
16-7x16-0
vaulted clg

Great Rm
19-6x23-10

Brkfst
14-9x13-0
vaulted clg

vaulted clg

Br 2
12-0x11-0

Kitchen
14-4x12-11
vaulted clg

Dn

L

Menu
Desk

R

P

Entry

Dining
12-0x15-0
tray clg

Laundry

W D

Br 3
12-0x11-5

L

Study
14-4x11-0
vaulted clg

Porch

Garage
22-4x20-4

Patio

53'-8"

69'-0"

Plan #529-0719
Price Code D

Total Living Area: 2,483 Sq. Ft.

Home has 3 bedrooms, 2 baths, 2-car side entry garage and basement foundation.

Special features

- A large entry porch with open brick arches and palladian door welcomes guests

- The vaulted great room features an entertainment center alcove and ideal layout for furniture placement

- Dining room is extra large with a stylish tray ceiling

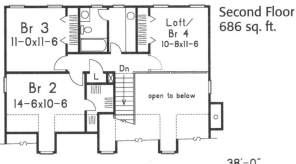

Second Floor
686 sq. ft.

Br 3
11-0x11-6

Loft/
Br 4
10-8x11-6

Dn

L

Br 2
14-6x10-6

open to below

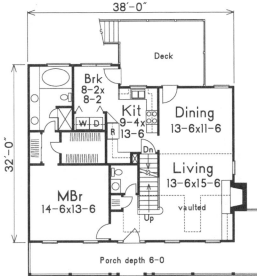

38'-0"

Deck

Brk
8-2x
8-2

Kit
9-4x
13-6

Dining
13-6x11-6

W D

R

Dn

32'-0"

Living
13-6x15-6

MBr
14-6x13-6

vaulted

Up

First Floor
1,132 sq. ft.

Porch depth 6-0

Plan #529-0598
Price Code C
<u>Total Living Area:</u> 1,818 Sq. Ft.

Home has 4 bedrooms, 2 1/2 baths, 2-car drive under garage and basement foundation.

Special features
- Breakfast room is tucked behind the kitchen and has laundry closet and deck access
- Living/dining area combination share vaulted ceiling and fireplace
- Master bedroom has two closets, large double-bowl vanity and separate tub and shower
- Large front porch wraps around home

LOWE'S
Signature SERIES

Plan #529-0307
Price Code E

Total Living Area: 3,153 Sq. Ft.

Home has 4 bedrooms, 3 1/2 baths, 2-car drive under garage and basement foundation, drawings also include crawl space and slab foundations.

Special features
- Master suite with full amenities
- Energy efficient design with 2" x 6" exterior walls
- Covered breezeway and front and rear porches
- Full-sized workshop and storage with garage below, a unique combination

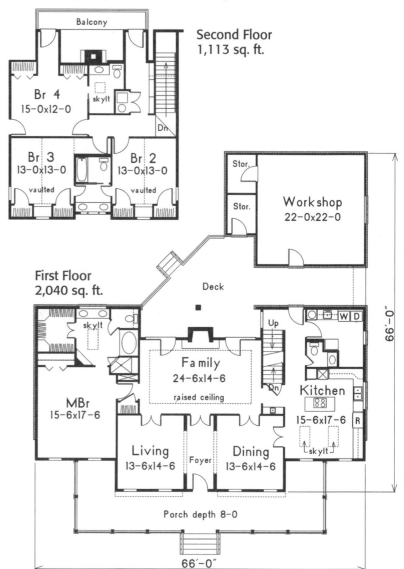

Second Floor 1,113 sq. ft.

Balcony

Br 4
15-0x12-0

skylt

Br 3
13-0x13-0
vaulted

Br 2
13-0x13-0
vaulted

Dn

Stor.

Stor.

Workshop
22-0x22-0

First Floor 2,040 sq. ft.

Deck

skylt

W D

Family
24-6x14-6
raised ceiling

Up

Dn

Kitchen
15-6x17-6

skylt

MBr
15-6x17-6

Living
13-6x14-6

Foyer

Dining
13-6x14-6

R

Porch depth 8-0

66'-0"

66'-0"

LOWE'S

Signature SERIES

URNIER INC. HAO

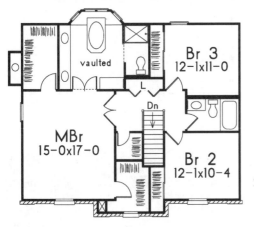

Br 3
12-1x11-0

vaulted

Dn

MBr
15-0x17-0

Br 2
12-1x10-4

Second Floor
1,046 sq. ft.

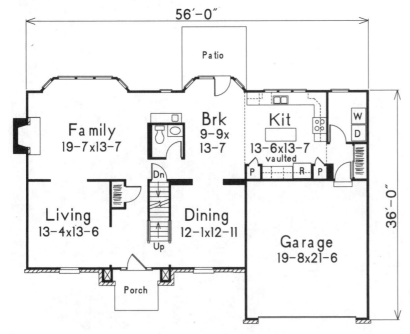

56'-0"

Patio

Family
19-7x13-7

Brk
9-9x
13-7

Kit
13-6x13-7
vaulted

W
D

Dn

P   R   P

Living
13-4x13-6

Dining
12-1x12-11

Up

Garage
19-8x21-6

36'-0"

Porch

First Floor
1,355 sq. ft.

Plan #529-0169
Price Code D

Total Living Area: 2,401 Sq. Ft.

Home has 3 bedrooms, 2 1/2 baths, 2-car garage and basement foundation, drawings also include slab and crawl space foundations.

Special features

- Striking front facade with handsome main entry and brick quoins
- Master bedroom has two walk-in closets, dressing rooms, elegant double-door entry and deluxe bath
- Full bay windows located on both floors create a great view from the rear of this home
- Spacious kitchen features a studio ceiling, double pantry, a large work island and planning center

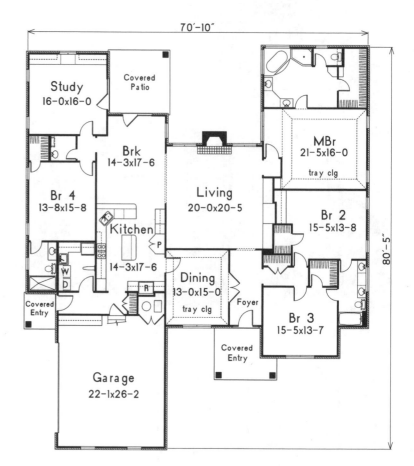

Plan #529-0803
Price Code F

Total Living Area: 3,366 Sq. Ft.

Home has 4 bedrooms, 3 1/2 baths, 2-car side entry garage and crawl space foundation, drawings also include slab foundation.

Special features

- Wonderful covered patio off secluded study and breakfast area
- Separate dining area for entertaining
- Spacious master suite has enormous private bath with walk-in closet

Signature SERIES

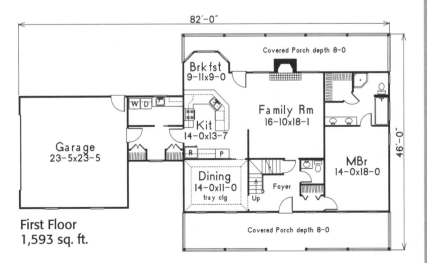

Second Floor
951 sq. ft.

Rec Rm
16-10x24-5

Br 2
14-0x16-5

Br 3
14-0x11-1

sloped clg   Dn

Plan #529-0801
Price Code D

Total Living Area: 2,544 Sq. Ft.

Home has 3 bedrooms, 2 1/2 baths, 2-car side entry garage and basement foundation, drawings also include crawl space and slab foundations.

Special features

- Central family room becomes gathering place
- Second floor family room is a great game room for children
- First floor master suite secluded from main living areas

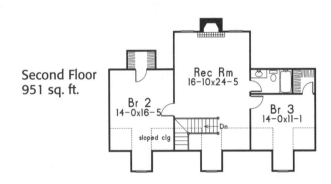

82'-0"

Covered Porch depth 8-0

Brk fst
9-11x9-0

W D

Family Rm
16-10x18-1

Kit
14-0x13-7

Garage
23-5x23-5

R   P

46'-0"

Dining
14-0x11-0
tray clg

Up   Foyer

MBr
14-0x18-0

First Floor
1,593 sq. ft.

Covered Porch depth 8-0

Plan #529-0735
Price Code F

| Total Living Area: | 3,657 Sq. Ft. |

Home has 4 bedrooms, 3 1/2 baths, 3-car side entry garage and basement foundation.

Special features

- Dramatic two-story foyer has a stylish niche, a convenient powder room and French doors leading to parlor

- State-of-the-art kitchen includes a large walk-in pantry, breakfast island, computer center and 40' vista through family room with walk-in wet bar

- Vaulted master bath features marble steps and Roman columns that lead to a majestic-sized whirlpool tub with marble deck surround and grandscale palladian window

- A jack and jill bath, hall bath, loft area and huge bedrooms comprise the second floor

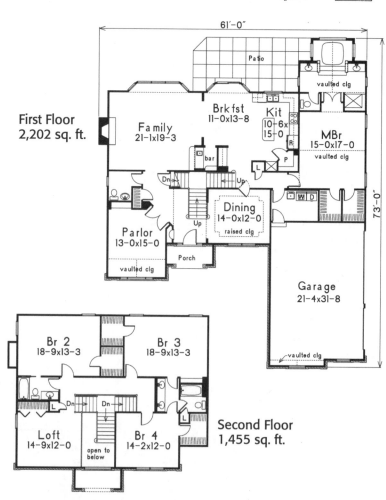

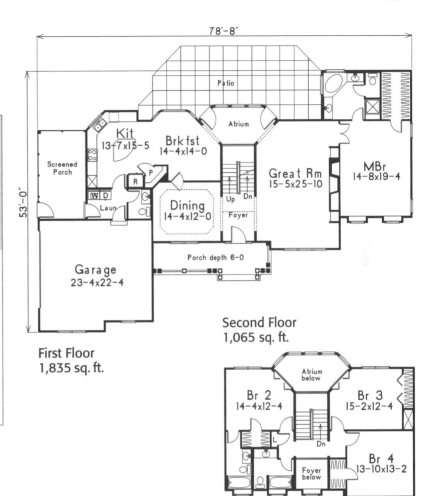

78'-8"

53'-0"

Patio

Kit
13-7x15-5

Brk fst
14-4x14-0

Atrium

Screened
Porch

Great Rm
15-5x25-10

MBr
14-8x19-4

P
R

W D

Laun

Dining
14-4x12-0

Up Dn

Foyer

Garage
23-4x22-4

Porch depth 6-0

First Floor
1,835 sq. ft.

Second Floor
1,065 sq. ft.

Atrium
below

Br 2
14-4x12-4

Br 3
15-2x12-4

L

Dn

Foyer
below

Br 4
13-10x13-2

Plan #529-0736
Price Code E
Total Living Area: 2,900 Sq. Ft.

Home has 4 bedrooms, 3 1/2 baths, 2-car side entry garage and basement foundation.

Special features

■ Elegant entry foyer leads to balcony overlook of vaulted two-story atrium

■ Spacious kitchen features an island breakfast bar, walk-in pantry, bayed breakfast room and adjoining screened porch

■ Two large second floor bedrooms and stair balconies overlook a sun drenched two-story vaulted atrium

Signature SERIES

Plan #529-0797

Price Code E

Total Living Area: 2,651 Sq. Ft.

Home has 3 bedrooms, 2 baths, 2-car side entry garage and basement foundation, drawings also include crawl space and slab foundations.

Special features

- Vaulted family room is open, yet cozy
- Masterfully designed kitchen and breakfast room
- Separated bedrooms provide plenty of privacy
- Master suite includes two walk-in closets for added storage

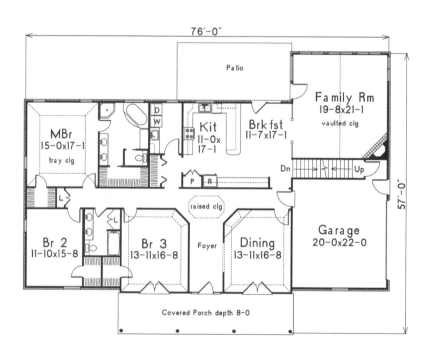

Great Media Room

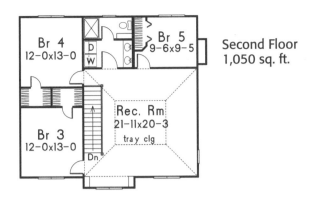

Br 4
12-0x13-0

Br 5
9-6x9-5

Second Floor
1,050 sq. ft.

Br 3
12-0x13-0

Rec. Rm
21-11x20-3
tray clg

Dn.

First Floor
1,700 sq. ft.

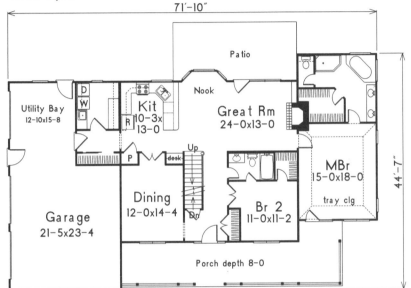

71'-10"

Patio

Utility Bay
12-10x15-8

Kit
10-3x 13-0

Nook

Great Rm
24-0x13-0

Dining
12-0x14-4

Up
desk

MBr
15-0x18-0
tray clg

Garage
21-5x23-4

Br 2
11-0x11-2

Dn

44'-7"

Porch depth 8-0

Plan #529-0805
Price Code E

Total Living Area: 2,750 Sq. Ft.

Home has 5 bedrooms, 3 1/2 baths, 2-car side entry garage and basement foundation, drawings also include crawl space and slab foundations.

Special features

- Oversized rooms throughout
- 9' ceiling on first floor
- Unique utility bay workshop off garage
- Spacious master suite with luxurious bath
- Optional sixth bedroom plan also included

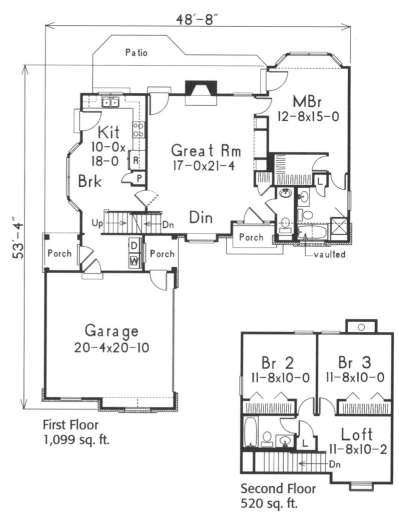

Plan #529-0482
Price Code B
<u>Total Living Area:</u>   1,619 Sq. Ft.

Home has 3 bedrooms, 2 1/2 baths, 2-car side entry garage and basement foundation.

Special features

- Elegant home features three quaint porches and a large rear patio
- Grandscale great room offers dining area, fireplace and built-in alcove and shelves, a natural entertainment center
- First floor master bedroom suite has walk-in closet, luxury bath, bay window and access to rear patio
- Breakfast room with bay window contains stairs that lead to second floor bedrooms and loft

First Floor
1,099 sq. ft.

Second Floor
520 sq. ft.

Signature SERIES

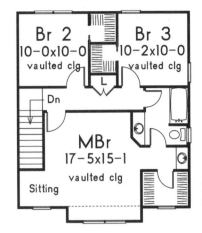

Br 2
10-0x10-0
vaulted clg

Br 3
10-2x10-0
vaulted clg

Dn

L

MBr
17-5x15-1
vaulted clg

Sitting

Second Floor
667 sq. ft.

Plan #529-0795
Price Code A
Total Living Area: 1,399 Sq. Ft.

Home has 3 bedrooms, 1 1/2 baths, 1-car garage and basement foundation, drawings also include crawl space or slab foundations.

Special features
- Living room overlooks dining area through arched columns
- Laundry room contains handy half bath
- Spacious master bedroom includes sitting area, walk-in closet and plenty of sunlight

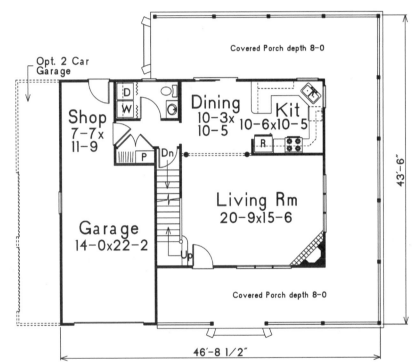

Covered Porch depth 8-0

Opt. 2 Car Garage

D
W

Shop
7-7x
11-9

P

Dn

Dining
10-3x
10-5

Kit
10-6x10-5

R

Living Rm
20-9x15-6

Garage
14-0x22-2

Up

Covered Porch depth 8-0

First Floor
732 sq. ft.

43'-6"

46'-8 1/2"

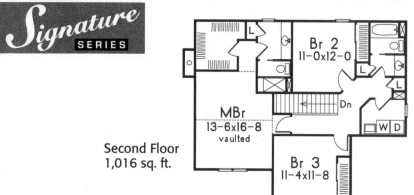

Second Floor
1,016 sq. ft.

MBr
13-6x16-8
vaulted

Br 2
11-0x12-0

Dn

W D

Br 3
11-4x11-8

Plan #529-0488
Price Code C
Total Living Area: 2,059 Sq. Ft.

Home has 3 bedrooms, 2 1/2 baths, 2-car garage and walk-out basement foundation.

Special features

- Large desk and pantry add to the breakfast room
- Laundry is located on second floor near bedrooms
- Vaulted ceiling in master suite
- Mud room is conveniently located near garage

Family
13-6x15-8

Brk
11-0x12-0

Kit
11-0x
12-0

R

Up

P

Dn

Entry

Dining
13-6x11-6

Garage
21-4x23-4

Porch depth 7-0

45'-8"

50'-0"

First Floor
1,043 sq. ft.

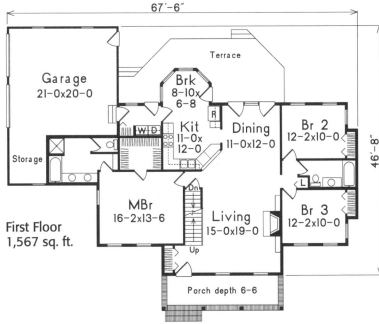

First Floor
1,567 sq. ft.

67'-6"

46'-8"

Garage
21-0x20-0

Storage

Terrace

Brk
8-10x
6-8

Kit
11-0x
12-0

W D

Dining
11-0x12-0

Br 2
12-2x10-0

MBr
16-2x13-6

Living
15-0x19-0

Br 3
12-2x10-0

Dn

Up

Porch depth 6-6

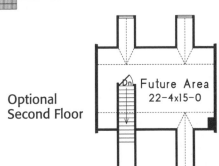

Optional
Second Floor

Future Area
22-4x15-0

Dn

Plan #529-0678
Price Code B

Total Living Area: 1,567 Sq. Ft.

Home has 3 bedrooms, 2 baths,
2-car side entry garage and basement
foundation, drawings also include slab
foundation.

Special features

- Living room flows into dining room
  shaped by an angled pass-through
  into the kitchen

- Cheerful, windowed dining area

- 338 square feet of optional living
  area is available on the second floor

- Master suite separated from other
  bedrooms for privacy

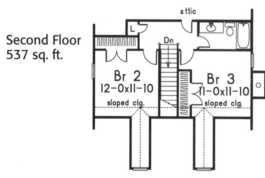

Second Floor
537 sq. ft.

attic

Br 2
12-0x11-10
sloped clg.

Br 3
11-0x11-10
sloped clg.

Dn

L

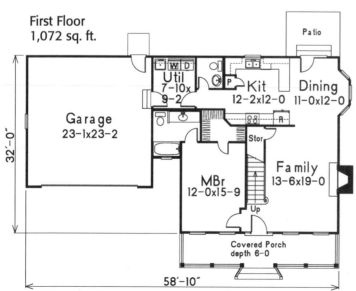

First Floor
1,072 sq. ft.

32'-0"

58'-10"

Patio

Util
7-10x
9-2

W D

P

Kit
12-2x12-0

Dining
11-0x12-0

Garage
23-1x23-2

Stor

MBr
12-0x15-9

Family
13-6x19-0

Up

Covered Porch
depth 6-0

Plan #529-0686
Price Code B

Total Living Area: 1,609 Sq. Ft.

Home has 3 bedrooms, 2 1/2 baths,
2-car garage and slab foundation.

Special features

- Kitchen captures full use of space with pantry, ample cabinets and workspace
- Master bedroom is well-secluded with walk-in closet and private bath
- Large utility room includes sink and extra storage
- Attractive bay window in dining area provides light

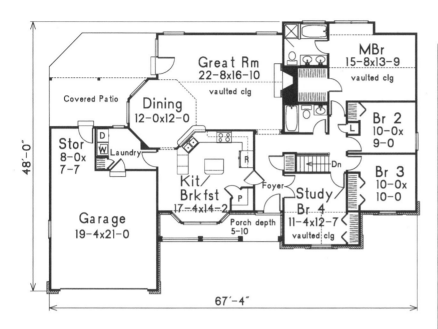

Great Rm
22-8x16-10
vaulted clg

MBr
15-8x13-9
vaulted clg

Covered Patio

Dining
12-0x12-0

Br 2
10-0x
9-0

Stor
8-0x
7-7

D
W Laundry

48'-0"

**Kit/
Brkfst**
17-4x14-2

P

Foyer

Dn

Br 3
10-0x
10-0

**Study
Br 4**
11-4x12-7
vaulted clg

Garage
19-4x21-0

Porch depth
5-10

67'-4"

Plan #529-0706
Price Code B

Total Living Area: 1,791 Sq. Ft.

Home has 4 bedrooms, 2 baths, 2-car garage and basement foundation.

Special features

- Vaulted great room and octagon-shaped dining area enjoy views of covered patio
- Kitchen features a pass-through to dining area, center island, large walk-in pantry and breakfast room with large bay window
- Master bedroom is vaulted with sitting area
- Extra storage in garage

LOWE'S

Signature **SERIES**

KURT KAUSS
OVIEDO-FLA.

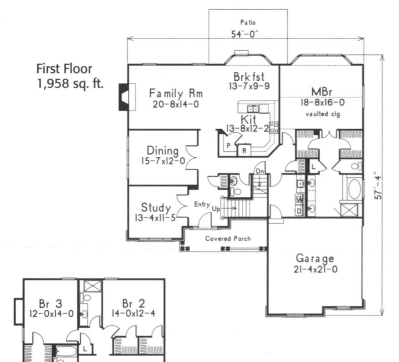

Patio

54'-0"

First Floor
1,958 sq. ft.

Family Rm
20-8x14-0

Brkfst
13-7x9-9

MBr
18-8x16-0
vaulted clg

Kit
13-8x12-2

Dining
15-7x12-0

P R

Dn

Study
13-4x11-5

Entry Up

57'-4"

Covered Porch

Garage
21-4x21-0

Br 3
12-0x14-0

Br 2
14-0x12-4

L

Playroom/
Loft
19-5x18-9

Dn

Br 4
12-0x14-3

Second Floor
1,180 sq. ft.

Plan #529-0720
Price Code E

Total Living Area: 3,138 Sq. Ft.

Home has 4 bedrooms, 3 1/2 baths, 2-car side entry garage and basement foundation.

Special features

- Impressive stair descends into large entry and study through double-doors

- Private dining is spacious and secluded

- Family room, master suite and laundry are among the many generously-sized rooms

- Three large bedrooms, two baths and four walk-in closets compose the second floor

LOWE'S

Signature SERIES

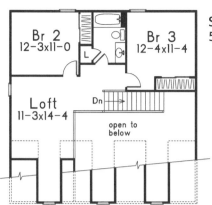

Second Floor
565 sq. ft.

Br 2
12-3x11-0

Br 3
12-4x11-4

Loft
11-3x14-4

Dn

open to below

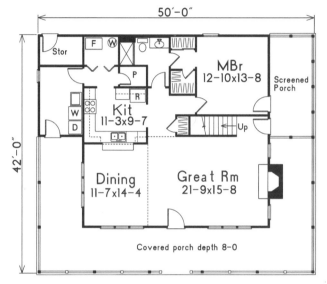

50'-0"

42'-0"

Stor

F W

MBr
12-10x13-8

Screened Porch

P

R

Kit
11-3x9-7

W
D

Up

Dining
11-7x14-4

Great Rm
21-9x15-8

Covered porch depth 8-0

First Floor
1,314 sq. ft.

Plan #529-0768
Price Code C
Total Living Area: 1,879 Sq. Ft.

Home has 3 bedrooms, 2 baths and crawl space foundation.

Special features

■ Open floor plan on both floors makes home appear larger

■ Loft area overlooks great room or can become an optional fourth bedroom

■ Large walk-in pantry in kitchen and large storage in rear of home with access from exterior

Plan #529-0751
Price Code A

Total Living Area: 1,278 Sq. Ft.

Home has 3 bedrooms, 1 bath, 2-car garage and walk-out basement foundation.

Special features

- Excellent U-shaped kitchen with garden window opens to an enormous great room with vaulted ceiling, fireplace and two skylights

- Vaulted master bedroom offers double entry doors, access to a deck and bath and two walk-in closets

- The bath has a double-bowl vanity and dramatic step-up garden tub with a lean-to greenhouse window

- 805 square feet of optional living area on lower level with family room, bedroom #4 and bath

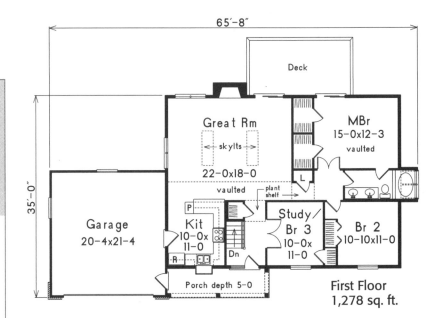

65'-8"

Deck

Great Rm
skylts
22-0x18-0
vaulted

MBr
15-0x12-3
vaulted

35'-0"

Garage
20-4x21-4

P

Kit
10-0x
11-0

plant shelf

Study/
Br 3
10-0x
11-0

Br 2
10-10x11-0

Dn

R

Porch depth 5-0

First Floor
1,278 sq. ft.

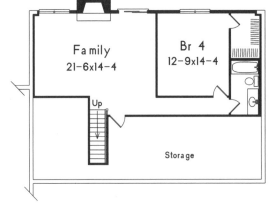

Family
21-6x14-4

Br 4
12-9x14-4

Up

Storage

Optional
Lower Level

Floridian Architecture With Mother-In-Law Suite

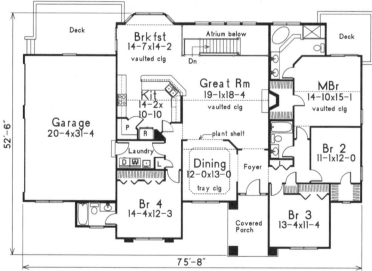

Deck

Brkfst
14-7x14-2
vaulted clg

Atrium below

Dn

Deck

Great Rm
19-1x18-4
vaulted clg

Kit
14-2x
10-10

MBr
14-10x15-1
vaulted clg

P

R

plant shelf

Garage
20-4x31-4

Br 2
11-1x12-0

Laundry

D W L

Dining
12-0x13-0
tray clg

Foyer

52'-6"

Br 4
14-4x12-3

Br 3
13-4x11-4

Covered Porch

75'-8"

First Floor
2,408 sq. ft.

Atrium
Up

Sitting
12-5x10-6

Family Rm
19-1x24-10

Wet Bar

Office/ Br 5
14-1x17-6

**Optional
Lower Level**

Unfinished Area

Plan #529-0730
Price Code D
Total Living Area: 2,408 Sq. Ft.

Home has 4 bedrooms, 3 baths, 3-car side entry garage and walk-out basement foundation.

Special features

- Large vaulted great room overlooks atrium and window wall, adjoins dining room, spacious breakfast room with bay and pass-through kitchen

- A special private bedroom with bath, separate from other bedrooms, is perfect for mother-in-law suite or children home from college

- Atrium open to 1,100 square feet of optional living area below

Rear View

Optional Lower Level

Br 6
14-9x15-2

Up
Atrium

Family Rm
18-7x24-5

Br 5
12-4x15-2

Up

Wet Bar

F

Unfinished Area

Plan #529-0729
Price Code D
Total Living Area: 2,218 Sq. Ft.

Home has 4 bedrooms, 2 baths, 2-car garage and walk-out basement foundation.

Special features

- Vaulted great room has arched colonade entry, bay windowed atrium with staircase and a fireplace
- Vaulted kitchen enjoys bay doors to deck, pass-through breakfast bar and walk-in pantry
- Breakfast room offers bay window and snack bar open to kitchen with laundry nearby
- Atrium open to 1,217 square feet of optional living area below

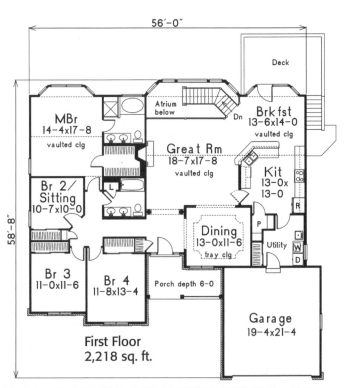

56'-0"

Deck

MBr
14-4x17-8
vaulted clg

Atrium below

Dn

Brkfst
13-6x14-0
vaulted clg

Great Rm
18-7x17-8
vaulted clg

Kit
13-0x
13-0

Br 2/ Sitting
10-7x10-0

L

Dining
13-0x11-6
tray clg

P

Utility

W
D

R

58'-8"

Br 3
11-0x11-6

Br 4
11-8x13-4

Porch depth 6-0

Garage
19-4x21-4

First Floor
2,218 sq. ft.

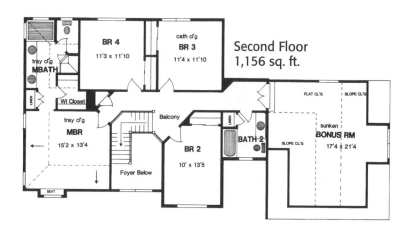

Second Floor
1,156 sq. ft.

BR 4
11'3 x 11'10

cath cl'g
BR 3
11'4 x 11'10

tray cl'g
MBATH

WI Closet

tray cl'g
MBR
15'2 x 13'4

Balcony

BR 2
10' x 13'5

BATH 2

FLAT CL'G

SLOPE CL'G

SLOPE CL'G

sunken
BONUS RM
17'4 x 21'4

Foyer Below

SEAT

Plan #529-JFD-20-2601-2
Price Code E

Total Living Area: 2,601 Sq. Ft.

Home has 4 bedrooms, 2 1/2 baths, 2-car side entry garage and basement foundation.

Special features

- Private study with double-door entrance makes perfect home office
- Large kitchen has convenient access from many parts of the home
- Sunken bonus room has an additional 364 square feet of living area

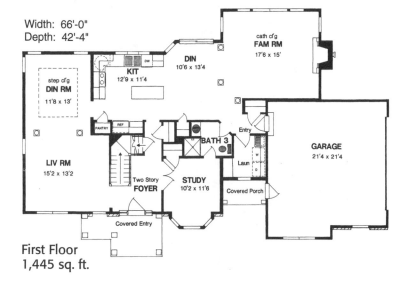

Width: 66'-0"
Depth: 42'-4"

cath cl'g
FAM RM
17'6 x 15'

DIN
10'6 x 13'4

KIT
12'9 x 11'4

DW

step cl'g
DIN RM
11'8 x 13'

PANTRY   REF

LIV RM
15'2 x 13'2

BATH 3

Entry

Laun
W

GARAGE
21'4 x 21'4

Two Story
FOYER

STUDY
10'2 x 11'6

Covered Porch

Covered Entry

First Floor
1,445 sq. ft.

MAXON

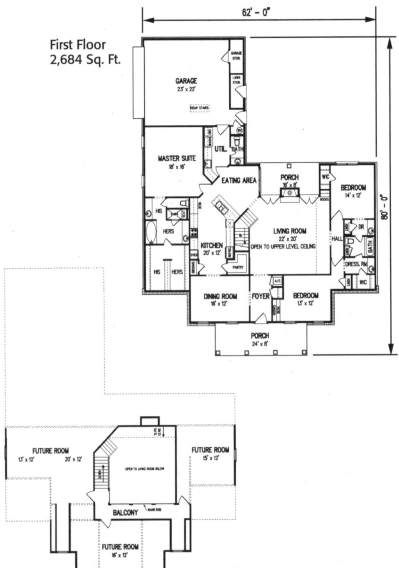

First Floor
2,684 Sq. Ft.

62' - 0"

80' - 0"

GARAGE
23' x 22'

GARAGE STOR.

LAWN STOR.

DROP STAIRS

UTIL.

BATH

MASTER SUITE
18' x 16'

EATING AREA

PORCH
16' x 8'

W/C

BEDROOM
14' x 12'

HIS

HERS

KITCHEN
20' x 12'

LIVING ROOM
22' x 20'
OPEN TO UPPER LEVEL CEILING

HALL

DR

BATH

PANTRY

DRESS. RM.

HIS

HERS

A/C

W/C

DINING ROOM
16' x 12'

FOYER

BEDROOM
13' x 12'

PORCH
24' x 8'

Plan #529-BF-2610

Price Code E

Total Living Area: 2,684 Sq. Ft.

Home has 3 bedrooms, 2 1/2 baths, 2-car garage and slab or crawl space foundation, please specify when ordering.

Special features

- Lots of future space on second floor
- Formal dining room off kitchen
- Enormous master suite with private bath and walk-in closet
- Optional second floor has an additional 926 square feet of living area

Optional
Second Floor

FUTURE ROOM
13' x 12'   20' x 12'

FUTURE ROOM
15' x 12'

OPEN TO LIVING ROOM BELOW

BALCONY   HAND RAIL

FUTURE ROOM
16' x 12'

Plan #529-FB-902
Price Code C

<u>Total Living Area:</u>   1,856 Sq. Ft.

Home has 3 bedrooms, 2 baths, 2-car side entry garage and walk-out basement, crawl space or slab foundation, please specify when ordering.

Special features

- Beautiful covered porch creates a Southern accent
- Kitchen has an organized feel with lots of cabinetry
- Large foyer has a grand entrance and leads into family room through columns and arched opening

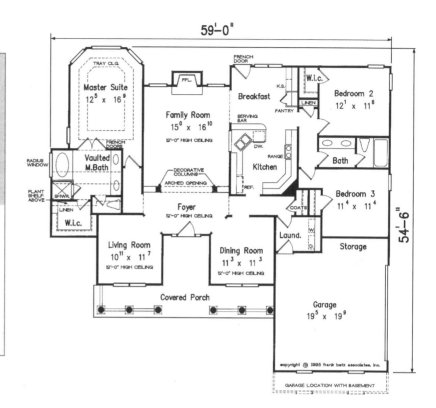

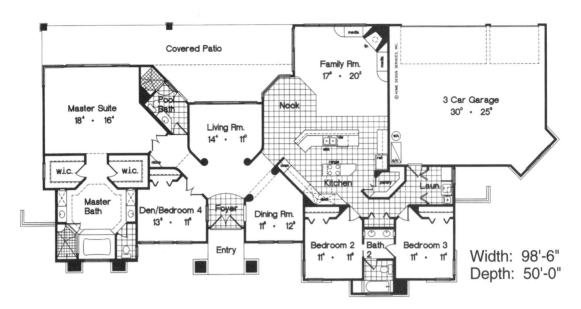

Covered Patio

Family Rm.
17⁴ · 20²

3 Car Garage
30⁰ · 25³

Master Suite
18⁴ · 16⁴

Pool Bath

Nook

Living Rm.
14⁴ · 11⁰

Kitchen

w.i.c.

w.i.c.

Master Bath

Den/Bedroom 4
13⁸ · 11⁰

Foyer

Dining Rm.
11⁴ · 12²

Laun.

Entry

Bedroom 2
11⁴ · 11⁴

Bath 2

Bedroom 3
11⁴ · 11⁴

Width: 98'-6"
Depth: 50'-0"

Plan #529-HDS-2597
Price Code D

Total Living Area: 2,597 Sq. Ft.

Home has 4 bedrooms, 3 baths, 3-car rear entry garage and slab foundation.

Special features
- Angled design creates unlimited views and spaces that appear larger
- Den/study is perfect home office or guest suite
- Island kitchen with view to nook and family spaces includes walk-in pantry
- Pool bath is shared by outdoor and indoor areas

J.N. HANSEN P.T.L.

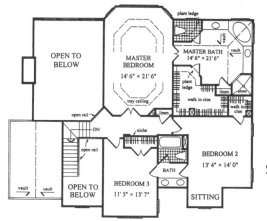

OPEN TO BELOW

MASTER BEDROOM
14' 6" × 21' 6"
tray ceiling

MASTER BATH
14' 6" × 21' 6"

plant ledge

vault

plant ledge

walk in clos

linen   shwr

walk in clos

open rail

DN

niche

open rail

BATH

BEDROOM 2
13' 4" × 14' 0"

vault   vault

OPEN TO BELOW

BEDROOM 3
11' 5" × 13' 7"

SITTING

Second Floor
1,265 sq. ft.

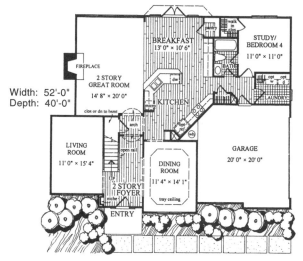

BREAKFAST
13' 0" × 10' 6"

STUDY/
BEDROOM 4
11' 0" × 11' 0"

FIREPLACE

2 STORY GREAT ROOM
14' 8" × 20' 0"

BATH

Width: 52'-0"
Depth: 40'-0"

KITCHEN

LAUNDRY

clos or dn to bsmt

arch

open rail

LIVING ROOM
11' 0" × 15' 4"

DINING ROOM
11' 4" × 14' 1"
tray ceiling

GARAGE
20' 0" × 20' 0"

2 STORY FOYER

niche

ENTRY

First Floor
1,486 sq. ft.

Plan #529-MG-96213
Price Code E

Total Living Area: 2,751 Sq. Ft.

Home has 4 bedrooms, 3 baths, 2-car side entry garage and basement foundation.

Special features

- Brick and stucco English cottage exterior
- Breakfast room situated near kitchen and great room
- Formal living and dining rooms off foyer
- First floor bedroom #4 has entrance to bath creating an ideal in-law suite

LOWE'S

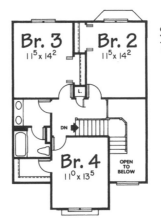

Second Floor
736 sq. ft.

Br. 3
11^5 x 14^2

Br. 2
11^5 x 14^2

Br. 4
11^0 x 13^5

DN

L.

OPEN TO BELOW

Plan #529-DBI-8012
Price Code D

Total Living Area: 2,266 Sq. Ft.

Home has 4 bedrooms, 2 1/2 baths, 3-car garage and basement foundation.

Special features

- Efficient kitchen opens into sunny breakfast room
- Box bay window in dining room adds interest
- Cozy great room with fireplace has 10' ceiling

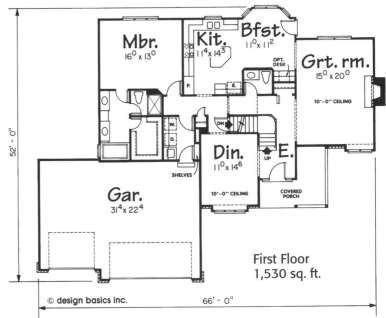

Mbr.
16^0 x 13^0

Kit.
11^4 x 14^3

Bfst.
11^0 x 11^2

Grt. rm.
15^0 x 20^0

10'-0" CEILING

OPT. DESK

P.

R.

W.

D.

DN

Din.
11^0 x 14^6

E.

UP

10'-0" CEILING

COVERED PORCH

SHELVES

Gar.
31^4 x 22^4

52' - 0"

66' - 0"

First Floor
1,530 sq. ft.

© design basics inc.

Second Floor
1,215 sq. ft.

Plan #529-MG-96183
Price Code E
Total Living Area: 2,737 Sq. Ft.

Home has 5 bedrooms, 4 baths, 2-car side entry garage and basement foundation.

Special features
- T-stairs make any room easily accessible
- Two-story foyer and grand room create spacious feeling
- Master bedroom has gorgeous bay window and a sitting area
- Bedroom #4 has its own private bath

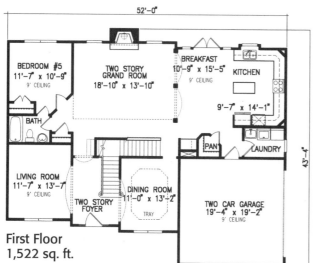

First Floor
1,522 sq. ft.

Width: 66'-4"
Depth: 74'-4"

Plan #529-HDS-2660-2
Price Code E
Total Living Area: 2,660 Sq. Ft.

Home has 4 bedrooms, 3 baths, 2-car side entry garage and slab foundation.

Special features

- Enormous family room with fireplace situated near breakfast nook and kitchen
- Spacious master suite has floor-to-ceiling windows and sitting area
- Well-designed kitchen with center island

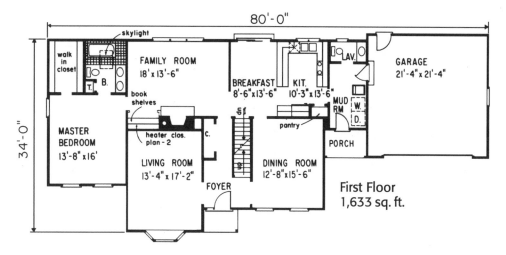

80'-0"

34'-0"

skylight

walk in closet

B.

T.

FAMILY ROOM
18' x 13'-6"

book shelves

heater clos.
plan - 2

c.

LIVING ROOM
13'-4" x 17'-2"

MASTER BEDROOM
13'-8" x 16'

FOYER

BREAKFAST
8'-6" x 13'-6"

KIT.
10'-3" x 13'-6"

LAV.

MUD RM

W.

D.

pantry

PORCH

DINING ROOM
12'-8" x 15'-6"

GARAGE
21'-4" x 21'-4"

First Floor
1,633 sq. ft.

Plan #529-1207
Price Code D

Total Living Area:	2,360 Sq. Ft.

Home has 4 bedrooms, 2 1/2 baths, 2-car garage and partial basement/crawl space foundation, drawings also include crawl space and slab foundations.

Special features

- Ample-sized living and dining rooms directly off foyer
- Family room enhanced with built-in bookshelves and cozy fireplace
- Master suite complemented with spacious walk-in closet and private bath with skylight

---

36'-0"

BEDROOM
13'-4" x 13'

B.

BEDROOM
11'-4" x 10'-4"

c.

c.

c.

ATTIC

BEDROOM
12'-8" x 10'-6"

Second Floor
727 sq. ft.

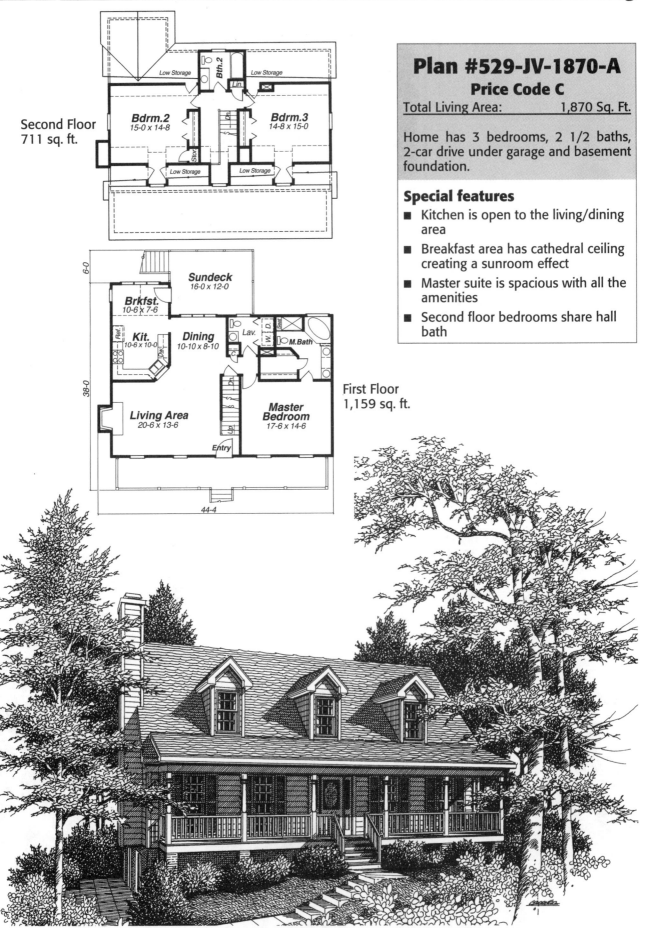

Second Floor
711 sq. ft.

Low Storage Bth.2 Low Storage

Bdrm.2
15-0 x 14-8

Bdrm.3
14-8 x 15-0

Lin.

Low Storage Low Storage

6-0

38-0

Sundeck
16-0 x 12-0

Brkfst.
10-6 x 7-6

Ref.

Kit.
10-6 x 10-0

DW

Dining
10-10 x 8-10

Lav.

W. D.

Seat

M.Bath

Living Area
20-6 x 13-6

Master Bedroom
17-6 x 14-6

Entry

44-4

First Floor
1,159 sq. ft.

Plan #529-JV-1870-A
Price Code C

Total Living Area: 1,870 Sq. Ft.

Home has 3 bedrooms, 2 1/2 baths, 2-car drive under garage and basement foundation.

Special features

- Kitchen is open to the living/dining area
- Breakfast area has cathedral ceiling creating a sunroom effect
- Master suite is spacious with all the amenities
- Second floor bedrooms share hall bath

SITTING
9'-9" x 3'-11"
8' CEILING

W.I.C.

VAULT

M.BATH

VAULT

BEDROOM 2
11'-11" x 11'-6"
8' CEILING

MASTER BEDROOM
14'-9" x 12'-11"
TRAY

W.I.C.

B#2

BEDROOM 4
11'-3" x 14'-0"
8' CEILING

W.I.C.

BEDROOM 3
12'-5" x 10'-1"
8' CEILING

LNDRY

TWO STORY
FOYER

SITTING
ROOM
8'-0" x 9'-5"
8' CEILING

Second Floor
1,199 sq. ft.

Plan #529-MG-9519-B
Price Code D

Total Living Area: 2,323 Sq. Ft.

Home has 4 bedrooms, 2 1/2 baths, 2-car garage and basement or slab foundation, please specify when ordering.

Special features

- Large open grand room, kitchen and breakfast area
- Elegant two-story foyer
- Inviting covered front porch
- Master bedroom and bedroom #3 include pleasant sitting areas

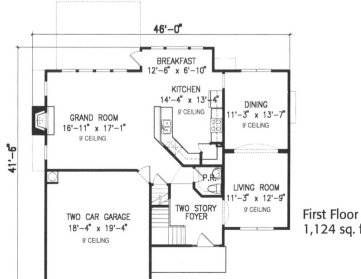

46'-0"

41'-6"

BREAKFAST
12'-6" x 6'-10"

KITCHEN
14'-4" x 13'-4"
9' CEILING

DINING
11'-3" x 13'-7"
9' CEILING

GRAND ROOM
16'-11" x 17'-1"
9' CEILING

P.R.

LIVING ROOM
11'-3" x 12'-9"
9' CEILING

TWO CAR GARAGE
18'-4" x 19'-4"
9' CEILING

TWO STORY
FOYER

First Floor
1,124 sq. ft.

J.N.HANSEN S.D.G.

Width: 70'-0"
Depth: 73'-4"

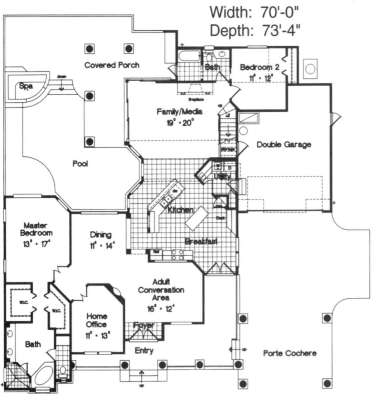

Covered Porch

Spa

Bath

Bedroom 2
11' · 12'

Family/Media
19' · 20'

fireplace

Double Garage

Pool

storage

Utility

Kitchen

Master
Bedroom
13' · 17'

Dining
11' · 14'

Breakfast

W.I.C.

W.I.C.

Adult
Conversation
Area
16' · 12'

Home
Office
11' · 13'

Foyer

Bath

Entry

Porte Cochere

First Floor
2,270 sq. ft.

Plan #529-HDS-2731
Price Code E

Total Living Area: 2,731 Sq. Ft.

Home has 3 bedrooms, 3 baths, 2-car
garage and slab foundation.

Special features

- Inviting wrap-around porch
- Master suite with well-appointed
  bath, double walk-in closets and
  access to home office
- Spacious kitchen with center island
  and view into family/media room

Second Floor
461 sq. ft.

Attic

Balcony

storage

Bedroom 3
14' · 26'

W.I.C.

storage

storage

Second Floor
1,270 sq. ft.

br3
11'4 x 11'

br4
12'4 x 16'8

SH

WHIRLPOOL TUB

OPEN TO
BELOW

OPEN RAILING

14'8 x 12'6
mbr

12' x 9'2
SITTING

12' x 12'
br2

Plan #529-SH-SEA-212
Price Code E

<u>Total Living Area:</u>   2,632 Sq. Ft.

Home has 4 bedrooms, 2 1/2 baths, 2-car garage and basement or crawl space foundation, please specify when ordering.

Special features

- Energy efficient home with 2" x 6" exterior walls

- Master bedroom has cheerful octagon-shaped sitting area

- Arched entrances create a distinctive living room with a lovely tray ceiling and help define the dining room

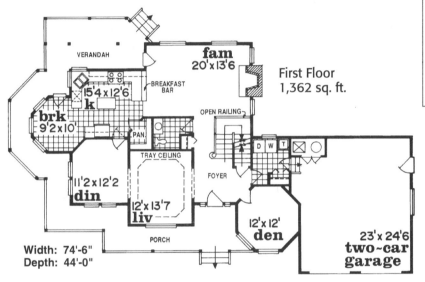

VERANDAH

fam
20' x 13'6

First Floor
1,362 sq. ft.

15'4 x 12'6
k

BREAKFAST
BAR

OPEN RAILING

brk
9'2 x 10'

PAN

D W T

TRAY CEILING

FOYER

11'2 x 12'2
din

12' x 13'7
liv

12' x 12'
den

23' x 24'6
**two-car
garage**

PORCH

Width: 74'-6"
Depth: 44'-0"

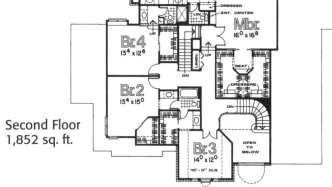

Second Floor
1,852 sq. ft.

Br 4
13⁴ x 12⁶

Br 2
13⁴ x 15⁰

Br 3
14⁰ x 12⁰

Mbr.
16⁰ x 16⁸

Sit.
12⁰ x 12⁰

WHIRLPOOL

LINEN

DRESSER

ENT. CENTER

SEAT

DRESSER

OPEN TO BELOW

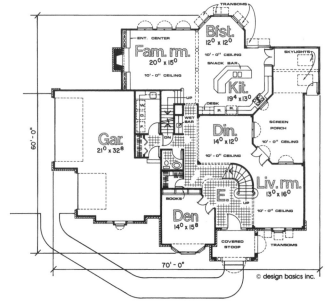

First Floor
1,923 sq. ft.

© design basics inc.

Fam. rm.
20⁰ x 15⁰

Bfst.
12⁰ x 12⁰

Kit.
19⁴ x 13⁰

Din.
14⁰ x 12⁰

Liv. rm.
13⁰ x 16⁰

Den
14⁰ x 15⁸

Gar.
21⁰ x 32⁸

SCREEN PORCH

ENT. CENTER

SNACK BAR

SKYLIGHTS

WET BAR

COVERED STOOP

TRANSOMS

60' - 0"

70' - 0"

Plan #529-DBI-2332
Price Code F

Total Living Area: 3,775 Sq. Ft.

Home has 4 bedrooms, 3 1/2 baths, 3-car side entry garage and basement foundation.

Special features

■ Screened porch off living and dining areas brings the outdoors in

■ Bookshelves flank the fireplace in the family room

■ Built-in bookshelves in den

■ Second floor master suite has bayed sitting area and wonderful bath

First Floor
1,810 sq. ft.

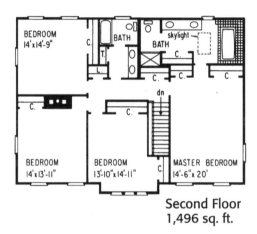

Second Floor
1,496 sq. ft.

Plan #529-1245
Price Code F

Total Living Area: 3,306 Sq. Ft.

Home has 4 bedrooms, 2 1/2 baths, 3-car side entry garage and basement foundation.

Special features

- Large living and family rooms center around a double masonry fireplace
- Kitchen features large island counter and built-in pantry
- Angled three-car garage provides extra space for workbench, bicycles, etc.
- Lavish and well-planned master bedroom and bath

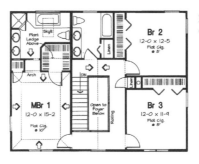

Second Floor
990 sq. ft.

Plan #529-GH-24713
Price Code D
Total Living Area:　　　2,269 Sq. Ft.

Home has 3 bedrooms, 3 baths, 2-car side entry garage and basement foundation.

Special features

- Master suite offers two closets and a skylight above the whirlpool tub
- Kitchen boasts an angled breakfast bar/extended counter and is open to the family room
- A decorative ceiling treatment adds architectural interest to the elegant dining room
- Centralized foyer gives access to the formal dining room

First Floor
1,279 sq. ft.

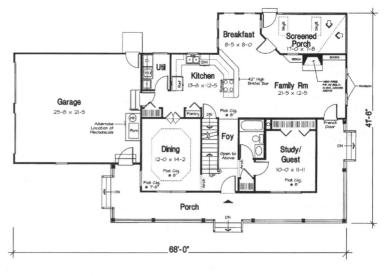

Second Floor
588 sq. ft.

Family Room Below

Bath

Bedroom 3
12^8 x 14^2

W.i.c.

STAIRS DN

OPEN RAIL

OVERLOOK

OPEN RAIL

LINEN

Foyer Below

Bedroom 2
12^0 x 11^0

W.i.c.

Opt. Bonus Room
12^5 x 18^2

Plan #529-FB-851
Price Code D

Total Living Area: 2,349 Sq. Ft.

Home has 4 bedrooms, 3 baths, 2-car garage and walk-out basement or crawl space foundation, please specify when ordering.

Special features

- Open and airy with two-story foyer and family room
- Den is secluded from the rest of the home and ideal as an office space
- Second floor bedrooms have walk-in closets and share a bath
- Optional bonus room has an additional 276 square feet of living area

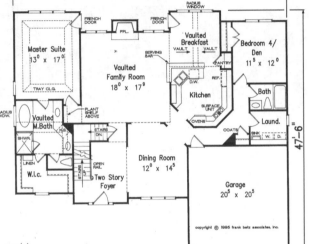

56'-0"

RADIUS WINDOW

FRENCH DOOR

FRENCH DOOR

FPL.

Master Suite
13^0 x 17^0

Vaulted Breakfast
VAULT VAULT

Bedroom 4/ Den
11^5 x 12^0

SERVING BAR

PANTRY

Vaulted Family Room
18^0 x 17^9

D.W.

REF.

Kitchen

TRAY CLG.

RADIUS WDW.

Vaulted M.Bath

PLANT SHELF ABOVE

SURFACE UNIT

Bath

SHWR.

STAIRS DN

OVENS

Laund.

COATS

SINK

W. D.

LINEN

W.i.c.

STAIRS UP

OPEN RAIL

Two Story Foyer

Dining Room
12^0 x 14^5

47'-6"

First Floor
1,761 sq. ft.

Garage
20^5 x 20^5

copyright © 1995 frank betz associates, inc.

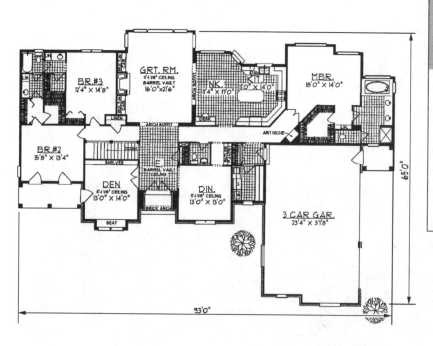

Plan #529-JA-74397
Price Code E

Total Living Area: 2,991 Sq. Ft.

Home has 3 bedrooms, 2 1/2 baths, 2-car side entry garage and basement foundation.

Special features

- Two additional bedrooms share a full bath and each have a walk-in closet
- Separate dining area provides a formal atmoshere while entertaining
- Great room has built-in cabinets surrounding fireplace

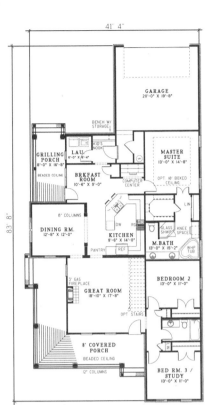

First Floor
1,845 sq. ft.

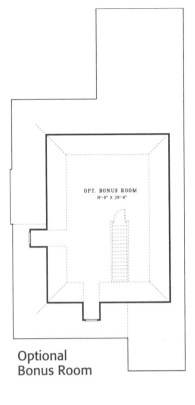

Optional
Bonus Room

Plan #529-NDG-321
Price Code C

__Total Living Area:__ 1,845 Sq. Ft.

Home has 3 bedrooms, 2 baths, 2-car rear entry garage and crawl space or slab foundation, please specify when ordering.

Special features

- Master suite has privacy from other bedrooms
- Dining room is convenient to kitchen and great room
- Breakfast room accesses outdoor grilling porch
- Optional bonus room is a great children's playroom
- Optional bonus room on second floor has an additional 1,191 square feet of living area

Plan #529-FB-743
Price Code C

Total Living Area: 1,978 Sq. Ft.

Home has 3 bedrooms, 2 1/2 baths, 2-car garage and walk-out basement or crawl space foundation, please specify when ordering.

Special features

- Elegant arched openings throughout interior
- Vaulted living room off foyer
- Master suite with cheerful sitting room and a private bath

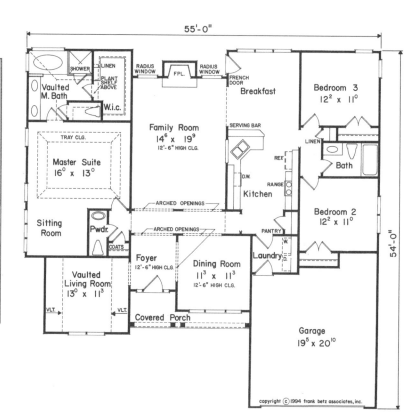

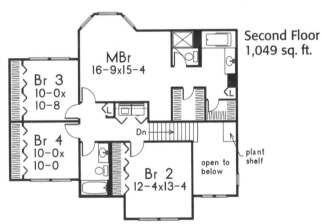

Second Floor
1,049 sq. ft.

MBr
16-9x15-4

Br 3
10-0x
10-8

Br 4
10-0x
10-0

Dn

Br 2
12-4x13-4

L

L

open to
below

plant
shelf

Plan #529-1308
Price Code D
Total Living Area: 2,280 Sq. Ft.

Home has 4 bedrooms, 2 1/2 baths,
2-car side entry garage and basement
foundation.

Special features
- Laundry area conveniently located
  on second floor
- Compact yet efficient kitchen
- Unique shaped dining room over-
  looks front porch
- Cozy living room enhanced with
  sloped ceilings and fireplace

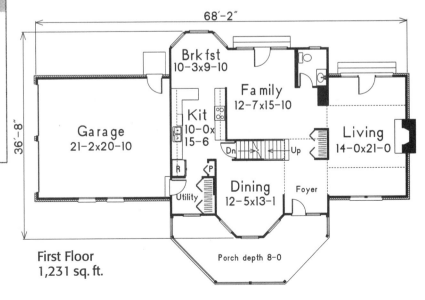

68'-2"

36'-8"

Brk fst
10-3x9-10

Family
12-7x15-10

Kit
10-0x
15-6

Garage
21-2x20-10

Living
14-0x21-0

Dn   Up

Utility

R   P

Dining
12-5x13-1

Foyer

First Floor
1,231 sq. ft.

Porch depth 8-0

Second Floor
791 sq. ft.

BEDRM 3
13-6 X 12-0

GAME ROOM
16-8 X 15-4

OPEN TO FOYER BELOW

BALCONY

BATH 3

SLOPE
PLANT LEDGE

LIN

BEDRM 4
11-4 X 11-4

WIDTH 64-2

DEPTH 62-0

COVERED PORCH

GREAT ROOM
19-4 X 17-6
12 FT CLG

MASTER BATH
9 FT CLG

COVERED PORCH

BRKFST RM
12-6 X 9-8
10 FT CLG

SEE THRU FP

KITCHEN
12-4 X 14-6
10 FT CLG

DINING ROOM
15-6 X 11-6
10 FT CLG

FOYER
10 FT CLG

MASTER BEDRM
16-8 X 14-8
9 FT CLG

UTIL
11-6 X 5-6

PANTRY

PORCH

BATH 2

BEDRM 2
11-4 X 11-8
9 FT CLG

GARAGE

COPYRIGHT LARRY E. BELK

STORAGE

First Floor
1,930 sq. ft.

Plan #529-LBD-27-6A
Price Code E
Total Living Area: 2,721 Sq. Ft.

Home has 4 bedrooms, 3 baths, 2-car side entry garage and basement, crawl space or slab foundation, please specify when ordering.

Special features
- Large foyer leads through arched columns into great room and dining room with see-through fireplace
- Sunny breakfast room has bay window
- Game room opens up second floor

COPYRIGHT 1993

Secondary Entrance

Second Floor
960 sq. ft.

Width: 64'-0"
Depth: 42'-0"

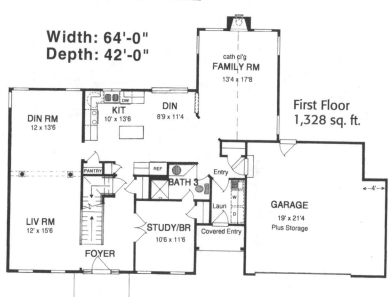

First Floor
1,328 sq. ft.

Plan #529-JFD-20-2288-1
Price Code D

Total Living Area: 2,288 Sq. Ft.

Home has 4 bedrooms, 2 1/2 baths, 2-car garage and basement foundation.

Special features

- Family room is cozy with large fireplace
- Formal living and dining rooms are separated from casual areas
- Double-door entry into study
- Master bedroom has private bath with double vanity and a separate shower

Plan #529-HDS-2962

Price Code E

Total Living Area: 2,962 Sq. Ft.

Home has 4 bedrooms, 3 baths, 3-car side entry garage and slab foundation.

Special features

- Vaulted breakfast nook adjacent to kitchen
- Bedroom #4 is an ideal guest suite with private bath
- Master suite includes see-through fireplace, bayed vanity and massive walk-in closet

Width: 66'-8"
Depth: 76'-8"

Second Floor
1,242 sq. ft.

TWO STORY GRAND ROOM

BEDROOM 2
11'-4" x 11'-5"

M. BATH

W.I.C.

B#2

TWO STORY FOYER

BEDROOM 4
11'-4" x 10'-4"

BEDROOM 3
12'-10" x 11'-4"
8' CEILING

MASTER BEDROOM
17'-0" x 13'-9"
TRAY

SITTING
8'-9" x 5'-7"

Plan #529-MG-96108
Price Code D
Total Living Area: 2,499 Sq. Ft.

Home has 4 bedrooms, 2 1/2 baths, 2-car garage and basement foundation.

Special features
- Brick traditional with covered front porch
- Master bedroom has private bath and a sitting room with extra storage
- Impressive two-story foyer
- Kitchen and breakfast room are spacious and have laundry room nearby

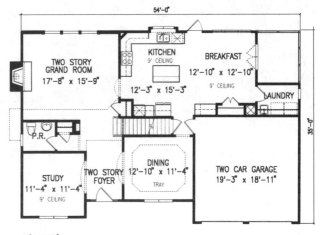

54'-0"

TWO STORY GRAND ROOM
17'-8" x 15'-9"

KITCHEN
9' CEILING

BREAKFAST
12'-10" x 12'-10"
9' CEILING

12'-3" x 15'-3"

LAUNDRY

P.R.

DINING
12'-10" x 11'-4"
TRAY

TWO STORY FOYER

TWO CAR GARAGE
19'-3" x 18'-11"

STUDY
11'-4" x 11'-4"
9' CEILING

35'-0"

First Floor
1,257 sq. ft.

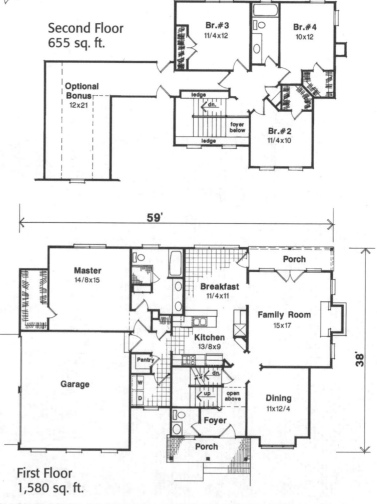

Second Floor
655 sq. ft.

Br.#3
11/4x12

Br.#4
10x12

Optional Bonus
12x21

ledge

dn.

foyer below

ledge

Br.#2
11/4x10

Plan #529-GM-2235
Price Code D

Total Living Area: 2,235 Sq. Ft.

Home has 4 bedrooms, 2 1/2 baths, 2-car side entry garage and basement foundation.

Special features

- Cheerful family room has double-doors leading to a covered porch
- Centrally located kitchen is convenient to all rooms on first floor
- Second floor bedrooms have large closets and lots of windows creating bright spaces

59'

38'

Master
14/8x15

Porch

Breakfast
11/4x11

Family Room
15x17

Kitchen
13/8x9

Pantry

Garage

W
D

dn.

up

open above

Dining
11x12/4

Foyer

Porch

First Floor
1,580 sq. ft.

Second Floor
651 sq. ft.

BEDROOM 2
13'-0" x 11'-6"

BEDROOM 3
13'-0" x 11'-6"

OPEN BELOW

LOFT
13'-8" x 11'-0"

LINEN

DN

First Floor
1,689 sq. ft.

DECK
35'-8" x 11'-7"

STORAGE
9'-10" x 6'-0"

PANTRY

LAUNDRY
11'-6" x 6'-0"

BRKFST
9'-5" x 11'-6"

KITCHEN
12'-4" x 11'-6"

DINING
13'-8" x 11'-6"

HERS

HIS

K/S

GARAGE
21'-8" x 21'-0"

FAMILY
18'-2" x 19'-6"

STAIRS TO BASEMENT

COATS

LIN

VAULT

OPEN TO DORMERS

UP

OFFICE/
BEDROOM
13'-8" x 11'-0"

TRAY CEILING

MASTER BDRM
15'-8" x 14'-10"

PORCH

◄74'-4'►

39'-4"
+DECK

Plan #529-AP-2317
Price Code D

Total Living Area: 2,340 Sq. Ft.

Home has 3 bedrooms, 2 1/2 baths, 2-car side entry garage and walk-out basement foundation.

Special features

- Large family room has vaulted ceiling, bookcases and an entertainment center which surrounds a brick fireplace
- Highly functional kitchen is easily accessible from many parts of this home
- The second floor consists of two secondary bedrooms each having direct access to the bath
- The loft can serve as a recreation area or fifth bedroom

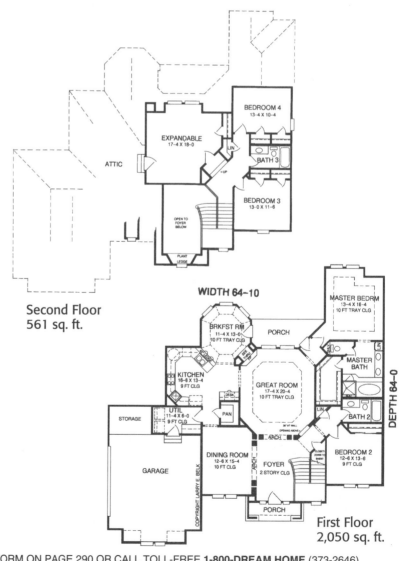

Second Floor
561 sq. ft.

WIDTH 64-10

DEPTH 64-0

First Floor
2,050 sq. ft.

Plan #529-LBD-26-24A
Price Code E
Total Living Area: 2,611 Sq. Ft.

Home has 4 bedrooms, 3 baths, 2-car side entry garage and basement, crawl space or slab foundation, please specify when ordering.

Special features
- Old world ambiance characterizes this European styled home
- Elegant stone entrance opens into two-story foyer
- Oversized great room features raised ceiling and see-through fireplace seen from the kitchen and breakfast room

Graceful Southern Hospitality

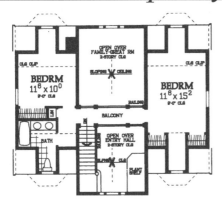

Second Floor
600 sq. ft.

OPEN OVER FAMILY-GREAT RM
2-STORY CLG
SLOPING CEILING

BEDRM
11⁸ x 10⁰
8'-0" CLG

BEDRM
11⁸ x 15²
8'-0" CLG

CLG CLP

CLG CLP

RAILING

BALCONY

BATH

OPEN OVER ENTRY HALL
2-STORY CLG

SLOPING CLG

LINEN CLS

50'0"

44'0"

WRAP-AROUND PORCH

RAILING

CLAW-FOOT TUB

MASTER BATH

WALK-IN CLOSET

FAMILY-GREAT RM
13⁰ x 14⁸
2-STORY CLG

EATING

COUNTRY KITCHEN
11⁸ x 15⁸

ISLAND

PANTRY

OVEN

DW

REF

MASTER SUITE
11⁸ x 19⁰

ENTRY HALL
2-STORY CLG

UP

DINING RM
11⁸ x 12⁰

POR RM

RAILING

WRAP-AROUND PORCH

First Floor
1,171 sq. ft.

Plan #529-HP-C619
Price Code B
Total Living Area: 1,771 Sq. Ft.

Home has 3 bedrooms, 2 1/2 baths, optional detached 2-car garage and basement foundation.

Special features
- Efficient country kitchen shares space with a bayed eating area
- Two-story family/great room is warmed by a fireplace in winter and open to outdoor country comfort in the summer with double French doors
- First floor master suite offers a bay window and access to the porch through French doors

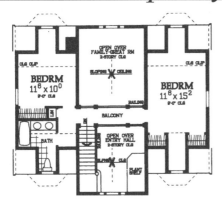

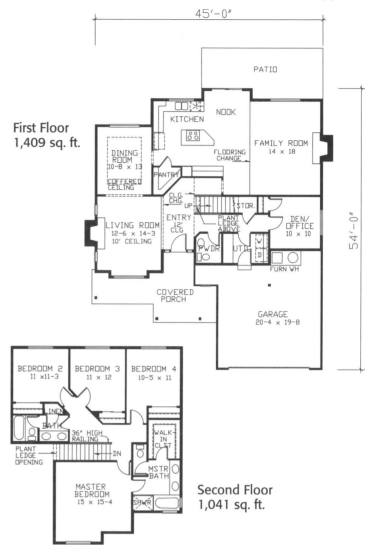

First Floor
1,409 sq. ft.

Second Floor
1,041 sq. ft.

Plan #529-GSD-2242
Price Code D
Total Living Area: 2,450 Sq. Ft.

Home has 4 bedrooms, 2 1/2 baths, 2-car garage and crawl space foundation.

Special features

- Oversized rooms throughout
- 12' ceiling height in entry adds drama
- Coffered ceiling in dining room is a unique touch
- Kitchen includes island, walk-in pantry and a nook ideal as a breakfast area

Second Floor
847 sq. ft.

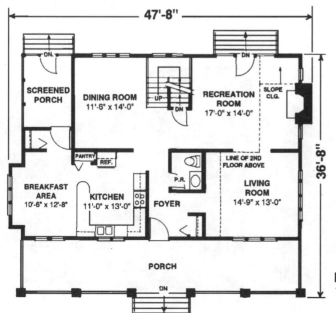

Plan #529-1305
Price Code C

Total Living Area: 2,009 Sq. Ft.

Home has 3 bedrooms, 2 1/2 baths and basement foundation.

Special features

- Spacious master bedroom has dramatic sloped ceiling and private bath with double sinks and walk-in closet
- Bedroom #3 has extra storage inside closet
- Versatile screened porch is ideal for entertaining year-round
- Large laundry area/powder room conveniently located adjacent to garage, just off kitchen
- Sunny breakfast area located near kitchen and screened porch for convenience

First Floor
1,162 sq. ft.

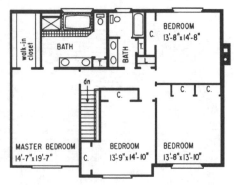

Second Floor
1,549 sq. ft.

Plan #529-1237
Price Code F

Total Living Area: 3,417 Sq. Ft.

Home has 4 bedrooms, 2 1/2 baths, 3-car side entry garage and partial basement/crawl space foundation, drawings also include crawl space foundation.

Special features
- Gourmet kitchen emphasizes function with built-in pantry, island counter and opening to breakfast room with large bay window.
- Large den is perfectly located for a quiet retreat
- In addition to three oversized bedrooms, the second floor includes an expansive master suite with huge bath and walk-in closet

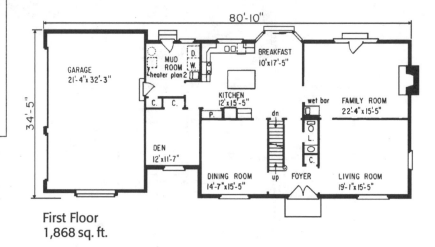

First Floor
1,868 sq. ft.

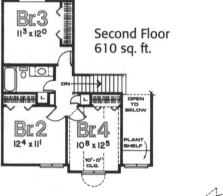

Second Floor
610 sq. ft.

Br.3
11³ x 12⁰

Br.2
12⁴ x 11¹

Br.4
10⁸ x 12⁵

DN

OPEN
TO
BELOW

PLANT
SHELF

10'-0"
CLG.

Plan #529-DBI-2285
Price Code C

Total Living Area: 2,115 Sq. Ft.

Home has 4 bedrooms, 2 1/2 baths, 3-car garage and basement foundation.

Special features

■ Cathedral ceiling in great room adds spaciousness

■ Two-story foyer is a grand entrance

■ Efficiently designed kitchen with breakfast area, snack bar and built-in desk

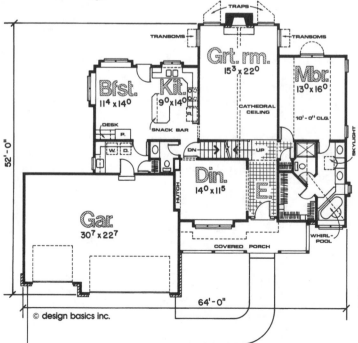

TRAPS

TRANSOMS

TRANSOMS

Grt. rm.
15³ x 22⁰

CATHEDRAL
CEILING

Mbr.
13⁰ x 16⁰

10'-0" CLG.

SKYLIGHT

Bfst.
11⁴ x 14⁰

Kit.
9⁰ x 14⁰

DESK

P.

SNACK BAR

W. D.

DN

UP

Din.
14⁰ x 11⁵

HUTCH

Gar.
30⁷ x 22⁷

WHIRL-
POOL

COVERED PORCH

© design basics inc.

52'-0"

64'-0"

First Floor
1,505 sq. ft.

Plan #529-MG-9510
Price Code D

Total Living Area: 2,379 Sq. Ft.

Home has 4 bedrooms, 2 1/2 baths, 2-car garage and basement foundation.

Special features

- Dining room accented with columns is open to grand room
- See-through fireplace enhances the family and grand rooms
- Second floor laundry room is convenient to all bedrooms

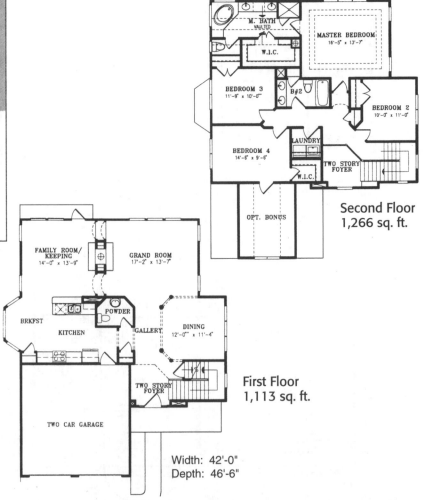

Second Floor
1,266 sq. ft.

First Floor
1,113 sq. ft.

Width: 42'-0"
Depth: 46'-6"

Second Floor
1,426 sq. ft.

First Floor
1,631 sq. ft.

© design basics inc.

Plan #529-DBI-2839
Price Code E
Total Living Area: 3,057 Sq. Ft.

Home has 4 bedrooms, 3 1/2 baths, 3-car side entry garage and basement foundation.

Special features
- Oversized rooms throughout
- Peaceful second floor master suite with dramatic bay window
- Living and dining rooms connect to screened veranda through beautiful double-doors

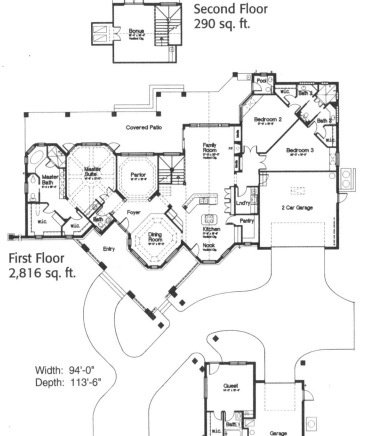

Sun Deck

Second Floor
290 sq. ft.

Bonus

First Floor
2,816 sq. ft.

Pool

Bath 2

Bedroom 2

Bath 3

Covered Patio

Family Room

Bedroom 3

w.i.c.

Master Suite

Parlor

Master Bath

Foyer

F.P.

Lnd'ry

2 Car Garage

w.i.c.

w.i.c.

Bath

Dining Room

Pantry

Kitchen

Entry

Nook

Width: 94'-0"
Depth: 113'-6"

Guest

w.i.c.

Bath

Garage

Guest House
330 sq. ft.

Plan #529-HDS-3436
Price Code F

Total Living Area:	3,436 Sq. Ft.

Home has 4 bedrooms, 4 baths, 2-car garage, 1-car garage and slab foundation.

Special features

- Unique angled rooms create an exciting feel
- Well-organized kitchen with island is adjacent to family room
- Beautiful sculptured ceilings in master suite
- Guest house is ideal as in-law suite or secluded home office

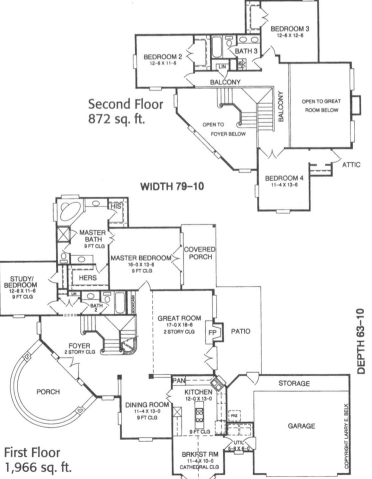

Second Floor
872 sq. ft.

BEDROOM 3
12-6 X 12-6

BEDROOM 2
12-6 X 11-6

BATH 3

LIN

BALCONY

BALCONY

OPEN TO GREAT
ROOM BELOW

OPEN TO
FOYER BELOW

ATTIC

BEDROOM 4
11-4 X 13-6

WIDTH 79-10

MASTER
BATH
9 FT CLG

HIS

MASTER BEDROOM
16-0 X 13-6
9 FT CLG

COVERED
PORCH

STUDY/
BEDROOM
12-6 X 11-6
9 FT CLG

HERS

BATH
2

FOYER
2 STORY CLG

GREAT ROOM
17-0 X 18-6
2 STORY CLG

FP

PATIO

PORCH

PAN

KITCHEN
12-0 X 13-0

STORAGE

DINING ROOM
11-4 X 13-0
9 FT CLG

FRZ

GARAGE

9 FT CLG

BRKFST RM
11-4 X 10-0
CATHEDRAL CLG

UTIL
5-8 X 6-0

DEPTH 63-10

COPYRIGHT LARRY E. BELK

First Floor
1,966 sq. ft.

Plan #529-LBD-28-1A
Price Code E
Total Living Area: 2,838 Sq. Ft.

Home has 4 bedrooms, 3 baths, 2-car garage and basement, crawl space or slab foundation, please specify when ordering.

Special features
- Elegant foyer is enormous and spotlights a grand staircase to the second floor
- Cozy study tucked away for privacy
- Sunny kitchen and breakfast area have cathedral ceilings

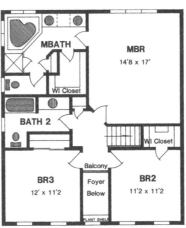

MBATH

MBR
14'8 x 17'

WI Closet

BATH 2

Second Floor
926 sq. ft.

WI Closet

BR3
12' x 11'2

Balcony
Foyer
Below

BR2
11'2 x 11'2

PLANT SHELF

Plan #529-JFD-20-1887-1
Price Code C

Total Living Area: 1,887 Sq. Ft.

Home has 3 bedrooms, 2 1/2 baths, 2-car garage and basement foundation.

Special features

■ Enormous great room is the heart of this home with an overlooking kitchen and dining room

■ Formal dining room has lovely bay window

■ Master bedroom has spacious bath with corner step-up tub, double vanity and walk-in closet

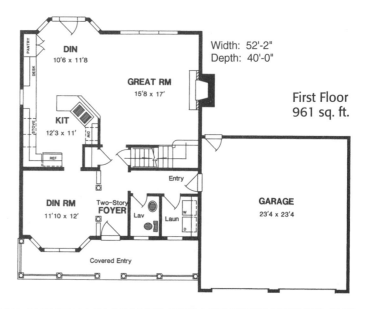

PANTRY

DIN
10'6 x 11'8

DESK

GREAT RM
15'8 x 17'

STOVE

KIT
12'3 x 11'

REF

DIN RM
11'10 x 12'

Two-Story
FOYER

Lav

Entry

Laun

Covered Entry

Width: 52'-2"
Depth: 40'-0"

First Floor
961 sq. ft.

GARAGE
23'4 x 23'4

Second Floor Hideaway

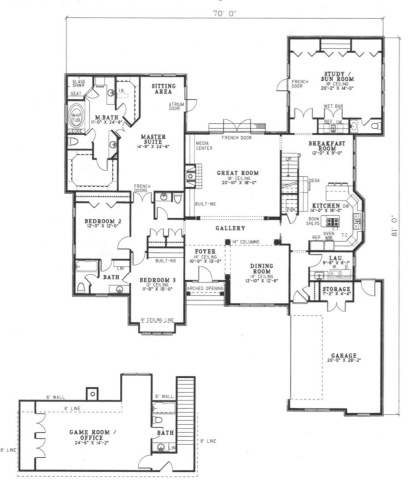

70' 0"

81' 0"

GLASS
SHWR
SEAT

SITTING
AREA

M.BATH
11'-0" X 24'-6"

WHP
TUB

ATRIUM
DOOR

LEDGE

MASTER
SUITE
14'-6" X 24'-8"

MEDIA
CENTER

FRENCH DOOR

FRENCH DOORS

BUILT-INS

GREAT ROOM
10' CEILING
20'-10" X 18'-0"

FRENCH
DOOR

STUDY /
SUN ROOM
10' CEILING
20'-2" X 14'-0"

WET BAR

REF. ICM

BREAKFAST
ROOM
12'-0" X 9'-0"

UP

DESK

KITCHEN DW
14'-0" X 16'-0"

BEDROOM 2
12'-0" X 12'-0"

BATH

GALLERY

BUILT-INS

BEDROOM 3
12' CEILING
11'-8" X 15'-0"

LIN.

FOYER
14' CEILING
10'-0" X 13'-0"

14" COLUMNS

DINING
ROOM
14' CEILING
12'-10" X 12'-6"

ARCHED OPENING

BOOK
SHLVS

OVEN
MW

REF. MW

T.C.

LAU.
9'-8" X 6'-?"

W.
D.

STORAGE
7'-? X 4'-4"

9' CEILING LINE

GARAGE
20'-0" X 28'-2"

First Floor
3,051 sq. ft.

6' WALL

8' LINE

6' WALL

8' LINE

GAME ROOM /
OFFICE
24'-6" X 14'-2"

BATH

LIN.

8' LINE

Second Floor
517 sq. ft.

Plan #529-NDG-322
Price Code F

Total Living Area: 3,568 Sq. Ft.

Home has 3 bedrooms, 3 1/2 baths, 2-car side entry garage and slab or crawl space foundation, please specify when ordering.

Special features

- Elegant great room has fireplace and built-in media center
- Study/sunroom off breakfast area has lots of storage, a half bath and a wet bar
- Master suite includes private bath, sitting area and a spacious walk-in closet

© Michael E. Nelson
NELSON DESIGN GROUP, LLC

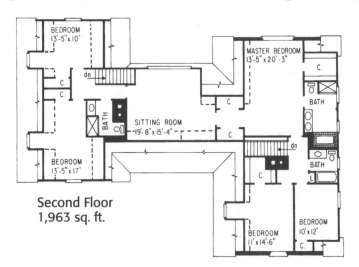

Second Floor
1,963 sq. ft.

Plan #529-1242
Price Code F

Total Living Area: 3,641 Sq. Ft.

Home has 5 bedrooms, 4 baths, 3-car side entry garage and basement foundation.

Special features

■ Secluded family room includes large fireplace, patio sliding doors and easy access to kitchen and dining room

■ The front of the home consists of a formal living room and an adjacent library for quiet time

■ Focal point of second floor is a large central sitting room perfect for children's play area or an office

■ Covered front porch adds charm to the design

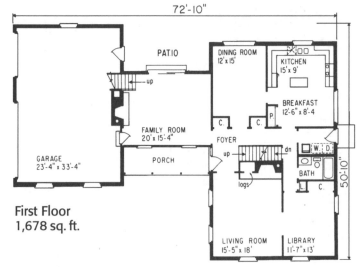

First Floor
1,678 sq. ft.

LOWE'S

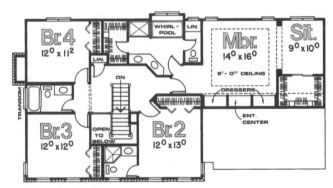

Second Floor
1,345 sq. ft.

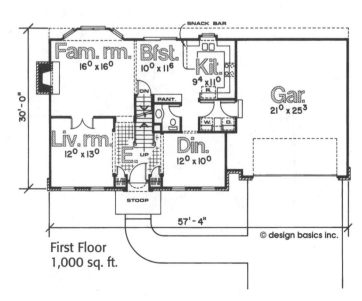

First Floor
1,000 sq. ft.

© design basics inc.

Plan #529-DBI-2316
Price Code D

Total Living Area: 2,345 Sq. Ft.

Home has 4 bedrooms, 3 1/2 baths, 2-car garage and basement foundation.

Special features
- Traditional styling with extras
- Master suite has private sitting area
- Family room with fireplace and bay window
- Formal living room with double-door entrance off family room
- Kitchen with snack bar counter for extra seating

Plan #529-HDS-3556
Price Code F

Total Living Area: 3,556 Sq. Ft.

Home has 4 bedrooms, 3 1/2 baths, 3-car side entry garage and slab foundation.

Special features

- Curved portico welcomes guests
- Master suite has see-through fireplace, wet bar, private bath and sitting area opening to covered patio
- Cozy family room with fireplace has adjacent summer kitchen outdoors on patio

Width: 85'-0"
Depth: 85'-0"

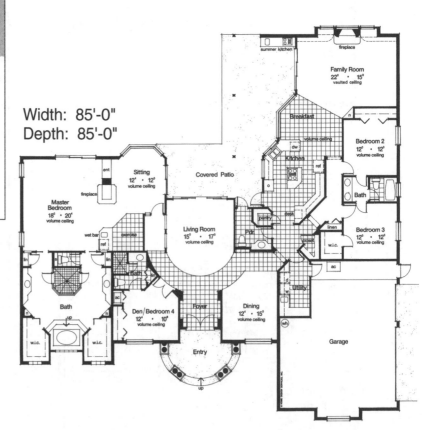

Plan #529-JV-2788-A
Price Code E

Total Living Area: 2,788 Sq. Ft.

Home has 3 bedrooms, 2 1/2 baths, 2-car side entry garage and basement foundation.

Special features

- Georgian grandeur with this elegant ranch design
- Spacious screened porch just beyond breakfast area stretches casual space to the outdoors
- A home office located conveniently off the living area could easily convert to a fourth bedroom

© 1996, Jannis Vann & Associates, Inc.

Sundeck 19-8 x 14-0

Screen Porch 20-0 x 14-0

Master Bdrm. 13-6 x 22-0

M.Bath

Paneled Ceiling 14' High

Kitchen 13-0 x 13-8

Laund.

Brkfst./ Keeping 10-8 x 19-6

Bdrm.3 11-6 x 11-0

Living Area 18-8 x 25-6

Ent.Center

Lav.

Bath 2

Linen

Dining Rm. 14-0 x 17-6 (11'-0" Ceiling)

Double Garage 21-8 x 21-4

Bdrm.2 12-6 x 11-8

Home Office 15-6 x 11-6 (11'-0" Ceiling)

Foyer 7-6 x 11-6 (11'-0" Ceiling)

60-5

82-4

Plan #529-CHD-23-10
Price Code D

Total Living Area: 2,350 Sq. Ft.

Home has 3 bedrooms, 2 1/2 baths, 2-car side entry garage and walk-out basement, slab or crawl space foundation, please specify when ordering.

Special features

■ Luxurious master suite with large bath and enormous walk-in closet

■ Built-in hutch in breakfast room is eye-catching

■ Terrific study located in its own private hall with half bath includes two closets and a bookcase

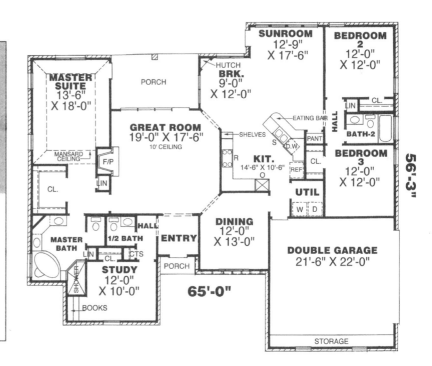

WIDTH 40'-0"
DEPTH 66'-6"

GARAGE
19-6 × 29-10

COVERED
PORCH

First Floor
1,495 sq. ft.

FURN

UTIL

WH

COPYRIGHT 1999 GSDG, INC.

FAMILY ROOM
VAULTED CEILING
13-6×14-6

PLANT
LEDGE
ABOVE

MASTER
BATH

PWDR

WALK-IN
CLST

UP

NOOK

EATING
COUNTER

PHONE
DESK

MASTER
BEDROOM
13-8×14

ENTRY
OPEN TO
ABOVE

ENTRY

BUTLER'S
PANTRY

KITCHEN

COVERED
PORCH

DINING
ROOM
13-4×12-2
VAULTED

TRELLIS

VAULTED
CEILING
LINE

ATTIC
STOR.

OPEN
BELOW

PLANT
LEDGE

BEDROOM 2
11-6 × 11-2

STOR

DN

OPEN
RAILING

OPEN
RAILING

BATH

OPEN
RAILING

PLAYROOM
13-2 × 19-2

STOR.
LINEN

BEDROOM 3
11-6 × 12

OPEN
TO
BELOW

SLOPED
CLG

Second Floor
927 sq. ft.

Plan #529-GSD-2107
Price Code D

Total Living Area: 2,422 Sq. Ft.

Home has 3 bedrooms, 2 1/2 baths, 3-car side entry garage and crawl space foundation.

Special features

- Covered porches invite guests into home
- Convenient and private first floor master suite
- Family room has vaulted ceiling
- 10' ceiling in dining room has formal feel
- Kitchen has walk-in pantry and eating bar

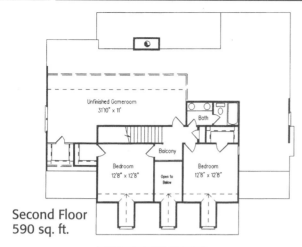

Second Floor
590 sq. ft.

Unfinished Gameroom
31'10" x 11'

Bath

Balcony

Bedroom
12'8" x 12'8"

Open to Below

Bedroom
12'8" x 12'8"

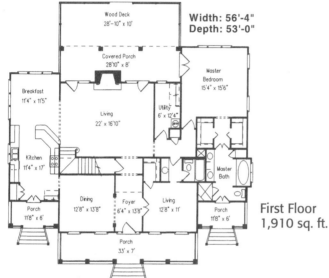

Wood Deck
28'-10" x 10'

Covered Porch
28'10" x 8'

Width: 56'-4"
Depth: 53'-0"

Breakfast
11'4" x 11'5"

Master Bedroom
15'4" x 15'6"

Living
22' x 16'10"

Utility
6' x 12'4"

Kitchen
11'4" x 17'

Master Bath

Porch
11'8" x 6'

Dining
12'8" x 13'8"

Foyer
6'4" x 13'8"

Living
12'8" x 11'

Porch
11'8" x 6'

Porch
33' x 7'

First Floor
1,910 sq. ft.

Plan #529-CHP-2543-A-42
Price Code D

Total Living Area: 2,500 Sq. Ft.

Home has 3 bedrooms, 2 1/2 baths and basement, slab or crawl space foundation, please specify when ordering.

Special features

- Master suite has its own separate wing with front porch, double walk-in closets, private bath and access to back porch and patio
- Large unfinished game room on second floor
- Living area is oversized and has a fireplace

Second Floor
909 sq. ft.

BONUS AREA
17'-8" X 16'-0"
380 SQ.FT.

BED RM. 2
16'-4" X 9'-2"

BED RM. 3
9'-8" X 12'-2"

8' LINE

GLASS BLOCKS

WHP TUB

MASTER BATH
15'-6" X 9'-0"

LIN

GRILLING PORCH
14'-0" X 6'-0"

KITCHEN
11'-0" X 10'-0"

DW

NOOK
7'-0" X 9'-0"

LAU.

STORAGE
10'-0" X 6'-0"

MASTER SUITE
11'-6" X 14'-0"

RG.

REF.

ISLAND

GARAGE
19'-8" X 19'-4"

GAS FIREPLACE

UP

8' COLUMNS

DINING
10'-2" X 14'-0"

GREAT RM.
15'-6" X 16'-0"

FOYER

PRCH

47' 0"

50' 0"

First Floor
1,155 sq. ft.

Plan #529-NDG-300
Price Code C
Total Living Area: 2,064 Sq. Ft.

Home has 3 bedrooms, 2 1/2 baths, 2-car garage and crawl space or slab foundation, please specify when ordering.

Special features
- Great room with fireplace is cozy and warm
- Master suite has private bath with many luxuries
- Well-designed kitchen has center island allowing extra seating for dining
- Second floor includes bonus room with an additional 380 square feet of living area

Second Floor
652 sq. ft.

Plan #529-1415
Price Code D

Total Living Area: 2,506 Sq. Ft.

Home has 3 bedrooms, 2 1/2 baths, 2-car garage and partial basement/crawl space foundation.

Special features

- Uniquely designed porch invites you into huge foyer with angled stair leading to second floor
- Great room feature doors on opposite sides of fireplace leading to patios at rear of home
- Large kitchen-in-a-bay has abundance of counter space, stove top island, and huge pantry
- Master bedroom has bay window, walk-in closet and private bath

First Floor
1,854 sq. ft.

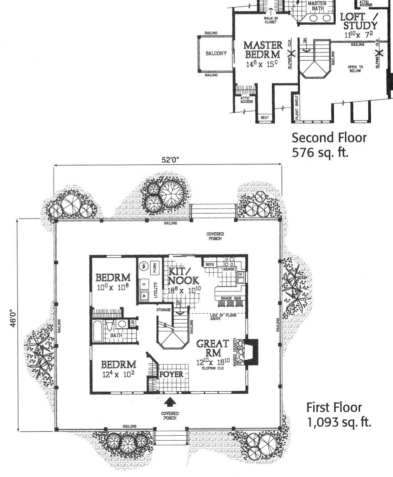

Plan #529-HP-C681

Price Code B

Total Living Area: 1,669 Sq. Ft.

Home has 3 bedrooms, 2 baths and crawl space foundation.

Special features

- Generous use of windows adds exciting visual elements to the exterior as well as plenty of natural light to the interior

- Two-story great room has a raised hearth

- Second floor loft/study would easily make a terrific home office

Second Floor
576 sq. ft.

First Floor
1,093 sq. ft.

Second Floor
1,099 sq. ft.

MASTER BATH &
DRESSING AREA

MASTER
BALCONY

MASTER BEDROOM
15'-0" x 13'-0"

BATH

BEDROOM
11'-11" x 13'-0"

BEDROOM
12'-0" x 11'-6"

DN.

Plan #529-1296
Price Code D
Total Living Area: 2,406 Sq. Ft.

Home has 3 bedrooms, 2 1/2 baths and basement foundation.

Special features
- Master suite has a beautiful fireplace, private balcony, enormous walk-in closet and private bath with dressing area
- Unique kitchen-in-a-bay is spacious and attaches to breakfast area and formal dining area that has a covered porch and fireplace
- First floor activity area has see-through fireplace, bookcases and covered veranda nearby

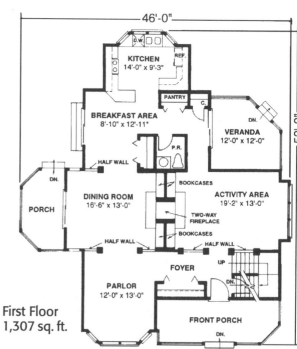

46'-0"

52'-2"

KITCHEN
14'-0" x 9'-3"

REF.

PANTRY

C.

BREAKFAST AREA
8'-10" x 12'-11"

DN.

VERANDA
12'-0" x 12'-0"

P.R.

HALF WALL

DN.

BOOKCASES

DINING ROOM
16'-6" x 13'-0"

ACTIVITY AREA
19'-2" x 13'-0"

PORCH

TWO-WAY
FIREPLACE

BOOKCASES

HALF WALL

HALF WALL

FOYER

UP

PARLOR
12'-0" x 13'-0"

DN.

First Floor
1,307 sq. ft.

FRONT PORCH

DN.

Bright And Cheery Sunroom

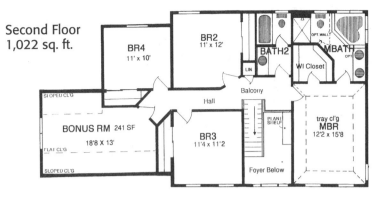

Second Floor
1,022 sq. ft.

BR4
11' x 10'

BR2
11' x 12'

BATH2

MBATH
OPT. WALL
OPT.

WI Closet

SLOPED CL'G

Balcony

Hall

tray cl'g
MBR
12'2 x 15'8

BONUS RM 241 SF
18'8 X 13'

FLAT CL'G

BR3
11'4 x 11'2

PLANT SHELF

SLOPED CL'G

Foyer Below

Plan #529-JFD-20-2211-1
Price Code D

Total Living Area: 2,211 Sq. Ft.

Home has 4 bedrooms, 2 1/2 baths, 2-car garage and basement foundation.

Special features

- Spacious sun room has three walls of windows and access outdoors

- Family room has open view into kitchen and dining area

- Large master bedroom has private luxurious bath with step-up tub

- Bonus room has an additional 241 square feet of living area

Width: 56'-8"
Depth: 44'-4"

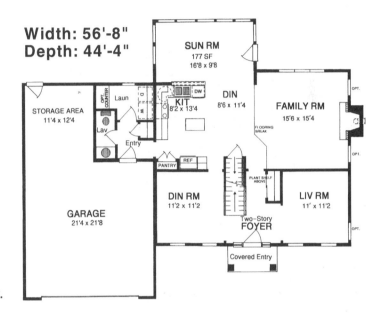

SUN RM
177 SF
16'8 x 9'8

STORAGE AREA
11'4 x 12'4

OPT. COUNTER

Laun

KIT
8'2 x 13'4

DW

DIN
8'6 x 11'4

FAMILY RM
15'6 x 15'4

OPT.

FLOORING BREAK

OPT.

Lav

Entry

REF

PANTRY

PLANT SHELF ABOVE

DIN RM
11'2 x 11'2

LIV RM
11' x 11'2

GARAGE
21'4 x 21'8

Two-Story
FOYER

OPT.

Covered Entry

First Floor
1,189 sq. ft.

M. MAXON

Plan #529-GH-24736

Price Code C

Total Living Area: 2,044 Sq. Ft.

Home has 3 bedrooms, 2 1/2 baths, 2-car side entry garage and basement, crawl space or slab foundation, please specify when ordering.

Special features

■ Formal dining area easily accesses kitchen through double-doors

■ Two-car garage features a workshop area for projects or extra storage

■ Second floor includes loft space ideal for office area and a handy computer center

■ Colossal master bedroom with double walk-in closets, private bath bay window seat

Second Floor
641 sq. ft.

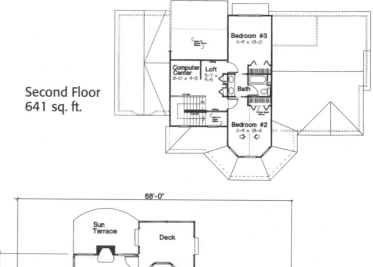

First Floor
1,403 sq. ft.

Plan #529-GSD-2686
Price Code F

Total Living Area: 3,502 Sq. Ft.

Home has 4 bedrooms, 2 full baths, 2 half baths, 3-car side entry garage and basement or crawl space foundation, please specify when ordering.

Special features

- 12' ceiling in dining room
- Interior column accents and display niches
- Living and family rooms have see-through fireplace
- Master bath has his and hers walk-in closets

COPYRIGHT 1999 GSDG

Second Floor
782 sq. ft.

Width: 89'-6"
Depth: 60'-2"

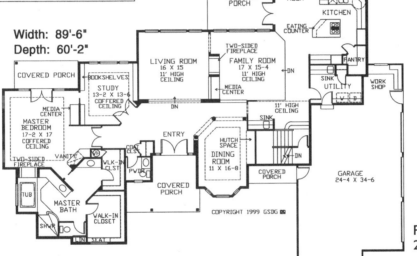

COPYRIGHT 1999 GSDG

First Floor
2,720 sq. ft.

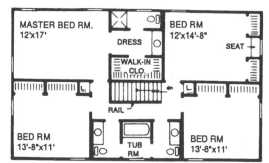

Second Floor
1,200 sq. ft.

MASTER BED RM.
12'x17'

DRESS

BED RM
12'x14'-8"

SEAT

WALK-IN
CLO.

dn

RAIL

BED RM
13'-8"x11'

TUB
RM

BED RM
13'-8"x11'

Plan #529-P-124
Price Code E

Total Living Area: 2,760 Sq. Ft.

Home has 4 bedrooms, 2 1/2 baths, 2-car side entry garage and basement foundation.

Special features

- A grand entry includes two guest closets and view of handcrafted stair to second floor

- Kitchen filled with many amenities including a built-in pantry, menu desk and a peninsula which defines the breakfast area

- A full bath and two closets accompany a first floor office or fifth bedroom located off foyer

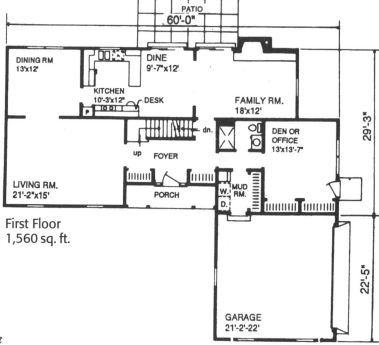

PATIO
60'-0"

DINING RM
13'x12'

DINE
9'-7"x12'

KITCHEN
10'-3"x12'

DESK

FAMILY RM.
18'x12'

dn.

up   FOYER

DEN OR
OFFICE
13'x13'-7"

29'-3"

LIVING RM.
21'-2"x15'

PORCH

W.
D.

MUD
RM.

First Floor
1,560 sq. ft.

GARAGE
21'-2'-22'

22'-5"

Plan #529-CHP-2443-A-67
Price Code D
Total Living Area: 2,450 Sq. Ft.

Home has 4 bedrooms, 2 1/2 baths, 2-car side entry garage and crawl space or slab foundation, please specify when ordering.

Special features

- Computer room is situated between bedrooms for easy access

- Two covered porches one in front and one in rear of home

- Master bedroom includes double walk-in closets in bath with luxurious step-up tub

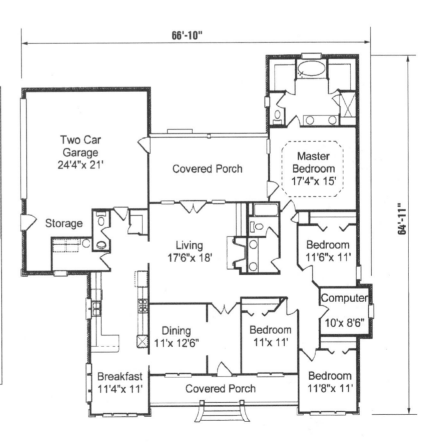

LOWE'S

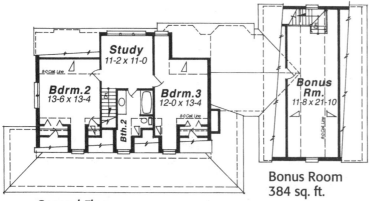

Study
11-2 x 11-0

8-0 Ceil. Line

Bdrm.2
13-6 x 13-4

Bdrm.3
12-0 x 13-4

Bth.2

8-0 Ceil. Line

Bonus Rm.
11-8 x 21-10

8-0 Ceil. Line

Bonus Room
384 sq. ft.

Second Floor
729 sq. ft.

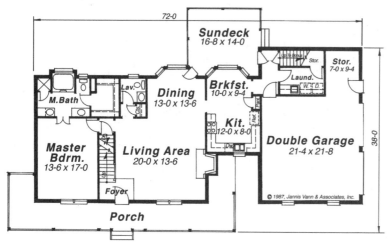

72-0

Sundeck
16-8 x 14-0

Stor.

Stor.
7-0 x 9-4

Laund.
W F D

Lav.

Dining
13-0 x 13-6

Brkfst.
10-0 x 9-4

M.Bath

Kit.
12-0 x 8-0

Double Garage
21-4 x 21-8

Master Bdrm.
13-6 x 17-0

Living Area
20-0 x 13-6

Foyer

38-0

© 1987, Jannis Vann & Associates, Inc.

Porch

First Floor
1,362 sq. ft.

Plan #529-JV-2091-A
Price Code D

Total Living Area: 2,475 Sq. Ft.

Home has 3 bedrooms, 2 1/2 baths, 2-car side entry garage and walk-out basement foundation.

Special features

- Country feeling with wrap-around porch and dormered front
- Open floor plan with living and dining areas combining has access to a sun deck
- First floor master bedroom with many luxuries

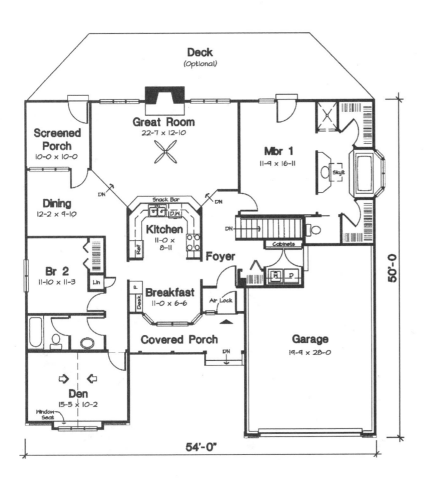

Deck
(Optional)

Screened
Porch
10-0 x 10-0

Great Room
22-7 x 12-10

Mbr 1
11-9 x 16-11

Skylt

Dining
12-2 x 9-10

DN

Snack Bar
D.W.

Kitchen
11-0 x 8-11

Ref

DN

DN

Cabinets

50-0

Br 2
11-10 x 11-3

Lin

Foyer

R P

Desk P

Breakfast
11-0 x 6-6

Air Lock

Garage
19-9 x 28-0

Covered Porch

DN

Den
15-5 x 10-2

Window
Seat

54'-0"

Plan #529-GH-24714
Price Code B

Total Living Area: 1,771 Sq. Ft.

Home has 2 bedrooms, 2 baths, 2-car garage and basement, crawl space or slab foundation, please specify when ordering.

Special features

- Den has sloped ceiling and charming window seat
- Private master bedroom has access outdoors
- Central kitchen allows for convenient access when entertaining

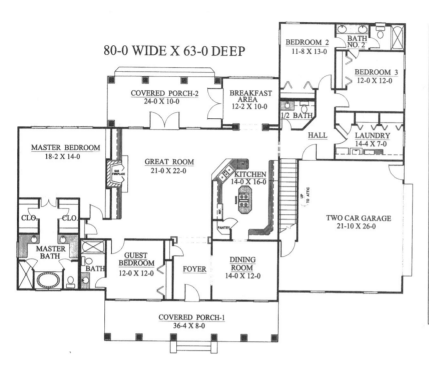

80-0 WIDE X 63-0 DEEP

BEDROOM 2
11-8 X 13-0

BATH NO. 2

BEDROOM 3
12-0 X 12-0

COVERED PORCH-2
24-0 X 10-0

BREAKFAST AREA
12-2 X 10-0

1/2 BATH

HALL

LAUNDRY
14-4 X 7-0

MASTER BEDROOM
18-2 X 14-0

GREAT ROOM
21-0 X 22-0

GAS FIREPLACE

KITCHEN
14-0 X 16-0

UP TO ATTIC

CLO.

CLO.

PANTRY

TWO CAR GARAGE
21-10 X 26-0

MASTER BATH

BATH

GUEST BEDROOM
12-0 X 12-0

FOYER

DINING ROOM
14-0 X 12-0

COVERED PORCH-1
36-4 X 8-0

Plan #529-DH-2600
Price Code E

Total Living Area: 2,669 Sq. Ft.

Home has 3 bedrooms, 3 1/2 baths, 2-car side entry garage and basement or slab foundation, please specify when ordering.

Special features

- Nice-sized corner pantry in kitchen
- Guest bedroom located off the great room with a full bath would make an excellent office
- Master bath has double walk-in closets, whirlpool bath and a large shower

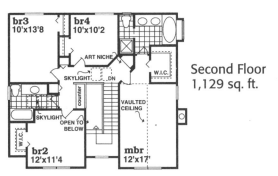

br3
10'x13'8

br4
10'x10'2

ART NICHE

SKYLIGHT   DN

W.I.C.

Second Floor
1,129 sq. ft.

SKYLIGHT

VAULTED
CEILING

counter

OPEN TO
BELOW

W.I.C.

br2
12'x11'4

mbr
12'x17'

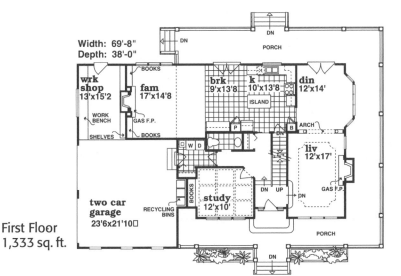

Width: 69'-8"
Depth: 38'-0"

DN

DN

PORCH

BOOKS

**wrk
shop**
13'x15'2

fam
17'x14'8

brk
9'x13'8

k
10'x13'8

din
12'x14'

WORK
BENCH

GAS F.P.

ISLAND

SHELVES

BOOKS

P

B

ARCH

W   D

liv
12'x17'

**two car
garage**
23'6x21'10

RECYCLING
BINS

BOOKS

study
12'x10'

DN   UP   DN

GAS F.P.

PORCH

First Floor
1,333 sq. ft.

DN

Plan #529-SH-SEA-307
Price Code D

Total Living Area: 2,462 Sq. Ft.

Home has 4 bedrooms, 2 1/2 baths,
2-car side entry garage and basement or
crawl space foundation, please specify
when ordering.

Special features

- Energy efficient 2" x 6" exterior
  walls

- The front study has beamed ceilings
  and also has built-ins

- French doors open from the breakfast and dining rooms to the
  spacious porch

Plan #529-SH-SEA-091

Price Code B

Total Living Area: 1,541 Sq. Ft.

Home has 3 bedrooms, 2 baths, 2-car garage and basement or crawl space foundation, please specify when ordering.

Special features

- Dining area offers access to a screened porch for outdoor dining and entertaining
- A country kitchen features a center island and a breakfast bay for casual meals
- Great room is warmed by a woodstove

Width: 87'-0"
Depth: 39'-0"

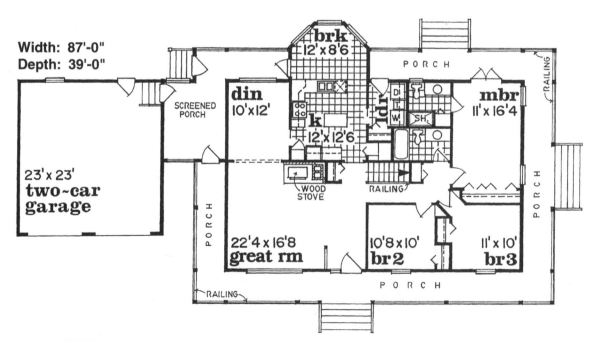

SCREENED PORCH

brk
12' x 8'6"

PORCH

din
10' x 12'

RAILING

mbr
11' x 16'4"

k
12' x 12'6"

ldr

D
W

SH.

PORCH

23' x 23'
two~car garage

WOOD STOVE

RAILING

PORCH

22'4 x 16'8
great rm

10'8 x 10'
br2

11' x 10'
br3

RAILING

PORCH

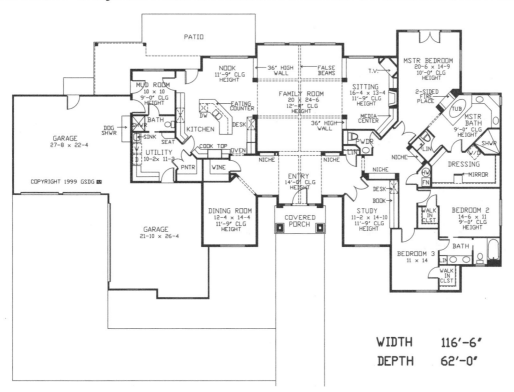

WIDTH 116'-6'
DEPTH 62'-0'

Plan #529-GSD-1017
Price Code F

Total Living Area: 3,671 Sq. Ft.

Home has 3 bedrooms, 2 full baths, 2 half baths, 4-car side entry garage and crawl space foundation.

Special features

- 14' high ceiling entry with display niches
- 11'-9" ceiling in dining room, nook, den and sitting room
- Kitchen has island eating counter, pantry and built-in desk
- Fireplace in master suite

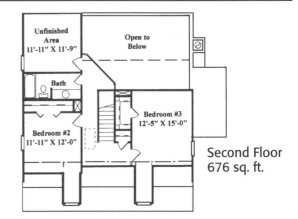

Second Floor
676 sq. ft.

Plan #529-CHP-2032-A-42
Price Code C

Total Living Area: 2,075 Sq. Ft.

Home has 3 bedrooms, 2 1/2 baths, 2-car side entry garage and slab or crawl space foundation, please specify when ordering.

Special features

■ Vaulted family room with fireplace

■ Sunny breakfast room

■ Private dining perfect for entertaining

■ Second floor includes two bedrooms, a bath and an unfinished area that would be perfect as a fourth bedroom, office or play area

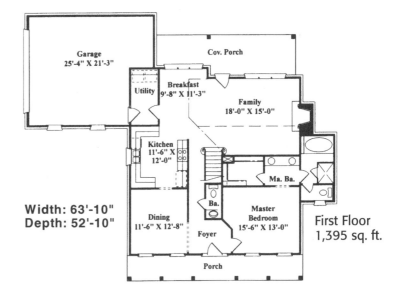

Width: 63'-10"
Depth: 52'-10"

First Floor
1,395 sq. ft.

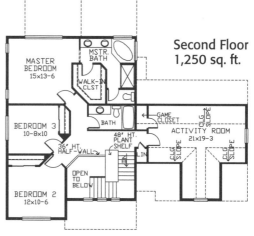

Second Floor
1,250 sq. ft.

MASTER BEDROOM 15×13-6

MSTR. BATH

WALK-IN CLST

BATH

GAME CLOSET

ACTIVITY ROOM 21×19-3

CLG SLOPE

CLG SLOPE

CLG SLOPE

CLG SLOPE

BEDROOM 3 10-8×10

36" HT. HALF WALL

48" HT. PLANT SHELF

LIN

OPEN TO BELOW

BEDROOM 2 12×10-6

Plan #529-GSD-2424
Price Code D

Total Living Area: 2,342 Sq. Ft.

Home has 3 bedrooms, 2 1/2 baths, 2-car garage and crawl space foundation.

Special features

- Display niches enhance two-story entry
- Arch accents in living and dining rooms
- Kitchen has eating bar, walk-in pantry and breakfast nook
- Spacious master suite has private bath with corner tub and dual sinks

UPPER FLOOR PLAN 'A'

NOOK 11×9

COVERED PATIO

EATING BAR

KITCHEN

PNTRY

FAMILY RM. 11×14-6

FURN

WH

First Floor
1,092 sq. ft.

DINING RM. 10-6×10

ARCH

LAUN.

GARAGE 23-8×24-4

48'-0"

PWDR

NICHE

ARCH

LIVING RM. 12×12-8

ENTRY

OPEN TO ABOVE

OPTIONAL FIREPLACE

COVERED PORCH

52'-0"

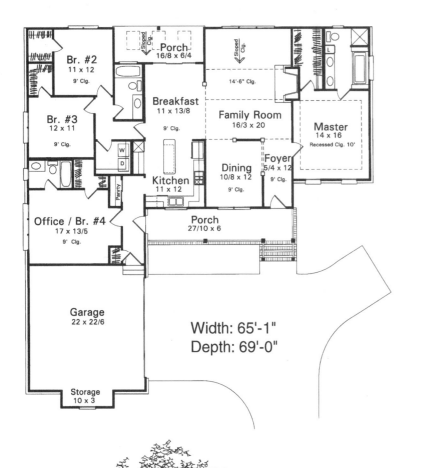

Br. #2
11 x 12
9' Clg.

Br. #3
12 x 11
9' Clg.

Porch
16/8 x 6/4

Sloped Clg.

Breakfast
11 x 13/8
9' Clg.

14'-6" Clg.

Sloped Clg.

Family Room
16/3 x 20

Master
14 x 16
Recessed Clg. 10'

W
D

Kitchen
11 x 12

Dining
10/8 x 12
9' Clg.

Foyer
5/4 x 12
9' Clg.

Pantry

Office / Br. #4
17 x 13/5
9' Clg.

Porch
27/10 x 6

Garage
22 x 22/6

Width: 65'-1"
Depth: 69'-0"

Storage
10 x 3

Plan #529-GM-2158
Price Code C

Total Living Area: 2,158 Sq. Ft.

Home has 4 bedrooms, 3 baths, 2-car side entry garage and crawl space or slab foundation, please specify when ordering.

Special features

- Private master suite has walk-in closet and bath
- Sloped ceiling in family room adds drama
- Secondary bedrooms include 9' ceilings and walk-in closets
- Covered porch adds a country touch

LOWE'S

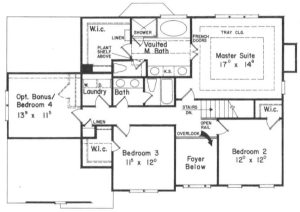

Second Floor
1,058 sq. ft.

First Floor
1,294 sq. ft.

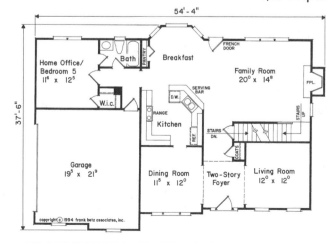

copyright © 1994 frank betz associates, inc.

Plan #529-FB-698
Price Code D

Total Living Area: 2,352 Sq. Ft.

Home has 4 bedrooms, 3 baths, 2-car side entry garage and walk-out basement or crawl space foundation, please specify when ordering.

Special features

- All bedrooms on second floor for privacy
- Kitchen and breakfast area flow into family room with fireplace
- Two-story foyer is open and airy
- Optional bonus room has an additional 168 square feet of living area

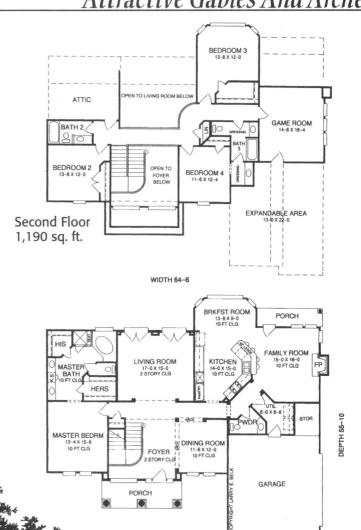

Second Floor
1,190 sq. ft.

WIDTH 64–6

Plan #529-LBD-31-20A
Price Code E

Total Living Area: 3,109 Sq. Ft.

Home has 4 bedrooms, 3 1/2 baths, 2-car side entry garage and basement, crawl space or slab foundation, please specify when ordering.

Special features

- Elegant two-story foyer
- Master suite has private bath with double closets
- Three large bedrooms plus a game room comprise second floor

First Floor
1,919 sq. ft.

DEPTH 55–10

Plan #529-1340
Price Code G

Total Living Area: 4,522 Sq. Ft.

Home has 4 bedrooms, 3 1/2 baths, 2-car garage and a partial basement/crawl space foundation.

Special features

- Large living room with cathedral ceiling views front terrace
- Kitchen, cheery breakfast room and huge family room combine creating an exciting space
- First floor master suite features a bath that defines luxury
- A second staircase serves the second floor's three bedrooms and mammoth bonus room

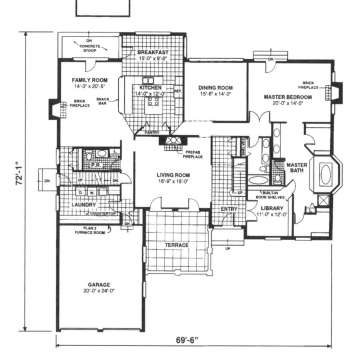

Second Floor
1,654 sq. ft.

First Floor
2,868 sq. ft.

LOWE'S

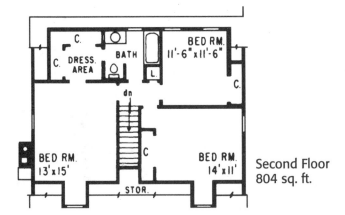

Second Floor 804 sq. ft.

BED RM. 13'x15'

BED RM. 14'x11'

STOR.

C.
DRESS. AREA
BATH
BED RM. 11'-6"x11'-6"
C.
C.
dn
C

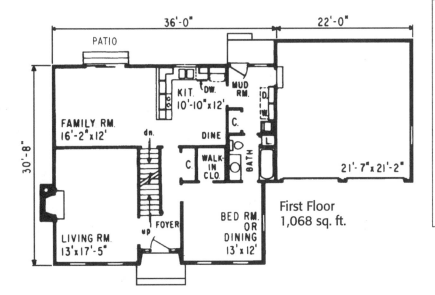

First Floor 1,068 sq. ft.

36'-0"
22'-0"
30'-8"

PATIO

FAMILY RM. 16'-2"x12'

KIT. 10'-10"x12'
DW.
MUD RM.

DINE
WALK-IN CLO.
C.
BATH

LIVING RM. 13'x17'-5"

FOYER
up
dn.

BED RM. OR DINING 13'x12'

21'-7" x 21'-2"

Plan #529-T-109
Price Code C

Total Living Area: 1,872 Sq. Ft.

Home has 4 bedrooms, 2 baths, 2-car garage and basement foundation, drawings also include crawl space and slab foundations.

Special features

- Recessed porch has entry door with sidelights and roof dormers adding charm
- Foyer with handcrafted stair adjoins living room with fireplace
- First floor bedroom with access to bath and laundry room is perfect for master suite or live-in parent
- Largest of three second floor bedrooms enjoys his and hers closets and private access to hall bath

Second Floor
1,314 sq. ft.

First Floor
1,866 sq. ft.

Plan #529-1315
Price Code E

Total Living Area: 3,180 Sq. Ft.

Home has 3 bedrooms, 2 1/2 baths, 2-car side entry garage and basement foundation.

Special features

- Majestic exterior through use of brick with projected window and corner quoins

- Two-story foyer with balcony overlook leads to an extravagant U-shaped stair built in bay window wall

- Preparing festive meals is irresistible in this kitchen and conveniently served in a sun-drenched breakfast room

- Other features include master suite sitting room, bedroom #3 balcony and coffered volume ceilings in living and dining rooms

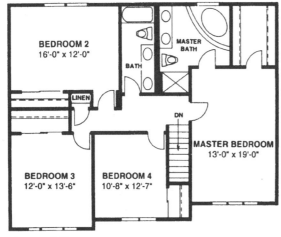

Second Floor
1,425 sq. ft.

BEDROOM 2
16'-0" x 12'-0"

MASTER BATH

BATH

LINEN

DN

MASTER BEDROOM
13'-0" x 19'-0"

BEDROOM 3
12'-0" x 13'-6"

BEDROOM 4
10'-8" x 12'-7"

UP

49'-0"

DW

REF

KITCHEN - DINETTE
25'-0" x 9'-10"

FAMILY ROOM
21'-4" x 13'-0"

LAUNDRY

31'-10"

DINING ROOM
12'-10" x 9'-0"

P.R.

DN

2 CAR GARAGE
20'-4" x 20'-0"

LIVING ROOM
20'-3" X 12'-3"

UP

First Floor
1,192 sq. ft.

Plan #529-1425
Price Code E

Total Living Area: 2,617 Sq. Ft.

Home has 4 bedrooms, 2 1/2 baths, 2-car garage and basement foundation.

Special features

- Combination dining and living rooms provide a relaxing atmosphere
- Kitchen/dinette area overlooks into large family room with fireplace
- Sunny master bedroom loaded with amenities like walk-in closet and luxurious private bath with step-up garden tub
- Covered front porch is a handy feature

Kitchen With Island Sink

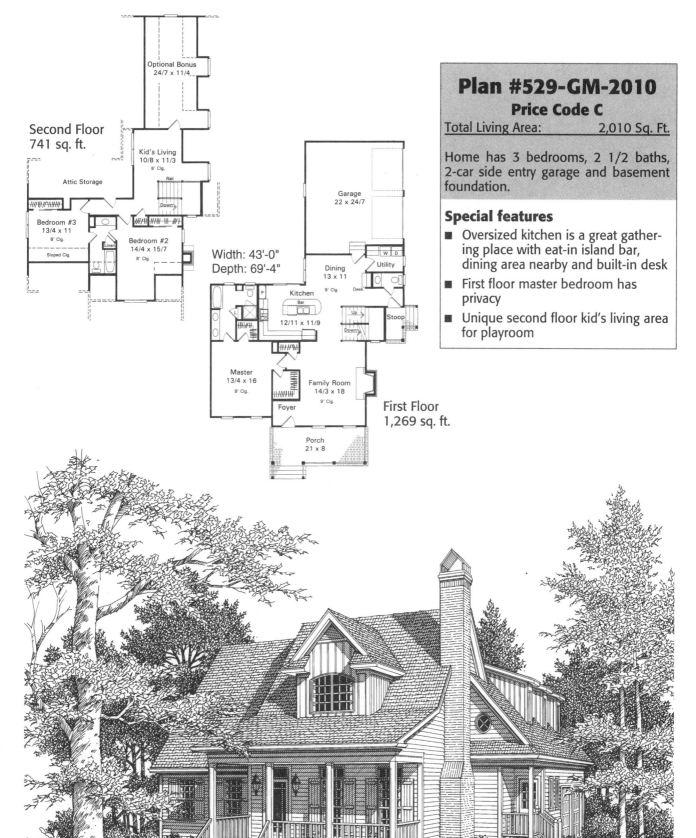

Optional Bonus
24/7 x 11/4

Second Floor
741 sq. ft.

Kid's Living
10/8 x 11/3
8' Clg.

Attic Storage

Rail

Down

Bedroom #3
13/4 x 11
8' Clg.

Linen

Bedroom #2
14/4 x 15/7
8' Clg.

Sloped Clg.

Garage
22 x 24/7

W | D

Width: 43'-0"
Depth: 69'-4"

Dining
13 x 11
9' Clg.

Utility

Desk

P

Kitchen
Bar
12/11 x 11/9

Up

Down

Stoop

Master
13/4 x 16
9' Clg.

Family Room
14/3 x 18
9' Clg.

Foyer

First Floor
1,269 sq. ft.

Porch
21 x 8

Plan #529-GM-2010
Price Code C

Total Living Area: 2,010 Sq. Ft.

Home has 3 bedrooms, 2 1/2 baths, 2-car side entry garage and basement foundation.

Special features

- Oversized kitchen is a great gathering place with eat-in island bar, dining area nearby and built-in desk
- First floor master bedroom has privacy
- Unique second floor kid's living area for playroom

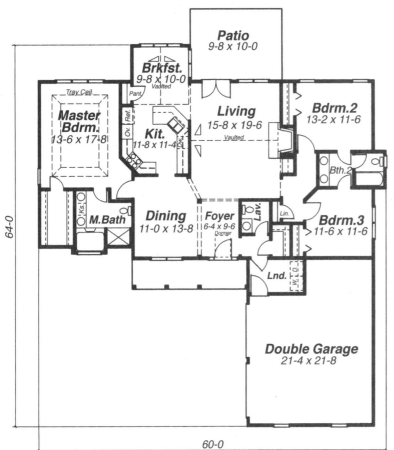

Patio
9-8 x 10-0

Brkfst.
9-8 x 10-0
Vaulted

Pant

Tray Ceil

Master Bdrm.
13-6 x 17-8

Ov. Ref.

Kit.
11-8 x 11-4

Dw.

Living
15-8 x 19-6
Vaulted

Bdrm.2
13-2 x 11-6

Bth.2

M. Bath

Wks.

Dining
11-0 x 13-8

Foyer
6-4 x 9-6
Dormer

Lav.

Lin.

Bdrm.3
11-6 x 11-6

Lnd.

W.T.D.

Double Garage
21-4 x 21-8

64-0

60-0

Plan #529-JV-1850-A
Price Code C

Total Living Area:	1,850 Sq. Ft.

Home has 3 bedrooms, 2 1/2 baths, 2-car side entry garage and crawl space or slab foundation, please specify when ordering.

Special features

- A dormer in the foyer adds natural light
- Master suite is tucked away from main traffic flow for privacy
- Alternate handicap accessible design is available that is 100% ADA compliant

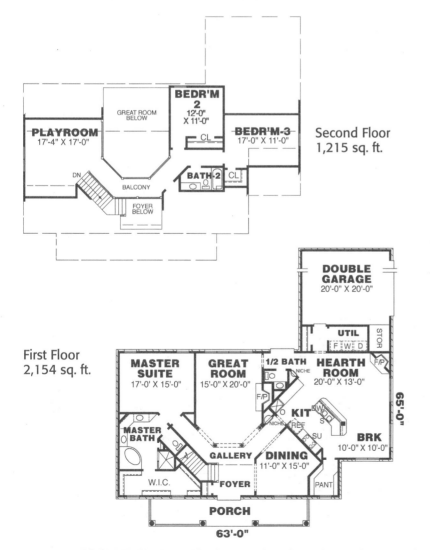

PLAYROOM
17'-4" X 17'-0"

GREAT ROOM BELOW

BEDR'M 2
12'-0" X 11'-0"

CL

BEDR'M-3
17'-0" X 11'-0"

Second Floor
1,215 sq. ft.

DN

BALCONY

BATH-2 CL

FOYER BELOW

First Floor
2,154 sq. ft.

DOUBLE GARAGE
20'-0" X 20'-0"

UTIL
F W D

STOR

MASTER SUITE
17'-0" X 15'-0"

GREAT ROOM
15'-0" X 20'-0"

1/2 BATH

HEARTH ROOM
20'-0" X 13'-0"

F/P

NICHE

F/P

MASTER BATH

KIT

W D

NICHE

REF

SU

BRK
10'-0" X 10'-0"

65'-0"

GALLERY

DINING
11'-0" X 15'-0"

W.I.C.

FOYER

PANT

PORCH

63'-0"

Plan #529-CHD-29-58
Price Code F

Total Living Area: 3,369 Sq. Ft.

Home has 3 bedrooms, 2 1/2 baths, 2-car side entry garage and walk-out basement foundation.

Special features

- Large playroom overlooks to great room below and makes a great casual family area
- Extra storage is located in garage
- Well-planned hearth room and kitchen are open and airy
- Foyer flows into unique diagonal gallery area creating a dramatic entrance into the great room

Second Floor
1,273 sq. ft.

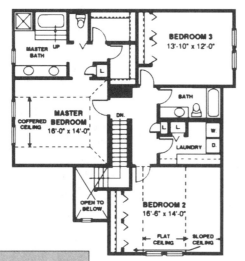

MASTER
BATH

UP

BEDROOM 3
13'-10" x 12'-0"

BATH

MASTER
BEDROOM
16'-0" x 14'-0"

COFFERED
CEILING

DN.

W

D.

LAUNDRY

OPEN TO
BELOW

BEDROOM 2
16'-6" x 14'-0"

FLAT
CEILING

SLOPED
CEILING

Plan #529-1294
Price Code E

Total Living Area: 2,645 Sq. Ft.

Home has 3 bedrooms, 2 1/2 baths,
2-car side entry garage and basement
foundation.

Special features

■ First floor activity area has a wall of
  windows creating a cheerful atmosphere

■ Formal living room has box bay
  window and a cozy fireplace

■ Bedroom #2 has a distinctive
  sloped ceiling

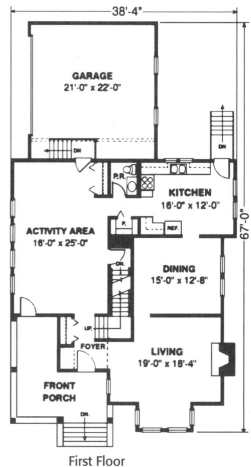

38'-4"

GARAGE
21'-0" x 22'-0"

DN.

DN.

67'-0"

P.R.

KITCHEN
16'-0" x 12'-0"

ACTIVITY AREA
16'-0" x 25'-0"

P.

REF.

DN.

DINING
15'-0" x 12'-8"

UP.

FOYER

LIVING
19'-0" x 18'-4"

FRONT
PORCH

DN.

First Floor
1,372 sq. ft.

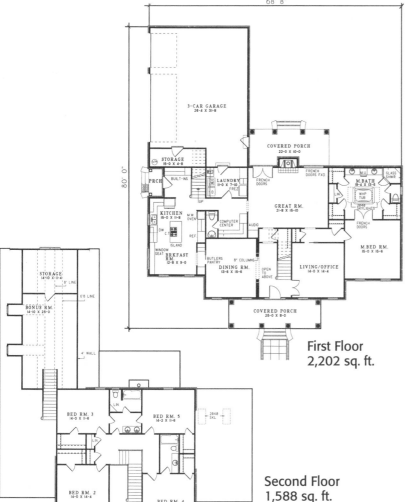

68' 8"

80' 0"

3-CAR GARAGE
28-4 X 31-8

STORAGE
16-0 X 4-8

PRCH

BUILT-INS

LAUNDRY
11-0 X 7-10
FREZ

FRENCH
DOORS

COVERED PORCH
22-0 X 10-0

FRENCH
DOORS FXD

M.U.

GLASS
SHWR

M.BATH
19-4 X 13-8

WHP
TUB

2848
SKYLIGHTS

KITCHEN
16-0 X 11-8

MW
OVEN

UP

COMPUTER
CENTER

AUDIO

GREAT RM.
21-8 X 15-10

FRENCH
DOORS

DW

REF

ISLAND

M.BED RM.
15-0 X 18-6

WINDOW
SEAT

BRKFAST
RM.
12-8 X 9-0

BUTLERS
PANTRY

8" COLUMNS

DINING RM.
13-8 X 15-8

OPEN
TO
ABOVE

LIVING/OFFICE
14-0 X 14-4

COVERED PORCH
28-0 X 8-0

First Floor
2,202 sq. ft.

STORAGE
14-10 X 11-4

8' LINE

6'8 LINE

BONUS RM.
14-10 X 25-0

4' WALL

BED RM. 3
14-0 X 11-8

LIN

BED RM. 5
14-2 X 11-8

2848
SKL

BED RM. 2
14-0 X 14-4

OPEN TO
BELOW

BED RM. 4
14-0 X 12-0

Second Floor
1,588 sq. ft.

Plan #529-NDG-147
Price Code F

Total Living Area: 3,790 Sq. Ft.

Home has 5 bedrooms, 3 1/2 baths, 3-car side entry garage and basement, walk-out basement, slab or crawl space foundation, please specify when ordering.

Special features

- Specially designed master bath has whirlpool tub in the center
- Great room has French doors leading to a covered porch
- Conveniently located computer center between kitchen and great room
- Second floor includes bonus room with 396 square feet of living area

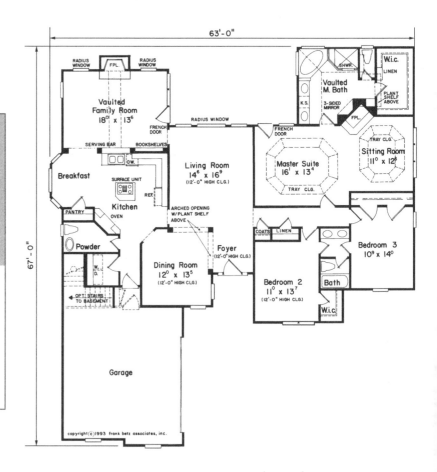

Plan #529-FB-599

Price Code D

Total Living Area: 2,236 Sq. Ft.

Home has 3 bedrooms, 2 1/2 baths, 2-car side entry garage and walk-out basement or crawl space foundation, please specify when ordering.

Special features

- Luxurious master suite has enormous sitting room with fireplace and vaulted private bath
- Cozy family room off kitchen/breakfast area
- Two secondary bedrooms share a bath

Second Floor
580 sq. ft.

Plan #529-HP-C675
Price Code B
Total Living Area: 1,673 Sq. Ft.

Home has 3 bedrooms, 2 baths, and crawl space foundation.

Special features

- Great room flows into the breakfast nook with outdoor access and beyond to an efficient kitchen

- Master suite on second floor has access to loft/study, private balcony and bath

- Covered porch surrounds the entire home for outdoor living area

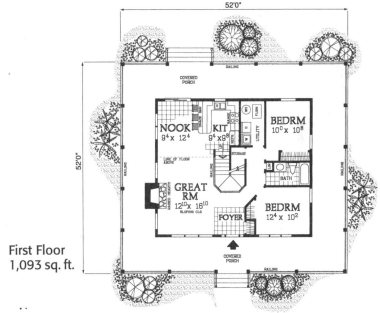

First Floor
1,093 sq. ft.

KOIZUMI/BUTLER

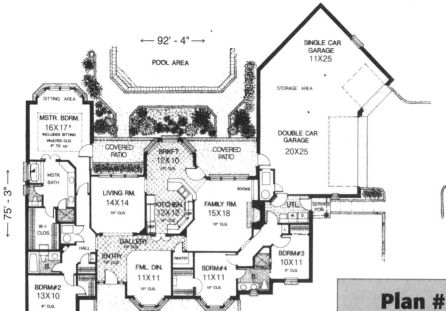

Plan #529-FDG-8729-L
Price Code D

Total Living Area: 2,529 Sq. Ft.

Home has 4 bedrooms, 3 baths, 3-car side entry garage and slab foundation.

Special features
- Breakfast and kitchen area are located between the family and living rooms for easy access
- Master bedroom includes sitting area, private bath and access to covered patio

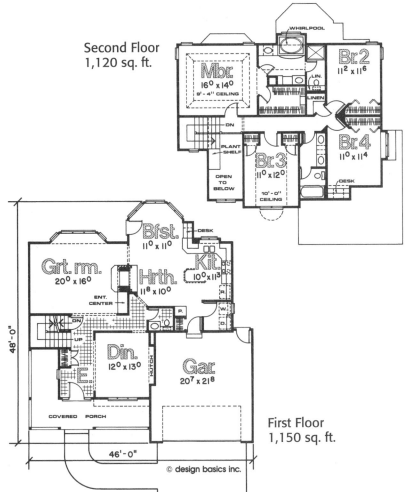

Second Floor
1,120 sq. ft.

WHIRLPOOL

Mbr.
16⁰ x 14⁰
9'-4" CEILING

Br. 2
11² x 11⁶

LIN.

LINEN

Br. 4
11⁰ x 11⁴

DN

PLANT SHELF

OPEN TO BELOW

Br. 3
11⁰ x 12⁰
10'-0" CEILING

DESK

Bfst.
11⁰ x 11⁰

DESK

Grt. rm.
20⁰ x 16⁰

Hrth.
11⁸ x 10⁰

Kit.
10⁰ x 11³

ENT. CENTER

DN

UP

P.

W.

D.

Din.
12⁰ x 13⁰

HUTCH

Gar.
20⁷ x 21⁸

COVERED   PORCH

48'-0"

46'-0"

© design basics inc.

First Floor
1,150 sq. ft.

Plan #529-DBI-2408
Price Code D

<u>Total Living Area:</u>   2,270 Sq. Ft.

Home has 4 bedrooms, 2 1/2 baths, 2-car garage and basement foundation.

Special features

- Great room and hearth room share see-through fireplace
- Oversized rooms throughout
- First floor has terrific floor plan for entertaining with large kitchen/breakfast area and adjacent great room

PATIO

DEN
12/0 X 10/8
(9' CLG.)

NOOK
9/2 X 10/0

VAULTED
FAMILY
16/6 X 21/4 +

LIVING
16/0 X 16/4
(13'-4" CLG.)

MASTER
15/8 X 15/8
(9' CLG.)

BR. 2
11/6 X 12/0

DESK

15/8 X 9/6 +

DINING
11/0 X 16/8

(13'-4" CLG.)

PANTRY

REF.

BR. 3
12/8 X 11/0

LIN

D. W.

GARAGE
20/6 X 19/8 +

◀ 84' ▶

▲
73'
▼

25/2 X 11/0

©Alan Mascord Design Associates, Inc.

Plan #529-AMD-1219
Price Code E

Total Living Area: 2,755 Sq. Ft.

Home has 3 bedrooms, 2 1/2 baths,
3-car side entry garage and crawl space
foundation.

Special features

- Contemporary design allows every
  room to take advantage of a rear
  view
- See-through fireplace and entertainment center separates formal living
  area from informal family area
- Master suite has its own wing

Dramatic U-Shaped Stairs

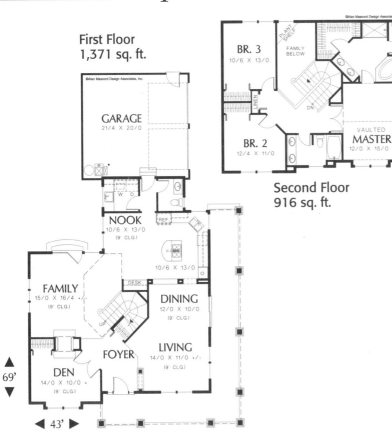

First Floor
1,371 sq. ft.

©Alan Mascord Design Associates, Inc.

GARAGE
21/4 X 20/0

W D

NOOK
10/6 X 13/0
(9' CLG.)

REF.

10/6 X 13/0

DESK

FAMILY
15/0 X 16/4 +/-
(9' CLG.)

DINING
12/0 X 10/0
(9' CLG.)

FOYER

LIVING
14/0 X 11/0 +/-
(9' CLG.)

DEN
14/0 X 10/0 +
(9' CLG.)

69'

43'

©Alan Mascord Design Associates, Inc.

BR. 3
10/6 X 13/0

PLANT SHELF

FAMILY BELOW

BR. 2
12/4 X 11/0

LINEN

DN

VAULTED
MASTER
12/0 X 15/0 +

Second Floor
916 sq. ft.

Plan #529-AMD-2229
Price Code D

Total Living Area: 2,287 Sq. Ft.

Home has 4 bedrooms, 2 1/2 baths, 2-car side entry garage and crawl space foundation.

Special features

- Wrap-around porch creates an inviting feeling
- First floor windows have transom windows above
- Den has see-through fireplace into the family area

Optional
Second Floor

Future Space
11⁰ • 20⁴

First Floor
2,551 sq. ft.

Plan #529-HDS-2551

Price Code D

Total Living Area: 2,551 Sq. Ft.

Home has 3 bedrooms, 3 baths, 2-car side entry garage and slab foundation.

Special features

- Archway joins formal living room and family area
- Master suite has private bath and access to covered patio
- Breakfast nook overlooks family room with corner fireplace
- Optional living area over garage has an additional 287 square feet of living area

Width: 70'-0"
Depth: 72'-0"

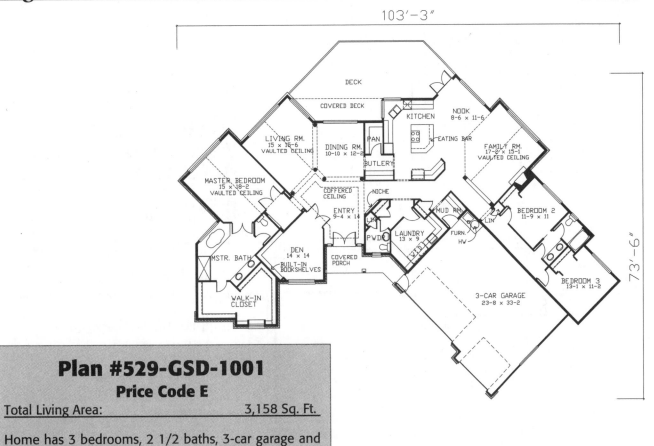

103'-3"

73'-6"

DECK

COVERED DECK

KITCHEN

NOOK
8-6 x 11-6

LIVING RM.
15 x 15-6
VAULTED CEILING

DINING RM.
10-10 x 12-2

PAN

EATING BAR

FAMILY RM.
17-2 x 15-1
VAULTED CEILING

BUTLERY

MASTER BEDROOM
15 x 18-2
VAULTED CEILING

COFFERED
CEILING

NICHE

ENTRY
9-4 x 14

MUD RM.

LIN

BEDROOM 2
11-9 x 11

MSTR. BATH

LIN

PWDR

LAUNDRY
13 x 9

FURN.

HW

DEN
14 x 14

BUILT-IN
BOOKSHELVES

COVERED
PORCH

BEDROOM 3
13-1 x 11-2

WALK-IN
CLOSET

3-CAR GARAGE
23-8 x 33-2

Plan #529-GSD-1001
Price Code E

Total Living Area: 3,158 Sq. Ft.

Home has 3 bedrooms, 2 1/2 baths, 3-car garage and
crawl space foundation.

Special features
- Coffered ceiling in entry
- Vaulted ceilings in living room, master bedroom
  and family room
- Interior columns accent the entry, living and dining
  areas
- Kitchen island has eating bar adding extra seating
- Master bath has garden tub and separate shower

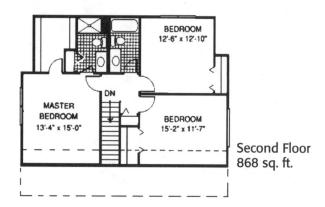

Second Floor
868 sq. ft.

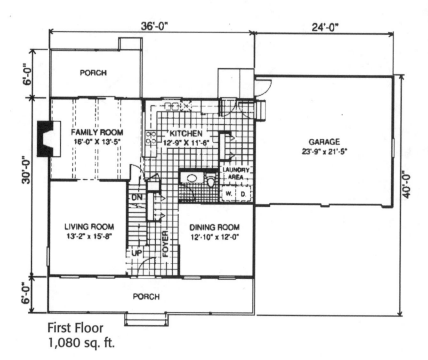

First Floor
1,080 sq. ft.

Plan #529-1347
Price Code C
Total Living Area: 1,948 Sq. Ft.

Home has 3 bedrooms, 2 1/2 baths, 2-car garage and basement foundation, drawings also include crawl space foundation.

Special features
- Large elongated porch for moonlit evenings
- Stylish family room features beamed ceiling
- Skillfully designed kitchen convenient to an oversized laundry area
- Second floor bedrooms all generously sized

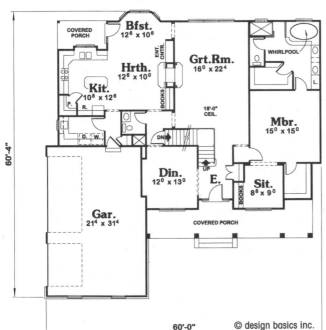

Br.2
11² x 11⁸

Br.3
11² x 12⁰

Br.4
11⁰ x 12⁰

OPEN TO BELOW

OPEN TO BELOW

DN

Second Floor
660 sq. ft.

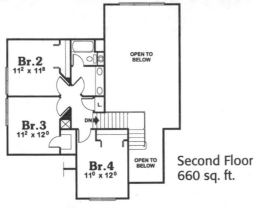

COVERED PORCH

Bfst.
12⁶ x 10⁶

Hrth.
12⁶ x 10⁰

Kit.
10⁸ x 12⁶

ENT. CNTR.

BOOKS

Grt.Rm.
16⁰ x 22⁴

WHIRLPOOL

18'-0" CEIL.

Mbr.
15⁰ x 15⁰

D. W.

DN

60'-4"

Gar.
21⁴ x 31⁴

Din.
12⁰ x 13⁰

E.

UP

Sit.
8⁸ x 9⁰

BOOKS

COVERED PORCH

60'-0"

© design basics inc.

First Floor
1,955 sq. ft.

Plan #529-DBI-5520

Price Code E

Total Living Area: 2,615 Sq. Ft.

Home has 4 bedrooms, 2 1/2 baths, 3-car side entry garage and basement foundation.

Special features

- Two-story great room is elegant with see-through fireplace into cozy hearth room
- Master suite has sitting area with built-in bookshelves
- Covered porch off breakfast area is a perfect place to spend quiet mornings

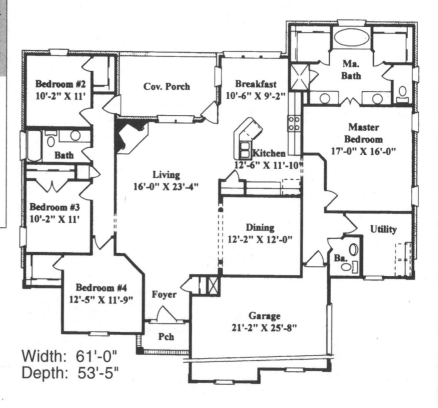

Plan #529-CHP-2243-A-29
Price Code D

Total Living Area: 2,246 Sq. Ft.

Home has 4 bedrooms, 2 1/2 baths, 2-car side entry garage and slab foundation.

Special features

- Enormous master bedroom and bath has all the amenities
- Covered rear porch accessible to all parts of the home
- Kitchen features island with sink, large pantry and plenty of cabinet space

Bedroom #2
10'-2" X 11'

Cov. Porch

Breakfast
10'-6" X 9'-2"

Ma.
Bath

Bath

Master
Bedroom
17'-0" X 16'-0"

Living
16'-0" X 23'-4"

Kitchen
12'-6" X 11'-10"

Bedroom #3
10'-2" X 11'

Dining
12'-2" X 12'-0"

Utility

Bedroom #4
12'-5" X 11'-9"

Foyer

Ba.

Pch

Garage
21'-2" X 25'-8"

Width: 61'-0"
Depth: 53'-5"

Second Floor
886 sq. ft.

ROOF ROOF
WALL BELOW
RECESSED ROOF
UPPER BREAKFAST RM BEDROOM
11¹⁰ x 11⁴
BEDROOM WALK-IN
11⁴ x 11⁴ CLOSET
LINEN CL
DN BATH
RAILING WHIRLPOOL
BATH
OPEN
BELOW DRESS. RM
UPPER MASTER WALK-IN
FOYER BEDROOM CLOSET
12⁴ x 16⁰
RECESSED ROOF
ROOF ROOF

32'8"

TERRACE
UP UP
BREAKFAST RM SCREENED
16⁸ x 10⁶ PORCH
11¹⁰ x 11²
SNACK BAR DESK
RANGE BC
KITCHEN DINING RM
16⁸ x 11² 12⁰ x 12⁸
DW PANTRY
REF'G PDR
RM
DN DN
OPEN CURIO
ABOVE CL
UP LIVING RM
FOYER 18⁴ x 14⁰
CURIO
VERANDA
RAILING RAILING
UP

50'0"

First Floor
1,111 sq. ft.

Plan #529-HP-C316
Price Code C

Total Living Area: 1,997 Sq. Ft.

Home has 3 bedrooms, 2 1/2 baths, and basement foundation.

Special features

- Screened porch leads to a rear terrace with access to the breakfast room

- Living and dining rooms combine adding spaciousness to the floor plan

- Other welcome amenities include boxed windows in breakfast and dining rooms, a fireplace in living room and a pass-through snack bar in the kitchen

Master Bdrm.
17-4 x 13-6
Tray Ceil.

Patio

Bdrm.4
11-2 x 11-4

Brkfst.
11-6 x 9-6

Family Rm.
20-2 x 15-2

Kit.
11-6 x 14-0

Bdrm.3
11-8 x 11-6

Double Garage
21-4 x 22-0

Dining
11-6 x 13-6
10'-0 Ceil.

Foyer
8-4 x 14-0
10'-0 Ceil.

Living
11-6 x 13-2
10'-0 Ceil.

Bdrm.2
13-4 x 11-6

Porch

72-10

63-5

Plan #529-JV-2542-A
Price Code D

Total Living Area: 2,542 Sq. Ft.

Home has 4 bedrooms, 2 1/2 baths, 2-car garage and basement, crawl space or slab foundation, please specify when ordering.

Special features

- Formal entry opens to living and dining rooms
- Private master suite features double closets and access to the outdoors
- Extra storage can be found throughout

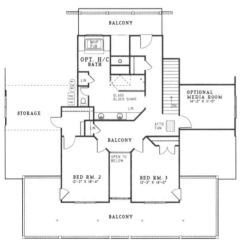

Second Floor
1,233 sq. ft.

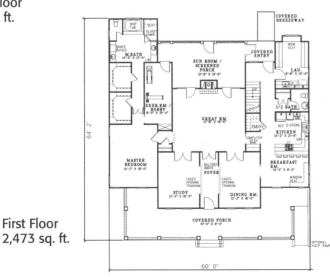

First Floor
2,473 sq. ft.

Plan #529-NDG-134
Price Code F

Total Living Area: 3,706 Sq. Ft.

Home has 3 bedrooms, 2 1/2 baths, 3-car detached garage and crawl space or slab foundation, please specify when ordering.

Special features

- Master suite has walk-in closets, a private bath and an exercise/hobby room that accesses a sun room

- Breakfast room with counter seating joins kitchen and dining area

Rear View

Second Floor
894 sq. ft.

Br 2
11-6 x 11-4

Br 3
11 x 11-4

linen

DN

railing

1/2 wall

open to below

Mstr Br
13-4 x 15

46'-8"

35'-8"

Dining
12-1 x 11-4

Kitchen
13 x 11-4

W
D

pantry

DN

Great Rm
14 x 21-8

UP

Garage
22 x 23-4

open to above

First Floor
891 sq. ft.

Plan #529-GH-24610
Price Code B

Total Living Area: 1,785 Sq. Ft.

Home has 3 bedrooms, 1 1/2 baths, 2-car garage and slab, basement or crawl space foundation, please specify when ordering.

Special features

■ Energy efficient home has 2" x 6" exterior walls

■ Large island in kitchen is ideal for dining

■ Vaulted master bedroom has private bath and walk-in closet

■ Two-story great room has a beautiful fireplace as a focal point

Plan #529-FB-1224
Price Code D

Total Living Area: 2,246 Sq. Ft.

Home has 4 bedrooms, 3 baths, 2-car side entry garage and walk-out basement or crawl space foundation, please specify when ordering.

Special features

- Two-story foyer
- Master suite has sitting area with bay window
- Breakfast area near kitchen
- Bedroom #4 easily converts to an office
- Optional bonus room has an additional 269 square feet of living area

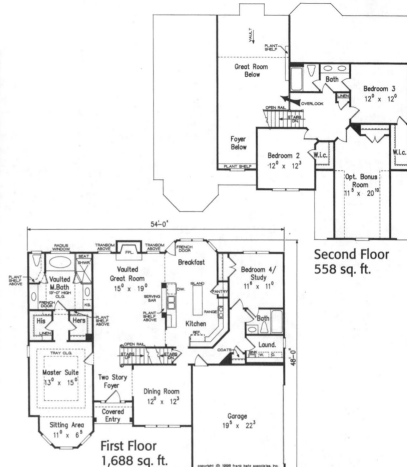

Second Floor
558 sq. ft.

First Floor
1,688 sq. ft.

Plan #529-DH-2352
Price Code D

Total Living Area: 2,352 Sq. Ft.

Home has 4 bedrooms, 2 baths, optional 2-car garage and crawl space or slab foundation, please specify when ordering

Special features

- Charming courtyard on the side of the home easily accesses the porch leading into the breakfast area
- French doors throughout home create a sunny atmosphere
- Master bedroom accesses covered porch

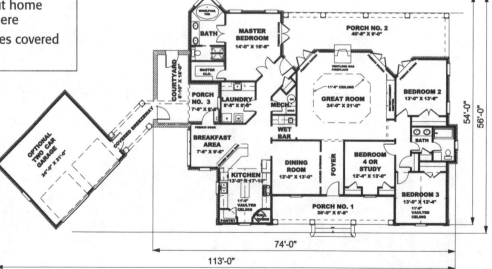

LOWE'S

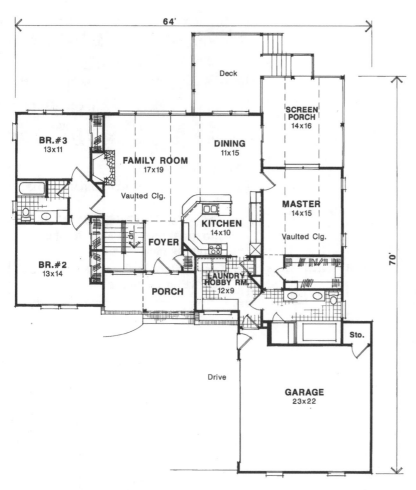

64'

Deck

SCREEN PORCH
14x16

BR.#3
13x11

FAMILY ROOM
17x19

DINING
11x15

Vaulted Clg.

MASTER
14x15

KITCHEN
14x10

Vaulted Clg.

FOYER

BR.#2
13x14

LAUNDRY
HOBBY RM.
12x9

PORCH

70'

Drive

Sto.

GARAGE
23x22

Plan #529-GM-1892
Price Code C

Total Living Area: 1,892 Sq. Ft.

Home has 3 bedrooms, 2 baths, 2-car side entry garage and basement foundation.

Special features

- Family room with vaulted ceiling has grand appeal
- Screened porch and deck off dining area allow for more entertaining area
- Large laundry/hobby room has lots of work space

First Floor
1,713 sq. ft.

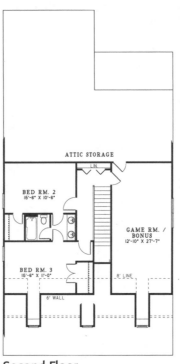

Second Floor
994 sq. ft.

Plan #529-NDG-307
Price Code E

Total Living Area: 2,707 Sq. Ft.

Home has 4 bedrooms, 3 baths, 2-car rear entry garage and slab or crawl space foundation, please specify when ordering.

Special features

- Double-doors lead into handsome study
- Kitchen and breakfast room flow into great room creating terrific gathering place
- Second floor includes bonus space perfect for game room

© Michael E. Nelson
NELSON DESIGN GROUP, LLC

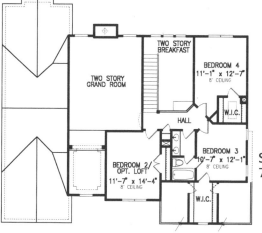

Second Floor
709 sq. ft.

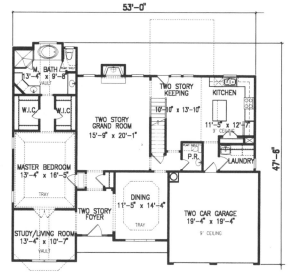

53'-0"

47'-6"

First Floor
1,751 sq. ft.

Plan #529-MG-96132
Price Code D

Total Living Area: 2,450 Sq. Ft.

Home has 4 bedrooms, 2 1/2 baths, 2-car garage and basement or slab foundation, please specify when ordering.

Special features

- Convenient first floor master bedroom has double walk-in closets and an optional sitting area/study
- Two-story breakfast and grand room are open and airy
- Laundry room has a sink and overhead cabinets for convenience

Second Floor
978 sq. ft.

Bed#2
11⁸x14

Bed#3
12⁸x13

BonusRm
14x17
234 Sq. Ft. Not
Included in Total
Square Footage

Balcony

Bed#4
12⁸x12

Open To
Entry
Below

First Floor
2,039 sq. ft.

Covered Patio

Covered
Patio

Brkfst
13⁸x11⁸

GreatRm
20⁸x17

MstrBed
16x17⁸

Kit
13x12

Gallery

Util

Cov
Porch

FmlDin
11x12

Ent

Study/
FmlLiv
12⁸x12

Cov
Por.

3-Car Gar
20⁸x30

62'-0"

77'-6 1/4"

Plan #529-FDG-8576-L
Price Code E

Total Living Area: 3,017 Sq. Ft.

Home has 4 bedrooms, 3 1/2 baths, 3-car side entry garage and slab foundation.

Special features

- Impressive two-story entry has curved staircase
- Family room has unique elliptical vault above window
- Master suite includes a private covered patio and bath with walk-in closet
- Breakfast area overlooks great room
- Bonus room has an additional 234 square feet of living area

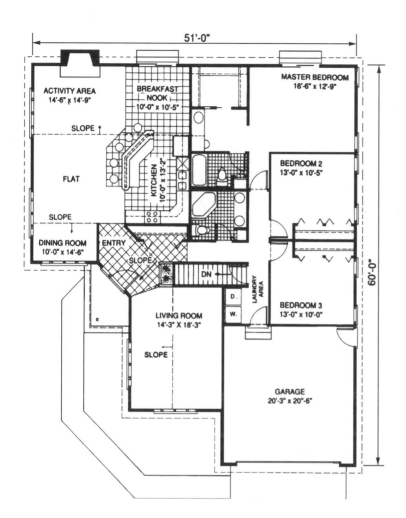

51'-0"

60'-0"

ACTIVITY AREA
14'-6" x 14'-9"

SLOPE ↑

FLAT

SLOPE

DINING ROOM
10'-0" x 14'-6"

BREAKFAST NOOK
10'-0" x 10'-5"

KITCHEN
10'-0" x 13'-2"

ENTRY

SLOPE

MASTER BEDROOM
16'-6" x 12'-9"

BEDROOM 2
13'-0" x 10'-5"

DN

D.

W.

LAUNDRY AREA

LIVING ROOM
14'-3" X 18'-3"

SLOPE

BEDROOM 3
13'-0" x 10'-0"

GARAGE
20'-3" X 20"-6"

Plan #529-1266
Price Code C

Total Living Area: 2,086 Sq. Ft.

Home has 3 bedrooms, 2 baths, 2-car garage and partial basement/crawl space foundation.

Special features

- An angled foyer leads to vaulted living room with sunken floor
- Dining room, activity room, nook and kitchen all have vaulted ceilings
- Skillfully designed kitchen features an angled island with breakfast bar
- Master bedroom is state-of-the-art with luxury bath and a giant walk-in closet

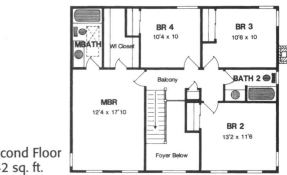

Second Floor
942 sq. ft.

Plan #529-JFD-20-2050-1
Price Code C
Total Living Area: 2,050 Sq. Ft.

Home has 4 bedrooms, 2 1/2 baths, 2-car garage and basement foundation.

Special features

- Angled dining area has lots of windows and opens into family room and kitchen

- All bedrooms located on second floor for privacy from living areas

- Master suite has private bath and a walk-in closet

Width: 64'-0"
Depth: 36'-0"

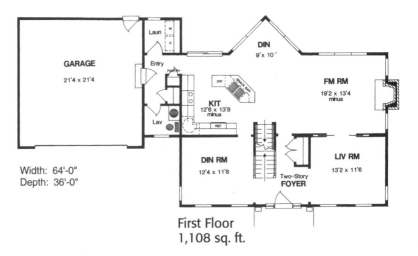

First Floor
1,108 sq. ft.

Plan #529-JA-64396
Price Code C

Total Living Area: 2,196 Sq. Ft.

Home has 3 bedrooms, 2 1/2 baths, 3-car garage and basement foundation.

Special features

- Covered front porch leads to the vaulted foyer which invites guests into the great room
- Master bedroom features walk-in closet, private bath with double vanity, spa tub and linen closet
- Large open kitchen

SCREEN PORCH
31'8" X 9'8"

M.B.R.
14'8" X 15'4"

GRT. RM.
VAULTED CEILING
17'8" X 22'0"

NK.
10'0" X 18'0"

KIT.
10'4" X 15'0"

DIN.
10'-1 1/8" CEILING
12'0" X 11'6"

VAULTED
CEILING

BR. #3
11'8" X 13'0"

BR. #2
10'-1 1/8" CEILING
13'0" X 13'4"

3 CAR GAR.
26'0" X 48'0"

58'8"

73'0"

FREILING

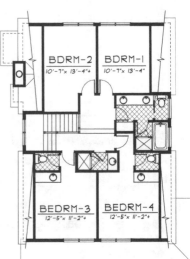

Second Floor
1,028 sq. ft.

BDRM-2
10'-7"x 13'-4"+

BDRM-1
10'-7"x 13'-4"+

BEDRM-3
12'-5"x 11'-2"+

BEDRM-4
12'-5"x 11'-2"+

Plan #529-DDI-100213
Price Code D
Total Living Area: 2,202 Sq. Ft.

Home has 5 bedrooms, 2 full baths, 2 half baths, 2-car drive under garage and basement or walk-out basement foundation, please specify when ordering.

Special features

- 9' ceilings on first floor
- Guest bedroom located on the first floor for convenience could easily be converted to an office area
- Large kitchen with oversized island overlooks dining area

Width: 34'-0" Depth: 46'-0"

DECK
10'-0"+ x 38'-0"

STORAGE

LIVING RM
15'-0"x 15'-0"

DINING
14'-0"x 10'-0"

ISLAND

PANTRY

KITCHEN
11'-0"x 11'-2"

GUEST
10'-2"x 11'-0"

MUD ROOM

COVERED PORCH

First Floor
1,174 sq. ft.

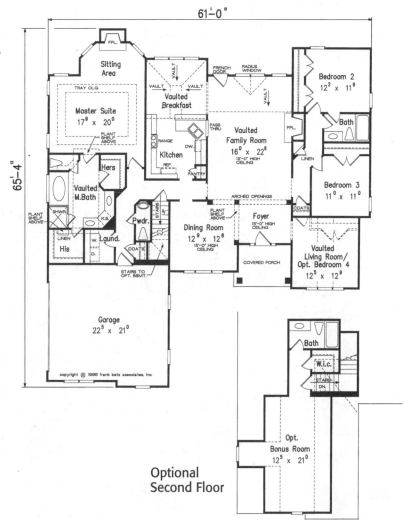

First Floor
2,311 sq. ft.

61'-0"

65'-4"

Sitting Area

FPL.

VAULT

FRENCH DOOR

RADIUS WINDOW

TRAY CLG.

Master Suite
17⁹ x 20⁰

PLANT SHELF ABOVE

Vaulted Breakfast

VAULT   VAULT

VAULT

Bedroom 2
12² x 11⁸

Hers

PASS THRU

RANGE   DW.

Kitchen

REF.   PANTRY

Vaulted Family Room
16⁰ x 22⁶
15'-0" HIGH CEILING

FPL.

LINEN

Bath

Vaulted M.Bath

PLANT SHELF ABOVE

K.S.

Pwdr.

STAIRS

ARCHED OPENINGS

PLANT SHELF ABOVE

Foyer
15'-0" HIGH CEILING

COATS

Bedroom 3
11⁰ x 11⁰

PLANT SHELF ABOVE

SHWR.

LINEN   w. Laund.

His   w.   D.

COATS

Dining Room
12⁹ x 12⁸
15'-0" HIGH CEILING

COVERED PORCH

Vaulted Living Room/
Opt. Bedroom 4
12⁵ x 12⁹

STAIRS TO OPT. BSMT.

Garage
22⁵ x 21⁰

copyright © 1996 frank betz associates, inc.

Plan #529-FB-969

Price Code D

Total Living Area: 2,311 Sq. Ft.

Home has 3 bedrooms, 2 1/2 baths, 2-car side entry garage and walk-out basement or crawl space foundation, please specify when ordering.

Special features

■ Fireplaces warm master suite and family room

■ Vaulted breakfast room near kitchen

■ Formal living room near dining room

■ Optional bonus room on second floor has an additional 425 square feet of living area

Bath

W.i.c.

STAIRS DN.

Opt. Bonus Room
12⁵ x 21⁰

Optional Second Floor

Width: 59'-10"
Depth: 60'-10"

Garage
23'-4" X 20'-7"

Ma. Bath

Patio

Ma. Bedroom
14'-3" X 17'-0"

Breakfast
9'-0" X 13'-0"

Util.

Living
20'-1" X 18'-0"

Kitchen
12'-7" X 12'-6"

Bath 2

Foyer

Dining
11'-4" X 13'-0"

Bath 3

Bedroom 2
10'-9" X 13'-0"

Bedroom 3
11'-6" X 11'-0"

Study
10'-8" X 12'-0"

Porch

Plan #529-CHP-2233-B-21
Price Code E
Total Living Area: 2,697 Sq. Ft.

Home has 3 bedrooms, 3 baths, 2-car side entry garage and slab foundation.

Special features
- Secluded study with full bath nearby is an ideal guest room or office
- Master bedroom has access to outdoor patio
- Additional 351 square feet of unfinished attic space

LOWE'S

Attic Storage

Stairs Down

Bedroom #3
14 x 12
8' Clg.

Linen

Bedroom #2
13/9 x 11/5
8' Clg.
Sloped Clg.

Second Floor
557 sq. ft.

Width: 48'-2"
Depth: 67'-5"

Garage & Storage
22 x 25/10

W
D

Rear Porch
18 x 7/10

Stairs Up

Pantry

Stairs Down

Kitchen
11/10 x 10/5

Breakfast
14/3 x 10/5
9' Clg.

Desk

Family Room
14 x 18/8
9' Clg.

Dining
11 x 11/5
9' Clg.

Master Bedroom
13/9 x 16/8
9' Clg.

Foyer
8/9 x 5/10

First Floor
1,409 sq. ft.

Front Porch
40 x 7/10

Plan #529-GM-1966
Price Code C

Total Living Area: 1,966 Sq. Ft.

Home has 3 bedrooms, 2 1/2 baths, 2-car side entry garage and basement foundation.

Special features

- Private dining room remains focal point when entering the home
- Kitchen and breakfast room join to create a functional area
- Lots of closet space in second floor bedrooms

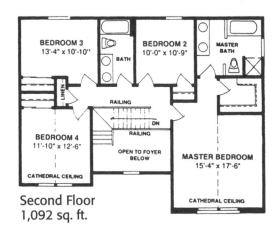

Second Floor
1,092 sq. ft.

Plan #529-1428
Price Code D
Total Living Area: 2,292 Sq. Ft.

Home has 4 bedrooms, 2 1/2 baths, 2-car garage and basement foundation.

Special features

- Wood-crafted staircase ascends into dramatic two-story foyer with second floor overlook

- Entertaining family will be delightful in the large family room with fireplace and views to the outdoors

- Open kitchen center island cabinet illustrates a carefully planned design

- Second floor master suite enjoys luxury bath and walk-in closet

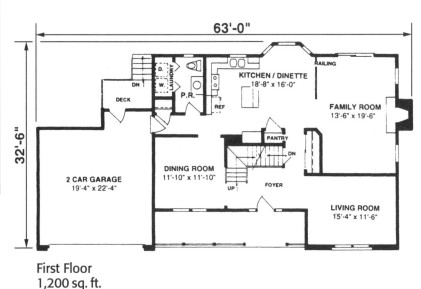

First Floor
1,200 sq. ft.

Plan #529-NDG-204

Price Code D

Total Living Area: 2,439 Sq. Ft.

Home has 4 bedrooms, 3 baths, 2-car garage and slab, crawl space, basement or walk-out basement foundation, please specify when ordering.

Special features

- Enter columned gallery area just before reaching family room with see-through fireplace
- Master suite has a corner whirlpool tub
- Double-door entrance into study

Plan #529-JA-73897
Price Code B

Total Living Area: 1,794 Sq. Ft.

Home has 3 bedrooms, 2 baths, 3-car garage and basement foundation.

Special features

- Elegant arched soffit connects the great room to the dining room
- Large kitchen has wrap-around counters, large pantry and center island
- Plenty of storage throughout

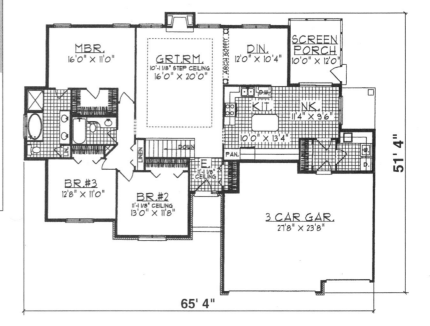

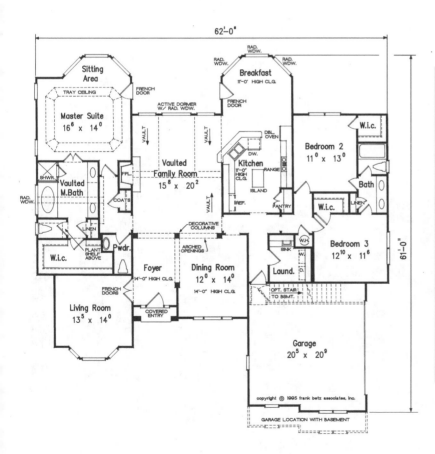

Plan #529-FB-930
Price Code D

Total Living Area: 2,322 Sq. Ft.

Home has 3 bedrooms, 2 1/2 baths, 2-car side entry garage and walk-out basement, crawl space or slab foundation, please specify when ordering.

Special features

- Vaulted family room has fireplace and access to kitchen
- Decorative columns and arched openings surround dining area
- Master suite has a sitting room and grand scale bath
- Kitchen includes island with serving bar

Plan #529-CHP-2443-A-38
Price Code D
Total Living Area: 2,481 Sq. Ft.

Home has 4 bedrooms, 2 1/2 baths, 2-car side entry garage and crawl space or slab foundation, please specify when ordering.

Special features
- All bedrooms separate from main living areas for privacy
- Enormous master bath with double walk-in closets
- Unique covered porch off living area and breakfast room
- Cozy fireplace with built-in bookshelves in living area

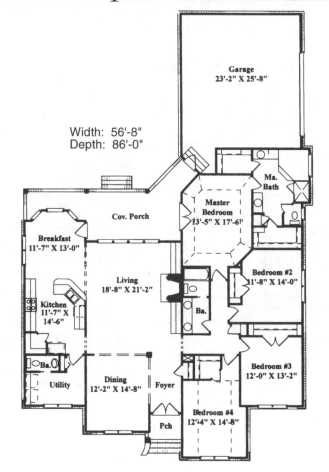

Width: 56'-8"
Depth: 86'-0"

Garage
23'-2" X 25'-8"

Ma. Bath

Master Bedroom
13'-5" X 17'-6"

Cov. Porch

Breakfast
11'-7" X 13'-0"

Living
18'-8" X 21'-2"

Bedroom #2
11'-8" X 14'-0"

Kitchen
11'-7" X 14'-6"

Ba.

Ba.

Bedroom #3
12'-0" X 13'-2"

Dining
12'-2" X 14'-8"

Foyer

Utility

Pch

Bedroom #4
12'4" X 14'-8"

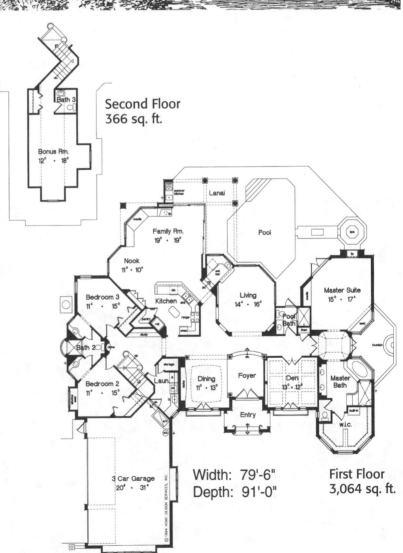

Second Floor
366 sq. ft.

Bath 3

Bonus Rm.
12⁰ · 18⁰

Plan #529-HDS-3430
Price Code F

Total Living Area: 3,430 Sq. Ft.

Home has 3 bedrooms, 3 1/2 baths, 3-car side entry garage and slab foundation.

Special features

- Den with balcony has coffered ceiling
- Master suite views private garden, shares see-through fireplace and accesses patio
- Living room with wet bar
- Summer kitchen allows for grilling and cooking in warmer months

Lanai

Family Rm.
19⁰ · 19⁰

Pool

Nook
11⁰ · 10⁴

Kitchen

Living
14⁴ · 16⁰

Master Suite
15⁰ · 17⁴

Bedroom 3
11⁴ · 15⁰

Pool Bath

Bath 2

Bedroom 2
11⁴ · 15⁰

Laun.

Dining
11⁰ · 13⁰

Foyer

Den
13⁰ · 12⁰

Master Bath

Entry

w.i.c.

3 Car Garage
20⁴ · 31⁴

Width: 79'-6"
Depth: 91'-0"

First Floor
3,064 sq. ft.

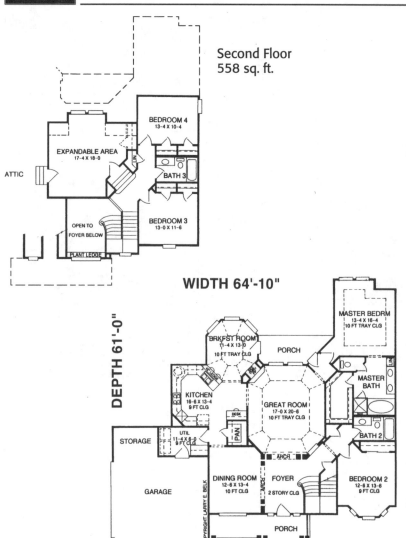

Second Floor
558 sq. ft.

ATTIC

BEDROOM 4
13-4 X 10-4

EXPANDABLE AREA
17-4 X 18-0

BATH 3

OPEN TO FOYER BELOW

BEDROOM 3
13-0 X 11-6

PLANT LEDGE

LIN

Plan #529-LBD-25-22A
Price Code D
Total Living Area: 2,586 Sq. Ft.

Home has 4 bedrooms, 3 baths, 2-car side entry garage and basement, crawl space or slab foundation, please specify when ordering.

Special features
- Great room has impressive tray ceiling and see-through fireplace into bayed breakfast room
- Master bedroom has walk-in closet and private bath

WIDTH 64'-10"

DEPTH 61'-0"

MASTER BEDRM
13-4 X 16-4
10 FT TRAY CLG

PORCH

BRKFST ROOM
11-4 X 13-0
10 FT TRAY CLG

MASTER BATH

KITCHEN
16-6 X 13-4
9 FT CLG

DESK

GREAT ROOM
17-0 X 20-6
10 FT TRAY CLG

PAN

BATH 2

UTIL
11-4 X 6-2
9 FT CLG

STORAGE

COPYRIGHT LARRY E. BELK

GARAGE

DINING ROOM
12-6 X 13-4
10 FT CLG

ARCH

FOYER
2 STORY CLG

ARCH

BEDROOM 2
12-6 X 13-6
9 FT CLG

First Floor
2,028 sq. ft.

PORCH

COPYRIGHT LARRY E. BELK

Second Floor
1,018 sq. ft.

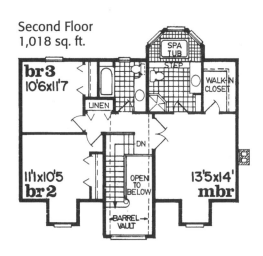

br3
10'6x11'7

LINEN

SPA TUB
STEP

WALK-IN CLOSET

DN

OPEN TO BELOW

11'1x10'5
br2

13'5x14'
mbr

BARREL VAULT

Plan #529-SH-SEA-078
Price Code D

Total Living Area: 2,389 Sq. Ft.

Home has 3 bedrooms, 2 1/2 baths, 2-car garage and basement or crawl space foundation, please specify when ordering.

Special features

- Energy efficient 2" x 6" exterior walls
- Full-width covered verandah invited outdoor relaxation
- Den can easily double as a guest room

First Floor
1,371 sq. ft.

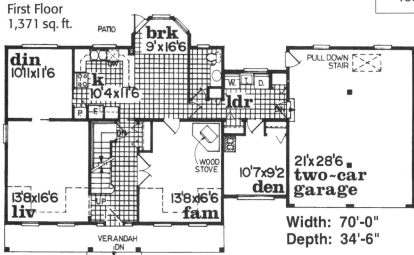

PATIO

brk
9' x 16'6

PULL DOWN STAIR

din
10'11x11'6

k
10'4x11'6

W. T. D.

ldr

P. F.

13'8x16'6
liv

UP

WOOD STOVE

13'8x16'6
fam

10'7x9'2
den

21'x28'6
two-car garage

VERANDAH
DN

Width: 70'-0"
Depth: 34'-6"

Width: 58'-6"
Depth: 72'-0"

Plan #529-HDS-2224
Price Code D

Total Living Area: 2,224 Sq. Ft.

Home has 4 bedrooms, 3 baths, 2-car side entry garage and slab foundation.

Special features

■ Vaulted living room with wet bar

■ Pass-through kitchen with V-shaped counter and walk-in pantry over- looks family room

■ Master suite with sitting area, two walk-in closets and a full bath with tub surrounded by windows

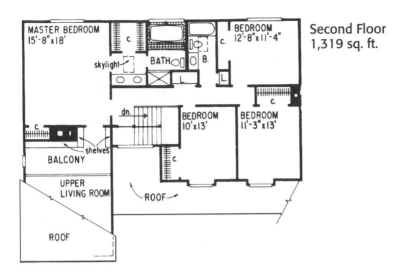

Second Floor
1,319 sq. ft.

MASTER BEDROOM
15'-8"x18'

skylight

BATH

BEDROOM
12'-8"x11'-4"

dn.

BEDROOM
10'x13'

BEDROOM
11'-3"x13'

shelves

BALCONY

UPPER
LIVING ROOM

ROOF

ROOF

ROOF

Plan #529-1218
Price Code E

Total Living Area: 2,751 Sq. Ft.

Home has 4 bedrooms, 2 1/2 baths, 2-car garage and partial basement/crawl space foundation, drawings also include crawl space foundation.

Special features
- Large palladian window in foyer welcomes the sun
- Spacious living room dominates design with sunken floor, sloped ceiling and see-through fireplace
- State-of-the-art kitchen features peninsula and built-in pantry
- Dramatic in size and design, the master bedroom boasts a balcony overlook of living room below

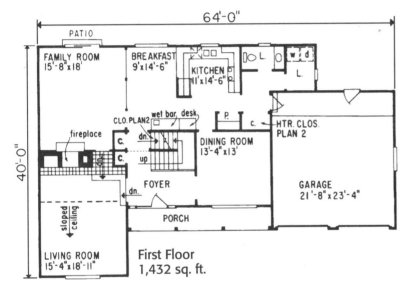

64'-0"

40'-0"

PATIO

FAMILY ROOM
15'-8"x18'

BREAKFAST
9'x14'-6"

KITCHEN
11'x14'-6"

w d

L.

CLO. PLAN 2

wet bar desk

fireplace

dn.

up

DINING ROOM
13'-4"x13'

P.

c.

HTR. CLOS.
PLAN 2

FOYER

dn.

GARAGE
21'-8"x23'-4"

sloped ceiling

PORCH

LIVING ROOM
15'-4"x18'-11"

First Floor
1,432 sq. ft.

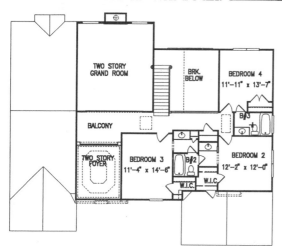

Second Floor
914 sq. ft.

TWO STORY
GRAND ROOM

BRK.
BELOW

BEDROOM 4
11'-11" x 13'-7"

B/3

BALCONY

TWO STORY
FOYER

BEDROOM 3
11'-4" x 14'-6"

B/2

BEDROOM 2
12'-2" x 12'-0"

W.I.C.

W.I.C.

M. BATH

HERS

HIS

TWO STORY
GRAND ROOM
17'-3" x 19'-5"

KITCHEN

BREAKFAST

MASTER
BEDROOM
14'-6" x 17'-2"

P.R.

PANTRY

LAUNDRY

TWO STORY
FOYER
9'-11" x 11'-11"

DINING
12'-4" x 14'

LIVING/
OPT. SITTING
17'-9" x 14'-1"

TWO CAR GARAGE

Width: 60'-0"
Depth: 52'-4"

First Floor
2,115 sq. ft.

Plan #529-MG-95107
Price Code E

Total Living Area: 3,029 Sq. Ft.

Home has 4 bedrooms, 3 1/2 baths, 2-car side entry garage and basement foundation.

Special features

- Brick traditional has dramatic arched entry and window wall
- Grand room has 1 1/2 story detailed fireplace
- Vaulted master bath has his and hers separate vanities and walk-in closets

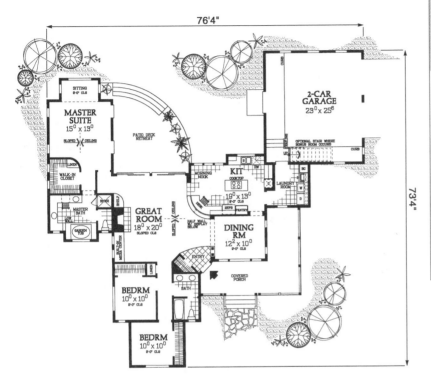

76'4"

73'4"

SITTING
8'-0" CLG

MASTER
SUITE
15⁰ x 13⁰
SLOPED CEILING

PATIO DECK
RETREAT

2-CAR
GARAGE
23⁰ x 25⁸

OPTIONAL STAIR WHERE
BONUS ROOM OCCURS

WALK-IN
CLOSET

MORNING
NOOK

KIT
COOKTOP
19⁰ x 13⁰
8'-0" CLG

LAUNDRY
ROOM

MASTER
BATH

GARDEN
TUB

GREAT
ROOM
18⁰ x 20⁰
SLOPED CLG

HALF WALL
DISPLAY
BELOW

PANTRY

DINING
RM
12² x 10⁰
8'-0" CLG

ENTRY

BEDRM
10⁰ x 10⁰
8'-0" CLG

BATH

COVERED
PORCH

BEDRM
10⁰ x 10⁰
8'-0" CLG

Plan #529-HP-C662
Price Code C
Total Living Area: 1,937 Sq. Ft.

Home has 3 bedrooms, 2 baths, 2-car side entry garage and crawl space foundation.

Special features

- Upscale great room offers a sloped ceiling, fireplace with extended hearth and built-in shelves for an entertainment center

- Gourmet kitchen includes a cooktop island counter and a quaint morning room

- Master suite features a sloped ceiling, cozy sitting room, walk-in closet and a private bath with whirlpool tub

Plan #529-1300

Price Code D

Total Living Area: 2,253 Sq. Ft.

Home has 3 bedrooms, 2 1/2 baths, 2-car garage and basement foundation.

Special features

- Great room joined by covered porch
- Secluded parlor provides area for peace and quiet or private office
- Sloped ceiling adds drama to master suite
- Great room and kitchen/breakfast area combine for large open living

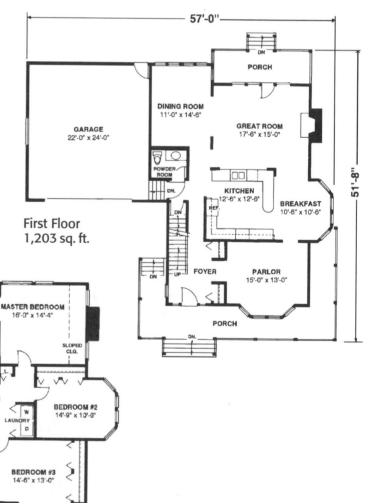

First Floor
1,203 sq. ft.

Second Floor
1,050 sq. ft.

Second Floor
902 sq. ft.

UPPER LIVING ROOM

UPPER FAMILY ROOM

dn

BATH

c.

c.

c.

STUDY AREA
11'-7"x16'-4"

BEDROOM
13'x15'

BEDROOM
12'-5"x17'-6"

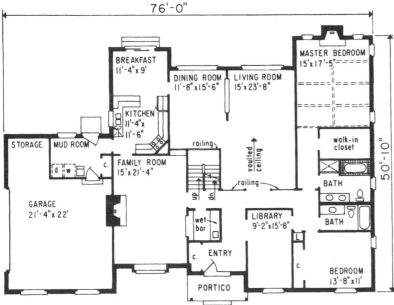

76'-0"

50'-10"

BREAKFAST
11'-4"x 9'

DINING ROOM
11'-8"x15'-6"

LIVING ROOM
15'x 23'-8"

MASTER BEDROOM
15'x 17'-5"

KITCHEN
11'-4"x 11'-6"

railing

vaulted ceiling

walk-in closet

STORAGE

MUD ROOM

d w

c.

FAMILY ROOM
15'x 21'-4"

railing

BATH

GARAGE
21'-4"x 22'

dn dn

wet bar

LIBRARY
9'-2"x15'-8"

BATH

c.

ENTRY

c.

PORTICO

BEDROOM
13'-8"x11'

First Floor
2,665 sq. ft.

Plan #529-1236
Price Code F

Total Living Area: 3,567 Sq. Ft.

Home has 4 bedrooms, 3 baths, 2-car garage and basement foundation.

Special features

- Master suite has cozy fireplace flanked by windows and a private bath
- Living and dining rooms adjoin for maximum convenience and versatility
- Special amenities include first floor library and second floor family room and study area

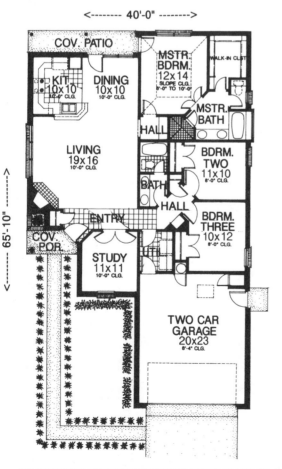

<-------- 40'-0" -------->

COV. PATIO

KIT.
10x10

DINING
10x10
10'-0" CLG.

MSTR.
BDRM.
12x14
SLOPE CLG.
8'-0" TO 10'-0"

WALK-IN CL'S'T.

MSTR.
BATH

HALL

LIVING
19x16
10'-0" CLG.

BDRM.
TWO
11x10
8'-0" CLG.

BATH

HALL

ENTRY

BDRM.
THREE
10x12
8'-0" CLG.

COV.
POR.

STUDY
11x11
10'-0" CLG.

UTIL.

65'-10"

TWO CAR
GARAGE
20x23
8'-4" CLG.

Plan #529-FDG-8673
Price Code B

Total Living Area: 1,604 Sq. Ft.

Home has 3 bedrooms, 2 baths, 2-car garage and slab foundation.

Special features

- Ideal design for a narrow lot
- Living and dining areas combine for a spacious feel
- Secluded study has double-doors for privacy
- Master bedroom has a spacious private bath

DEPTH 67–9

HERS | HIS

STEP MASTER BATH
11 FT TRAY CLG

SEAT

FP

PORCH
9 FT CLG

FAMILY ROOM
13–6 X 16–6
9 FT CLG

MASTER BEDRM
15–0 X 17–4
11 FT TRAY CLG

BEDRM 4
14–8 X 12–8
9 FT CLG

COVERED PORCH
9 FT CLG

BRKFST RM
10–8 X 11–6
9 FT CLG

BATH 2

42" LEDGE

LIVING ROOM
18–4 X 18–6
11 FT CLG

KITCHEN
13–6 X 11–4
9 FT CLG

PWDR

UTIL
12–6 X 5–8
9 FT CLG

GARAGE

PAN

BEDRM 3
11–0 X 13–4
9 FT CLG

BEDRM 2/
STUDY
11–6 X 13–0
11 FT TRAY CLG

FOYER
11 FT CLG

DINING ROOM
14–0 X 13–6
11 FT CLG

ARCH

COPYRIGHT LARRY E. BELK

PORCH
9 FT CLG

WIDTH 70–2

Plan #529-LBD-26-23A
Price Code E

Total Living Area: 2,678 Sq. Ft.

Home has 4 bedrooms, 2 1/2 baths, 2-car side entry garage and crawl space or slab foundation, please specify when ordering.

Special features
- Elegant arched opening graces entrance
- Kitchen has double ovens, walk-in pantry and an eating bar
- Master bedroom has beautiful bath spotlighting step-up tub

Width: 65'-8"
Depth: 73'-4"

Family Room
volume ceiling
17⁰ · 16⁰

fireplace

Breakfast

opt. summer kitchen

volume ceiling

Bedroom 2
volume ceiling
12⁰ · 11⁴

Covered Patio
volume ceiling

Kitchen

dw

Bath

lin

Living Room
volume ceiling
14⁰ · 17⁰

Master Bedroom
volume ceiling
13⁰ · 17⁰

Bath

ref

pan

lin

Bedroom 3
volume ceiling
12⁰ · 11⁴

Utility

w

d

ac   wh

Dining
volume ceiling
11⁰ · 14⁰

Foyer

Bedroom 4
Den/Study
volume ceiling
10⁰ · 11⁰

w.i.c.   w.i.c.

Bath

up

Double Garage

Entry

Plan #529-HDS-2244
Price Code D
Total Living Area: 2,362 Sq. Ft.

Home has 4 bedrooms, 3 baths, 2-car side entry garage and slab foundation.

Special features

- Versatile den/study adjacent to master suite entry and powder/pool bath
- Island kitchen overlooks nook and family room
- Foyer opens into formal living room

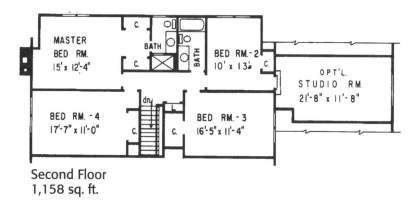

Second Floor
1,158 sq. ft.

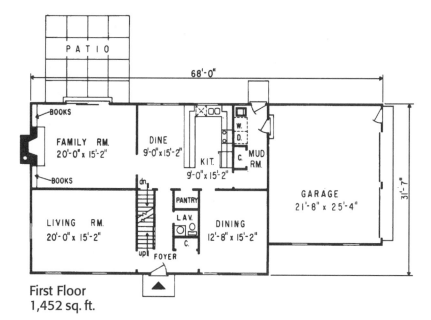

First Floor
1,452 sq. ft.

Plan #529-1079
Price Code E

Total Living Area:	2,610 Sq. Ft.

Home has 4 bedrooms, 2 1/2 baths, 2-car side entry garage and basement foundation.

Special features

- A 10' cabinet peninsula divides large dining area from a functional kitchen featuring an abundance of storage and counterspace
- Bookshelves flanking a masonry fireplace adorn the end of a spacious family room
- All second floor bedrooms have ample storage and an optional studio is available above garage
- Master bedroom includes his and her closets and a full bath

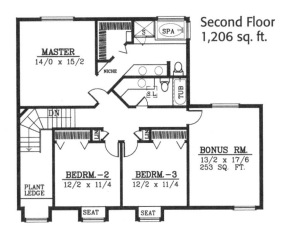

Second Floor
1,206 sq. ft.

MASTER
14/0 x 15/2

NICHE

SPA

S.L.

TUB

DN

PLANT
LEDGE

BEDRM.-2
12/2 x 11/4

BEDRM.-3
12/2 x 11/4

BONUS RM.
13/2 x 17/6
253 SQ. FT.

SEAT

SEAT

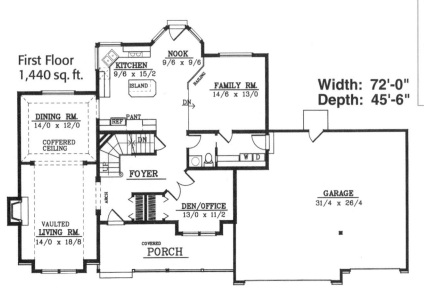

First Floor
1,440 sq. ft.

KITCHEN
9/6 x 15/2

ISLAND

NOOK
9/6 x 9/6

FAMILY RM.
14/6 x 13/0

RAILING

DINING RM.
14/0 x 12/0

COFFERED
CEILING

REF

PANT

DN

UP

DN

W

D

FOYER

VAULTED
LIVING RM.
14/0 x 18/8

ARCH

DEN/OFFICE
13/0 x 11/2

GARAGE
31/4 x 26/4

COVERED
PORCH

Width: 72'-0"
Depth: 45'-6"

Plan #529-DDI-100-219
Price Code E

Total Living Area: 2,646 Sq. Ft.

Home has 3 bedrooms, 2 1/2 baths,
3-car garage and basement foundation.

Special features

- Casual living areas of home located in the rear including a kitchen with eating bar overlooking an angled nook

- Private second floor master suite has a large walk-in closet, double sinks, spa tub and separate shower

- Two additional generous-sized bedrooms with dormered window seats and a large bonus room share a hall bath

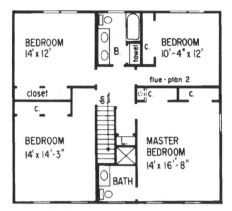

Second Floor
1,152 sq. ft.

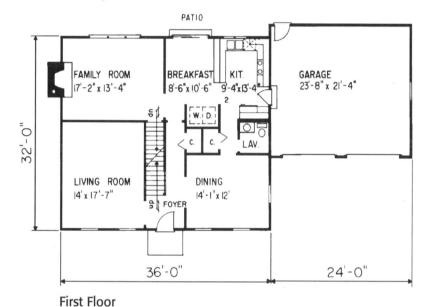

First Floor
1,152 sq. ft.

Plan #529-1209
Price Code D
Total Living Area: 2,304 Sq. Ft.

Home has 4 bedrooms, 2 1/2 baths, 2-car garage and basement foundation, drawings also include crawl space and slab foundations.

Special features

- Stately foyer with ascending stair and access to living and dining rooms
- Well-organized kitchen includes pass-through peninsula and spacious pantry
- Powder room adjacent to first floor laundry
- Roomy master bedroom enjoys double closets

Plan #529-1307
Price Code D

Total Living Area: 2,420 Sq. Ft.

Home has 4 bedrooms, 2 1/2 baths, 2-car garage and basement foundation.

Special features

- Master suite filled with extras like unique master bath and lots of storage
- Extending off great room is a bright sunroom with access to a deck
- Compact kitchen with nook creates useful breakfast area

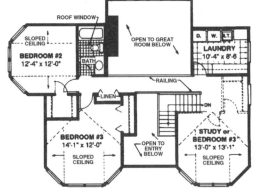

ROOF WINDOW

SLOPED CEILING

BEDROOM #2
12'-4" x 12'-0"

BATH

OPEN TO GREAT ROOM BELOW

D. W. LT.

LAUNDRY
10'-4" x 8'-6"

RAILING

LINEN

BEDROOM #3
14'-1" x 12'-0"

SLOPED CEILING

OPEN TO ENTRY BELOW

DN

STUDY or BEDROOM #3
13'-0" x 13'-1"

SLOPED CEILING

Second Floor
842 sq. ft.

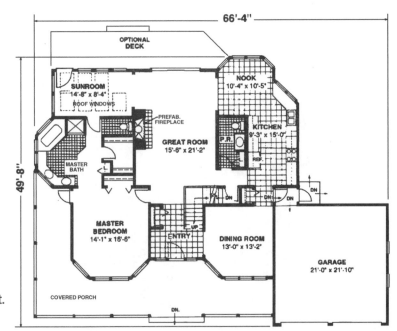

66'-4"

OPTIONAL DECK

SUNROOM
14'-8" x 8'-4"

ROOF WINDOWS

PREFAB. FIREPLACE

NOOK
10'-4" x 10'-5"

GREAT ROOM
15'-6" x 21'-2"

P.R.

KITCHEN
9'-3" x 15'-0"

REF.

49'-8"

MASTER BATH

MASTER BEDROOM
14'-1" x 16'-6"

ENTRY

UP

DN

DN

DN

DN

DINING ROOM
13'-0" x 13'-2"

GARAGE
21'-0" x 21'-10"

First Floor
1,578 sq. ft.

COVERED PORCH

DN.

BEDROOM #4
11'-6" x 11'-0"

D
W
LAUN.
L.T.

BEDROOM #3
12'-9" x 12'-6"

SLOPE CEILING

SLOPE CEILING

MASTER BATH

BATH

BEDROOM #2
11'-4" x 11'-6"

MASTER BEDROOM
17'-0" x 14'-6"

SLOPE CEILING

BALCONY

DN.

OPEN TO ENTRY
FOYER BELOW

Second Floor
1,215 sq. ft.

GARAGE
22'-0" x 23'-0"

DN.

DN.

BREAKFAST
10'-0" x 12'-6"

P.

FAMILY ROOM
14'-0" x 18'-6"

KITCHEN
12'-0" x 12'-6"

REF.

DN.

DINING ROOM
12'-0" x 11'-6"

PORCH

P.R.

LIVING ROOM
17'-0" x 14'-6"

OPEN TO SECOND
FLOOR CEILING

ENTRY

UP

DN.

PORCH

65'-4"

72'-10"

First Floor
1,345 sq. ft.

Plan #529-1309
Price Code D
Total Living Area: 2,562 Sq. Ft.

Home has 3 bedrooms, 2 1/2 baths, 2-car garage and basement foundation.

Special features

- Numerous bay windows create a design unlike any other
- Enormous master suite has private bath with step-up tub-in-a-bay
- Double stairways make any room easily accessible
- Cheerful breakfast room extends onto covered private porch

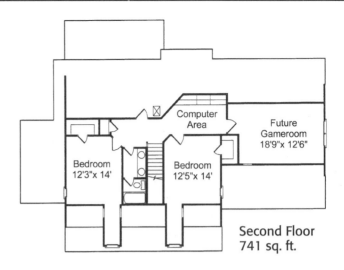

Second Floor
741 sq. ft.

Computer Area

Bedroom
12'3"x 14'

Bedroom
12'5"x 14'

Future
Gameroom
18'9"x 12'6"

Plan #529-CHP-2333-A-29
Price Code D

Total Living Area: 2,279 Sq. Ft.

Home has 3 bedrooms, 2 1/2 baths, 2-car side entry garage and slab or crawl space foundation, please specify when ordering.

Special features

- Kitchen overlooks living area with fireplace and lots of windows
- Conveniently located first floor master bedroom
- Second floor features computer area with future game room space

Covered Porch

Breakfast
10'x 10'

Living
21'x 15'6"

Two Car
Garage
22'8"x 21'4"

Master
Bedroom
13'x 17'8"

Dining
12'x 12'8"

First Floor
1,538 sq. ft.

Covered Porch

Width: 44'-10"
Depth: 47'-7"

Plan #529-AP-1914
Price Code C
Total Living Area: 1,992 Sq. Ft.

Home has 4 bedrooms, 3 baths, 2-car side entry garage and basement, crawl space or slab foundation, please specify when ordering.

Special features

- Interesting angled walls add drama to many of the living areas including family room, master bedroom and breakfast area

- Covered porch includes spa and an outdoor kitchen with sink, refridgerator and cooktop

- Enter majestic master bath to find a dramatic corner oversized tub

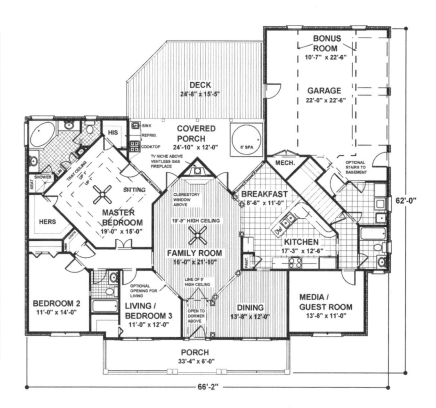

Easy Living

Plan #529-RDD-1753-9
Price Code B
Total Living Area: 1,753 Sq. Ft.

Home has 3 bedrooms, 2 baths and slab or crawl space foundation, please specify when ordering

Special features
■ Large front porch has charming appeal
■ Kitchen with breakfast bar overlooks morning room and accesses covered porch
■ Master suite with amenities like private bath, spacious closets and sunny bay window

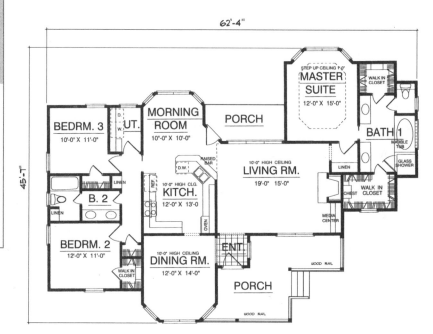

Columned Facade

© Michael E. Nelson
NELSON DESIGN GROUP, LLC

Plan #529-NDG-275

Price Code D

Total Living Area: 2,247 Sq. Ft.

Home has 3 bedrooms, 2 1/2 baths, 2-car side entry garage and basement, crawl space or slab foundation, please specify when ordering.

Special features

- Enormous great room with fireplace extends into a kitchen with center island

- Formal dining area is quiet, yet convenient to kitchen

- All bedrooms located on second floor maintain privacy

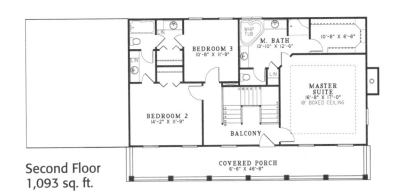

Second Floor
1,093 sq. ft.

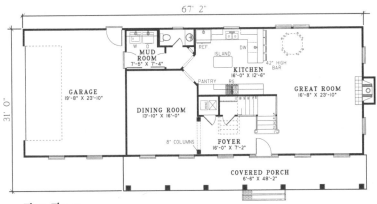

First Floor
1,154 sq. ft.

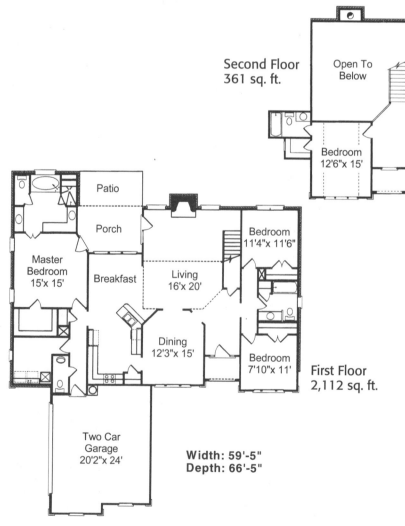

Second Floor
361 sq. ft.

Open To Below

Bedroom
12'6"x 15'

Plan #529-CHP-2444-A-2
Price Code D

Total Living Area: 2,473 Sq. Ft.

Home has 4 bedrooms, 3 1/2 baths, 2-car side entry garage and crawl space or slab foundation, please specify when ordering.

Special features

- Open floor plan makes this home incredibly spacious throughout
- Kitchen has lots of storage and cabinetry
- Practical fourth bedroom on second floor has lots of privacy for guest
- Master suite has direct access to porch and patio

Patio

Porch

Master Bedroom
15'x 15'

Breakfast

Living
16'x 20'

Bedroom
11'4"x 11'6"

Dining
12'3"x 15'

Bedroom
7'10"x 11'

First Floor
2,112 sq. ft.

Two Car Garage
20'2"x 24'

Width: 59'-5"
Depth: 66'-5"

Plan #529-1114
Price Code E
Total Living Area: 2,851 Sq. Ft.

Home has 4 bedrooms, 3 baths, 2-car garage and basement foundation, drawings also include crawl space and slab foundations.

Special features

- Foyer with double-door entrance leads to unique sunken living room with patio view
- Multi-purpose room perfect for home office, hobby room or fifth bedroom
- Master bedroom boasts abundant closet space and access to patio
- Family room has access to kitchen and features a fireplace flanked by windows

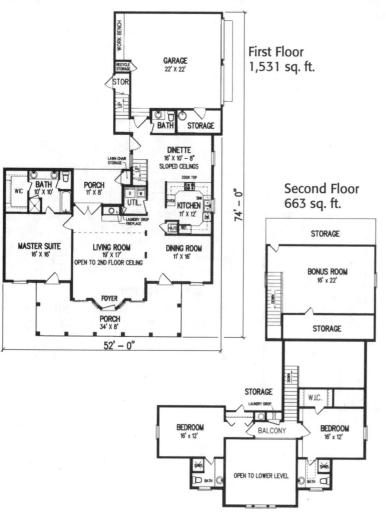

First Floor
1,531 sq. ft.

WORK BENCH

GARAGE
22' X 22'

RECYCLE STORAGE

STOR

UP

BATH   STORAGE

LAWN CHAIR STORAGE

DINETTE
16' X 10' – 8"
SLOPED CEILINGS

COOK TOP

KITCHEN
11' X 12'

OVEN   SINK

UTIL.

D   W

LAUNDRY DROP
FIREPLACE

REF.

BATH
10' X 10'

W/C

PORCH
11' X 8'

74' – 0"

Second Floor
663 sq. ft.

MASTER SUITE
16' X 16'

LIVING ROOM
19' X 17'
OPEN TO 2ND FLOOR CEILING

DINING ROOM
11' X 16'

FOYER

PORCH
34' X 8'

52' – 0"

STORAGE

BONUS ROOM
16' x 22'

DOWN

STORAGE

STORAGE

LAUNDRY DROP

DOWN

W.I.C.

BEDROOM
16' x 12'

BALCONY

BEDROOM
16' x 12'

BATH

OPEN TO LOWER LEVEL

BATH

Plan #529-BF-2108
Price Code C

<u>Total Living Area:</u>   2,194 Sq. Ft.

Home has 3 bedrooms, 3 1/2 baths, 2-car side entry garage and crawl space, slab or basement foundation, please specify when ordering.

Special features

- Energy efficient home with 2" x 6" exterior walls
- Utility room has laundry drop conveniently located next to kitchen
- Both second floor bedrooms have large closets and their own bath

PATIO

74'-10"

67'-10"

BREAKFAST 12'-6" x 12'-6"

FAMILY ROOM 15'-6" x 20'-6"

LIVING ROOM 14'x20'-6"

skylight

MASTER BEDROOM 21'x15'

45° chamfered ceiling

KITCHEN 12'-6" x 11'

railing

C

BATH

C

BEDROOM 12'-6" x 14'

C

L

B.

d w.

FOYER

C.

C.

C.

MUD ROOM

DINING ROOM 14'x16'

C.

C.

C.

BEDROOM 11'-8" x 13'-8"

BEDROOM 16'x12'-8"

STOR.

45° chamfered ceiling

C.

dn.

GARAGE 21'-4" x 23'-8"

Plan #529-1223
Price Code E

Total Living Area: 3,108 Sq. Ft.

Home has 4 bedrooms, 3 baths, 2-car side entry garage and partial basement/ crawl space foundation, drawings also include crawl space and slab foundations.

Special features

- Cheery living room glows with wide bow window
- Unusually large dining room features chamfered ceiling
- Located near kitchen is the spacious mud room with laundry facilities, full bath, coat closets, storage pantry and stairs to basement
- Master bedroom features a chamfered ceiling and bath with skylight

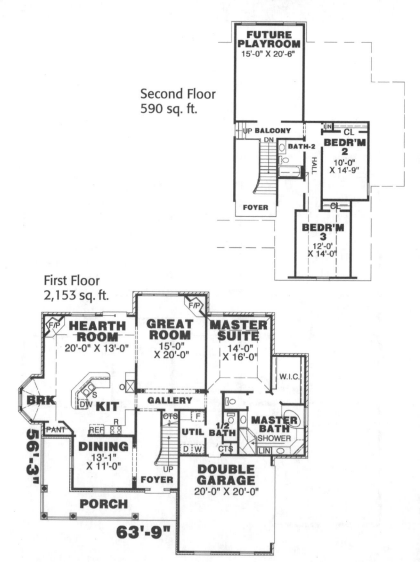

Second Floor
590 sq. ft.

FUTURE PLAYROOM
15'-0" X 20'-6"

UP BALCONY
DN
BATH-2
HALL
BEDR'M 2
10'-0" X 14'-9"
FOYER
CL
BEDR'M 3
12'-0' X 14'-0"

First Floor
2,153 sq. ft.

HEARTH ROOM
20'-0" X 13'-0"

GREAT ROOM
15'-0" X 20'-0"

MASTER SUITE
14'-0" X 16'-0"

W.I.C.

BRK
KIT
DW
PANT
GALLERY

MASTER BATH
SHOWER

REF
CTS
F
1/2 BATH
UTIL
CTS
LIN

DINING
13'-1" X 11'-0"

UP
D W

FOYER

DOUBLE GARAGE
20'-0" X 20'-0"

56'-3"

PORCH

63'-9"

Plan #529-CHD-27-35
Price Code E

Total Living Area: 2,743 Sq. Ft.

Home has 3 bedrooms, 2 1/2 baths, 2-car garage and slab foundation.

Special features

- 9' ceilings on first floor of this home
- Kitchen, breakfast and hearth rooms connect creating one large living space ideal for family living
- Master suite has its own wing with large private bath and walk-in closet
- Wrap-around porch in the front of the home makes a lasting impression
- Future playroom on the second floor has an additional 327 square feet of living area

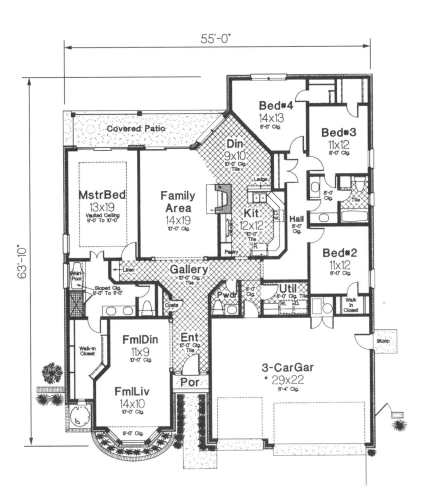

Plan #529-FDG-8526
Price Code D
Total Living Area: 2,370 Sq. Ft.

Home has 4 bedrooms, 2 1/2 baths, 3-car garage and slab foundation.

Special features
- Dramatic gallery located in front of family area
- Formal dining and living areas in the front of home are ideal for entertaining
- All bedrooms throughout this home have spacious walk-in closets

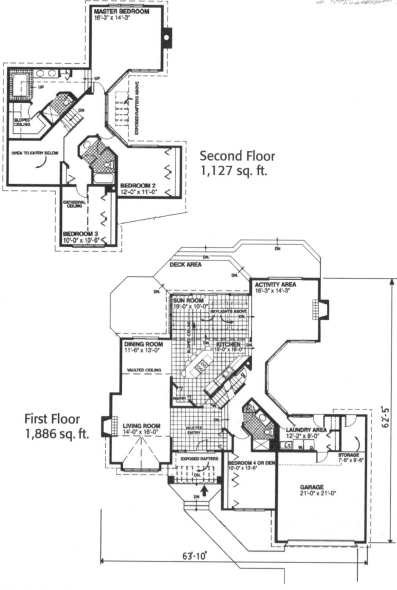

Plan #529-1258

Price Code E

Total Living Area: 3,013 Sq. Ft.

Home has 3 bedrooms, 3 baths, 2-car garage and partial basement/crawl space foundation.

Special features

- Varying roof lines create an exciting exterior look

- Unique interior has countless innovative features

- Large activity area and hall to laundry feature curving window wall which surrounds outdoor atrium

- Kitchen opens to a sun-drenched sunroom with sloping ceiling and skylights

- Master suite boasts a luxurious step-up vaulted bath with Roman tub, separate shower/toilet area and enormous walk-in closet

Second Floor
1,127 sq. ft.

First Floor
1,886 sq. ft.

LOWE'S

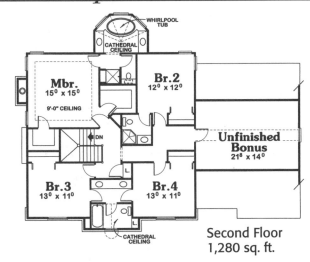

WHIRLPOOL
TUB

CATHEDRAL
CEILING

Mbr.
15⁰ x 15⁰

9'-0" CEILING

Br.2
12⁰ x 12⁰

DN

**Unfinished
Bonus**
21⁸ x 14⁰

Br.3
13⁰ x 11⁰

Br.4
13⁰ x 11⁰

L

CATHEDRAL
CEILING

Second Floor
1,280 sq. ft.

Bfst.
11⁰ x 11⁰

SNACK
BAR

Fam. Rm.
18⁰ x 15⁰

DESK

Kit.
11⁸ x 12⁰

P.

R.

W. D.

WET
BAR

SEAT

DN

Gar.
21⁸ x 29⁴

UP

OPTIONAL
COMPUTER
AREA

Liv.
14⁰ x 11⁰

E.

Din.
14⁰ x 11⁰

STOOP

44'-4"

58'-0"

© design basics inc.

First Floor
1,333 sq. ft.

Plan #529-DBI-4106
Price Code E

Total Living Area: 2,613 Sq. Ft.

Home has 4 bedrooms, 3 1/2 baths,
3-car side entry garage and basement
foundation.

Special features
- Traditional styling makes this home
  a favorite
- Well-designed living and family
  rooms connected by pass-through
  wet bar
- Master suite includes a dramatic
  private bath

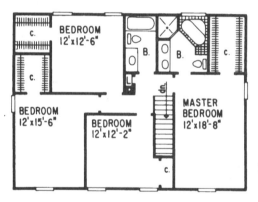

Second Floor
1,160 sq. ft.

Plan #529-1217
Price Code D

Total Living Area: 2,372 Sq. Ft.

Home has 4 bedrooms, 2 1/2 baths, 2-car garage and basement foundation, drawings also include crawl space and slab foundations.

Special features

- Spacious living room features opening to entry flanked by bookshelves
- Family room boasts an impressive fireplace and sunken living room
- Well-appointed kitchen includes snack counter
- Second floor bedrooms combine extravagant room sizes with lots of walk-in closets

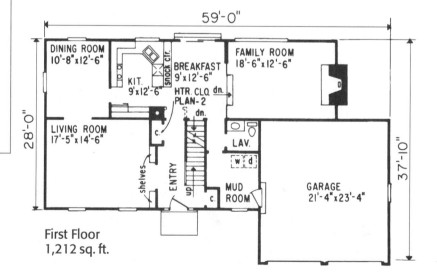

First Floor
1,212 sq. ft.

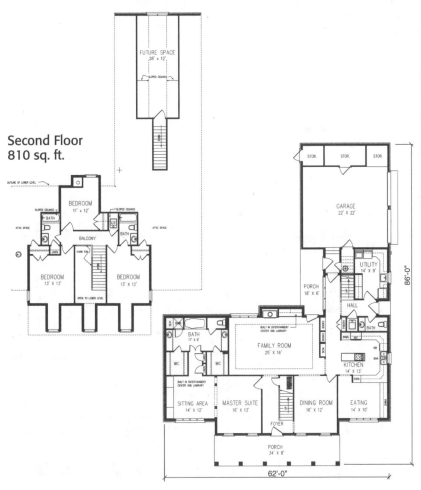

Second Floor
810 sq. ft.

FUTURE SPACE
28' x 12'
SLOPED CEILING

OUTLINE OF LOWER LEVEL

BEDROOM
11' x 12'
SLOPED CEILINGS   SLOPED CEILINGS

BATH   BATH
ATTIC SPACE   ATTIC SPACE
BALCONY
LINEN   HAND RAIL

BEDROOM
13' x 13'   BEDROOM
13' x 12'
OPEN TO LOWER LEVEL

STOR.   STOR.   STOR.

GARAGE
22' x 22'

UTILITY
14' x 9'

PORCH
18' x 6'

HALL

BATH

BATH
17' x 9'

BUILT IN ENTERTAINMENT
CENTER AND LIBRARY

FAMILY ROOM
25' x 16'

KITCHEN
14' x 13'

WIC   WIC

BUILT IN ENTERTAINMENT
CENTER AND LIBRARY

SITTING AREA
14' x 12'   MASTER SUITE
16' x 13'   DINING ROOM
16' x 12'   EATING
14' x 10'

FOYER

PORCH
34' x 8'

86'-0"

62'-0"

First Floor
2,202 sq. ft.

Plan #529-BF-3007
Price Code E

<u>Total Living Area:</u>   3,012 Sq. Ft.

Home has 4 bedrooms, 3 1/2 baths, 2-car side entry garage and crawl space, slab or basement foundation, please specify when ordering.

Special features

- Master suite has sitting area with entertainment center/library
- Utility room has a sink and includes lots of storage and counter space
- Future space above garage has an additional 336 square feet of living area

Plan #529-1264
Price Code E

Total Living Area: 2,773 Sq. Ft.

Home has 3 bedrooms, 3 baths, 2-car side entry garage and partial basement/ crawl space foundation, drawings also include slab foundation.

Special features

- Exposed roof rafters illuminate window seat of huge living room featuring built-in bookshelves, fireplace and cathedral ceilings
- Kitchen with cooktop island has breakfast bar opening to activity area with vaulted ceilings
- Laundry room, third bedroom and library with built-in bookshelves occupy the left portion of home
- Master suite features double-vanity bath with his and hers walk-in closets and double sliding glass doors leading to deck

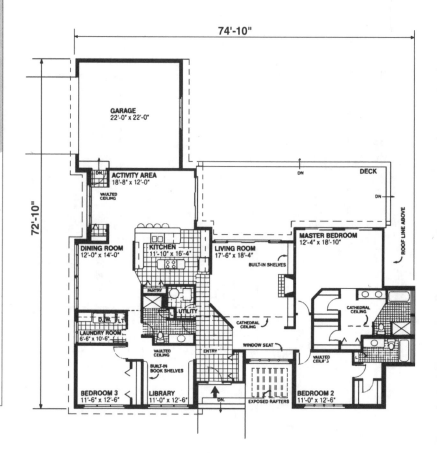

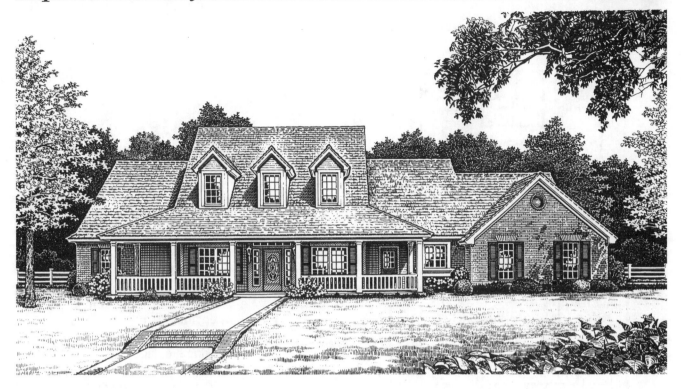

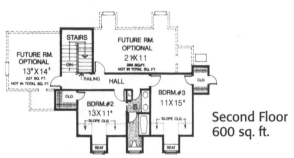

Second Floor
600 sq. ft.

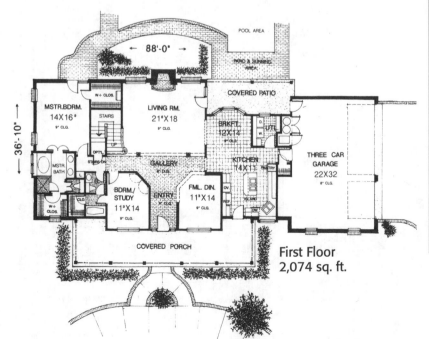

First Floor
2,074 sq. ft.

Plan #529-FDG-8753-L
Price Code E

Total Living Area: 2,674 Sq. Ft.

Home has 4 bedrooms, 3 baths, 3-car side entry garage and basement or slab foundation, please specify when ordering.

Special features

- First floor master bedroom has convenient location
- Kitchen and breakfast area have island and access to covered front porch
- Second floor bedrooms have dormer window seats for added charm
- Optional future room on second floor has an additional 520 square feet of living area

Second Floor
565 sq. ft.

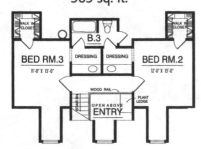

WALK IN CLOSET B.3 WALK IN CLOSET
BED RM.3
11'-0" X 13'-0"
DRESSING DRESSING
BED RM.2
12'-0" X 13'-0"
WOOD RAIL PLANT LEDGE
STAIR DN OPEN ABOVE
ENTRY

Plan #529-RDD-1895-9
Price Code C
Total Living Area: 1,895 Sq. Ft.

Home has 3 bedrooms, 2 1/2 baths, 2-car garage and basement, crawl space or slab foundation, please specify when ordering.

Special features
- Kitchen overlooks both the breakfast nook and living room for an open floor plan
- Living area has built-in bookshelves flanking fireplace
- Master suite has private bath and access to covered rear porch

70'-9"

43'-4"

PORCH
MASTER SUITE 12'-0" X 15'-0"
LIVING RM. 15'-0" X 17'-0"
NOOK 12'-0" X 10'-0"
B.2
GARAGE 22'-0" X 22'-0"
MEDIA CENTER
BOOKS
RAISED BAR
D.W.
KITCH. 12'-0" X 11'-6"
REF.
RANGE
UT.
W/H
BATH 1
MARBLE TUB
SHELF
GLASS SHOWER
STORAGE UNDER STAIR
ENTRY
STAIR UP
WALK IN CLOSET
DINING RM. 12'-0" X 12'-0"
PORCH

First Floor
1,330 sq. ft.

Width: 65'-0"
Depth: 56'-8"

Plan #529-HDS-2454
Price Code D

Total Living Area: 2,458 Sq. Ft.

Home has 4 bedrooms, 3 baths, 2-car garage and slab foundation.

Special features

- Formal dining and living rooms flank foyer
- Master bedroom with fireplace and private bath
- Cheerful and bright bayed breakfast area

COPYRIGHT LARRY E. BELK

Plan #529-LBD-27-23A
Price Code E
Total Living Area: 2,757 Sq. Ft.

Home has 4 bedrooms, 2 1/2 baths, 2-car side entry garage and basement, crawl space or slab foundation, please specify when ordering.

Special features
- Breakfast and family rooms combine creating terrific gathering place
- Luxurious master bedroom with private bath
- Sunny living room has two sets of double-doors leading to porch

WIDTH 69-6

LOWE'S

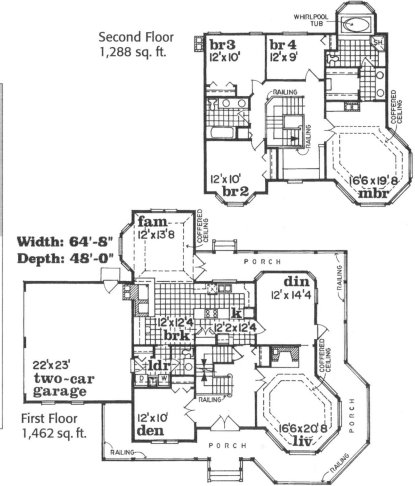

Second Floor
1,288 sq. ft.

br 3
12' x 10'

br 4
12' x 9'

WHIRLPOOL TUB

RAILING

SH

COFFERED CEILING

RAILING

RAILING

12' x 10'

br 2

16'6 x 19'8

mbr

Plan #529-SH-SEA-101
Price Code E

Total Living Area: 2,750 Sq. Ft.

Home has 4 bedrooms, 2 1/2 baths, 2-car side entry garage and basement or crawl space foundation, please specify when ordering.

Special features

- Spacious dining room is connected to kitchen for ease and also has access onto wrap-around porch
- Enter the master bedroom through double-doors and find a spacious walk-in closet and a private bath with whirlpool tub
- Secluded den has storage closet and double-doors making it an ideal place for a home office

Width: 64'-8"
Depth: 48'-0"

fam
12' x 13'8

COFFERED CEILING

PORCH

RAILING

din
12' x 14'4

22' x 23'
two-car
garage

12' x 12'4

k

12'2 x 12'4

brk

ldr

D W

RAILING

COFFERED CEILING

12' x 10'
den

RAILING

PORCH

16'6 x 20'8
liv

PORCH

RAILING

First Floor
1,462 sq. ft.

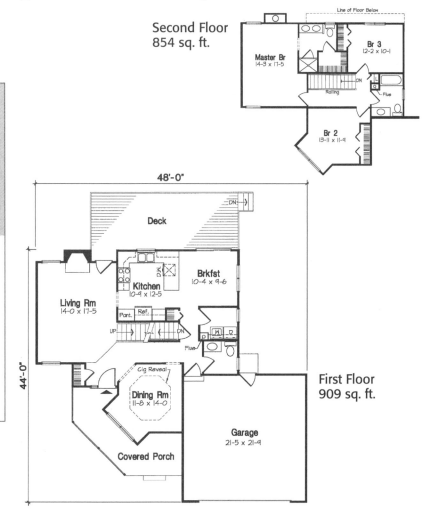

Second Floor
854 sq. ft.

First Floor
909 sq. ft.

Plan #529-GH-34901
Price Code C
Total Living Area: 1,763 Sq. Ft.

Home has 3 bedrooms, 2 1/2 baths, 2-car garage and basement foundation, drawings also include crawl space and slab foundations

Special features

- Dining room has a large box bay window and a recessed ceiling
- Living room includes a large fireplace
- Kitchen has plenty of workspace, a pantry and a double sink overlooking the deck
- Master suite features a large bath with walk-in closet

Rear View

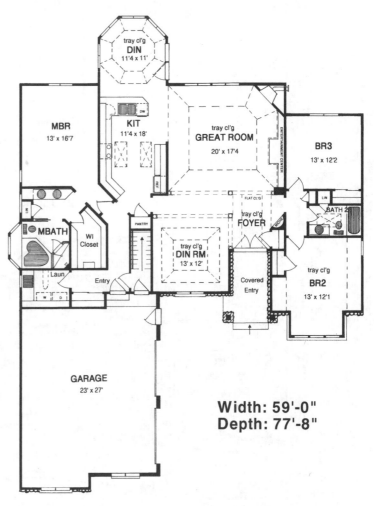

Plan #529-JFD-10-2178-2
Price Code C

Total Living Area: 2,178 Sq. Ft.

Home has 3 bedrooms, 2 baths, 2-car side entry garage and basement foundation.

Special features

- Large foyer leads to a sunny great room with corner fireplace and expansive entertainment center
- Kitchen and dining area are efficiently designed
- Master bedroom has private bath with step-up tub and a bay window

Width: 59'-0"
Depth: 77'-8"

Plan #529-1134
Price Code D

Total Living Area: 2,212 Sq. Ft.

Home has 3 bedrooms, 2 1/2 baths, 2-car garage and partial basement/crawl space foundation, drawings also include crawl space foundation.

Special features

- Louvered shutters, turned posts with railing and garage door detailing are a few inviting features
- Dining room is spacious and borders a well-planned U-shaped kitchen and breakfast room
- Colossal walk-in closet and over-sized private bath are part of a gracious master suite

MASTER BEDROOM
14'-10" x 14'-5"
BATH
BEDROOM
15'-10" x 12'-6"
BEDROOM
11'-4" x 12'-6"
C
C
dn

Second Floor
4 bedroom option
952 sq. ft.

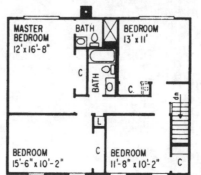

MASTER BEDROOM
12' x 16'-8"
BATH
BEDROOM
13' x 11'
BATH
C.
BEDROOM
15'-6" x 10'-2"
BEDROOM
11'-8" x 10'-2"
C
C
dn

Second Floor
3 bedroom option
952 sq. ft.

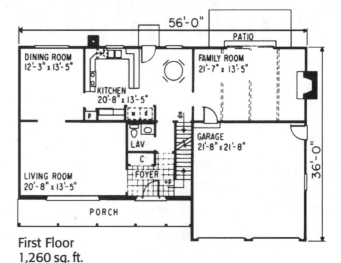

56'-0"

PATIO

DINING ROOM
12'-3" x 13'-5"
KITCHEN
20'-8" x 13'-5"
FAMILY ROOM
21'-7" x 13'-5"

LAV
GARAGE
21'-8" x 21'-8"
C
FOYER
up
36'-0"

LIVING ROOM
20'-8" x 13'-5"

PORCH

First Floor
1,260 sq. ft.

COPYRIGHT LARRY E. BELK

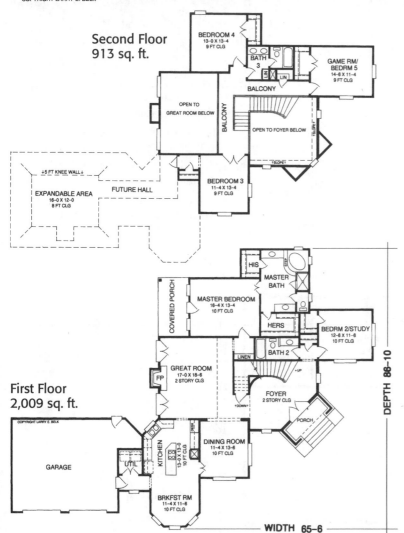

Second Floor
913 sq. ft.

BEDROOM 4
13-0 X 13-4
9 FT CLG

BATH 3

GAME RM/
BEDRM 5
14-6 X 11-4
9 FT CLG

OPEN TO
GREAT ROOM BELOW

BALCONY

OPEN TO FOYER BELOW

5 FT KNEE WALL

EXPANDABLE AREA
16-0 X 12-0
8 FT CLG

FUTURE HALL

BEDROOM 3
11-4 X 13-4
9 FT CLG

HIS

MASTER BATH

COVERED PORCH

MASTER BEDROOM
16-4 X 13-4
10 FT CLG

HERS

BEDRM 2/STUDY
12-6 X 11-6
10 FT CLG

LINEN

BATH 2

GREAT ROOM
17-0 X 18-6
2 STORY CLG

FP

FOYER
2 STORY CLG

PORCH

First Floor
2,009 sq. ft.

COPYRIGHT LARRY E. BELK

GARAGE

UTIL

KITCHEN
13-0 X 13-0
10 FT CLG

DINING ROOM
11-4 X 13-6
10 FT CLG

BRKFST RM
11-4 X 11-6
10 FT CLG

DEPTH 86-10

WIDTH 65-6

Plan #529-LBD-29-28A
Price Code E
Total Living Area: 2,922 Sq. Ft.

Home has 5 bedrooms, 3 baths, 2-car side entry garage and basement, crawl space or slab foundation, please specify when ordering.

Special features
- Elegant European styled home is breathtaking from every angle
- A gourmet island in kitchen has room for cooktop
- Master suite has private porch, his and hers walk-in closets and whirlpool tub

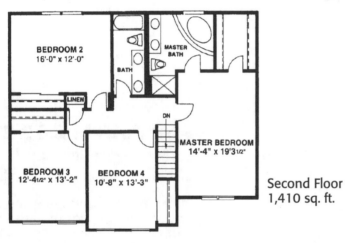

BEDROOM 2
16'-0" x 12'-0"

MASTER BATH

BATH

LINEN

DN

BEDROOM 3
12'-4½" x 13'-2"

BEDROOM 4
10'-8" x 13'-3"

MASTER BEDROOM
14'-4" x 19'3½"

Second Floor
1,410 sq. ft.

Plan #529-1426
Price Code E

Total Living Area: 2,602 Sq. Ft.

Home has 4 bedrooms, 2 1/2 baths, 3-car garage and basement foundation.

Special features
- Kitchen/dinette joined by family room produce central living space
- Living/dining combine for ideal entertainment space
- Master bedroom includes master bath with oversized step-up tub and enormous walk-in closet

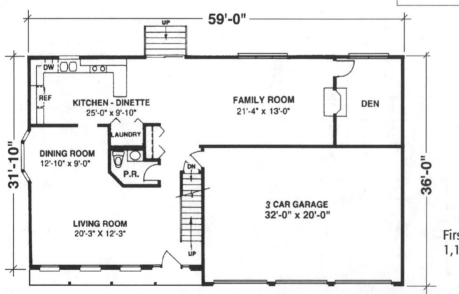

UP

59'-0"

DW

REF

KITCHEN - DINETTE
25'-0" x 9'-10"

FAMILY ROOM
21'-4" x 13'-0"

DEN

LAUNDRY

DINING ROOM
12'-10" x 9'-0"

P.R.

31'-10"

DN

LIVING ROOM
20'-3" X 12'-3"

3 CAR GARAGE
32'-0" x 20'-0"

36'-0"

UP

First Floor
1,192 sq. ft.

Second Floor
768 sq. ft.

First Floor
1,875 sq. ft.

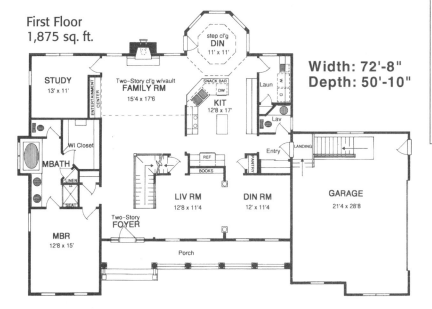

Width: 72'-8"
Depth: 50'-10"

Plan #529-JFD-20-2643-2
Price Code E

Total Living Area: 2,643 Sq. Ft.

Home has 4 bedrooms, 2 1/2 baths, 2-car side entry garage and basement foundation.

Special features

- Living and dining rooms combine to create a lovely area for entertaining
- Kitchen has snack bar which overlooks octagon-shaped dining area
- Family room is centrally located with entertainment center
- Private study at rear of home

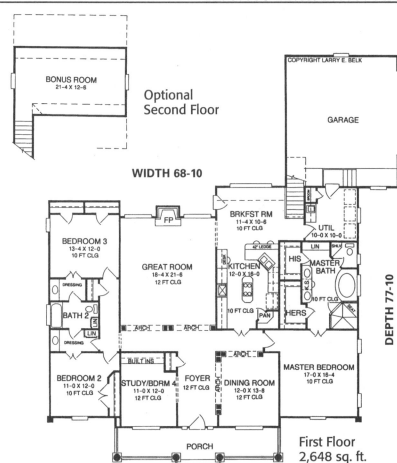

Optional Second Floor

BONUS ROOM
21-4 X 12-6

COPYRIGHT LARRY E. BELK

GARAGE

WIDTH 68-10

DEPTH 77-10

BRKFST RM
11-4 X 10-6
10 FT CLG

UTIL
10-0 X 10-0

BEDROOM 3
13-4 X 12-0
10 FT CLG

GREAT ROOM
18-4 X 21-6
12 FT CLG

42" LEDGE

KITCHEN
12-0 X 18-0

HIS

MASTER BATH

DRESSING

BATH 2

10 FT CLG

10 FT CLG

PAN

HERS

ARCH

ARCH

LIN

DRESSING

BUILT INS

ARCH

BEDROOM 2
11-0 X 12-0
10 FT CLG

STUDY/BDRM 4
11-0 X 12-0
12 FT CLG

FOYER
12 FT CLG

DINING ROOM
12-0 X 13-8
12 FT CLG

MASTER BEDROOM
17-0 X 16-4
10 FT CLG

PORCH

**First Floor
2,648 sq. ft.**

Plan #529-LBD-26-21A
Price Code E
Total Living Area: 2,648 Sq. Ft.

Home has 4 bedrooms, 2 baths, 2-car side entry garage and basement, crawl space or slab foundation, please specify when ordering.

Special features

- 12' ceilings give the study, dining room and great room a larger feel
- Kitchen features a 42' eating bar
- Study off the foyer is an ideal office space with built-in bookshelves
- Bonus room has an additional 270 square feet of living area

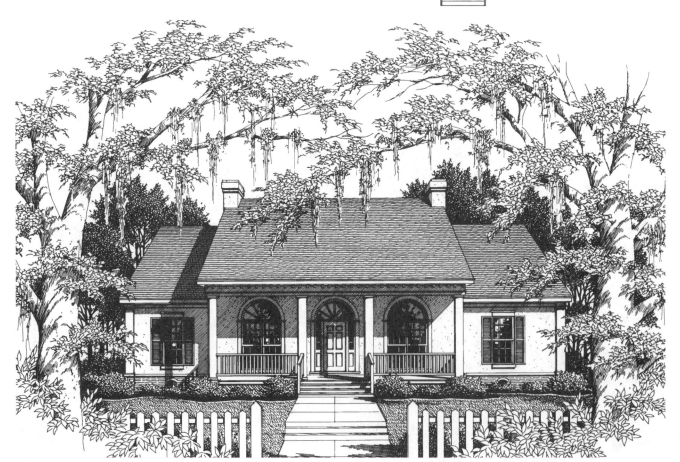

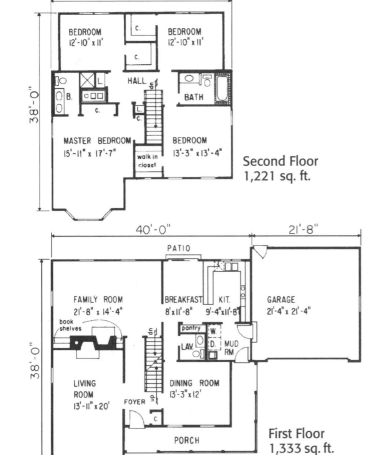

Second Floor
1,221 sq. ft.

First Floor
1,333 sq. ft.

Plan #529-1213
Price Code D

Total Living Area: 2,554 Sq. Ft.

Home has 4 bedrooms, 2 1/2 baths, 2-car garage and basement foundation, drawings also include crawl space and slab foundations.

Special features

- Dual fireplaces enhance family and living rooms
- All three bedrooms include spacious walk-in closets
- Double-bowl vanity in master bath for convenience

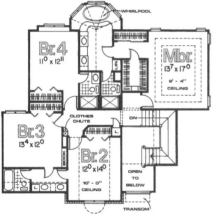

Second Floor
1,331 sq. ft.

Br. 4
11⁰ x 12¹¹

Mbr.
13⁷ x 17⁰
9' - 4"
CEILING

WHIRLPOOL

CLOTHES CHUTE

Br.3
13⁴ x 12⁰

Br. 2
12⁰ x 14⁰
10' - 0"
CEILING

DN.

OPEN TO BELOW

TRANSOM

First Floor
1,583 sq. ft.

59' - 4"

Bfst.
11³ x 12⁰

Kit.
15⁷ x 13³
SNACK BAR

Fam. rm.
19⁸ x 16⁸

DESK

W. D.
PANTRY

LAUNDRY
B.

DN.

Den
11⁰ x 12⁰

Din.
13⁰ x 14⁰

UP

Gar.
21³ x 31³

Liv. rm.
12⁰ x 14⁴

COVERED STOOP

11' - 8" CEILING

TRANSOMS

58' - 0"

© design basics inc.

Plan #529-DBI-2207
Price Code E
Total Living Area: 2,914 Sq. Ft.

Home has 4 bedrooms, 3 1/2 baths, 3-car side entry garage and basement foundation.

Special features
- Master bath has step-up whirlpool tub
- Cozy den makes ideal office or library
- Kitchen has plenty of eating space with large snack bar
- Fourth bedroom could be a nice guest room with private bath

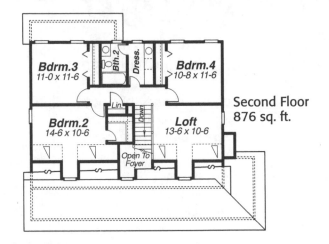

Bdrm.3
11-0 x 11-6

Bth.2

Dress.

Bdrm.4
10-8 x 11-6

Second Floor
876 sq. ft.

Bdrm.2
14-6 x 10-6

Lin.

Down

Loft
13-6 x 10-6

Open To Foyer

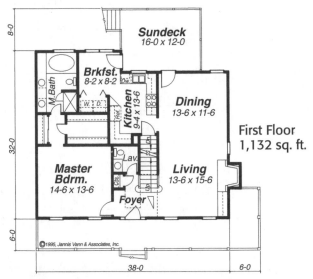

Sundeck
16-0 x 12-0

Brkfst.
8-2 x 8-2

M.Bath

W. D.

Kitchen
9-4 x 13-6

Dining
13-6 x 11-6

First Floor
1,132 sq. ft.

Master Bdrm.
14-6 x 13-6

Lav.

Cls.

Living
13-6 x 15-6

Foyer

©1995, Jannis Vann & Associates, Inc.

38-0

6-0

8-0

32-0

6-0

Plan #529-JV-2008-B
Price Code C

Total Living Area: 2,008 Sq. Ft.

Home has 4 bedrooms, 2 1/2 baths, 2-car drive under garage and basement foundation.

Special features

- Living and dining areas join to create wonderful space for entertaining
- Master bedroom includes bath with large tub and separate shower
- Second floor includes loft space perfect for home office or playroom

Our Blueprint Packages Offer...

Quality plans for building your future, with extras that provide unsurpassed value, ensure good construction and long-term enjoyment.

A quality home - one that looks good, functions well, and provides years of enjoyment - is a product of many things - design, materials, craftsmanship. But it's also the result of outstanding blueprints - the actual plans and specifications that tell the builder exactly how to build your home.

And with our BLUEPRINT PACKAGES you get the absolute best. A complete set of blueprints is available for every design in this book. These "working drawings," are highly detailed, resulting in two key benefits:

- *Better understanding by the contractor of how to build your home, and...*

- *More accurate construction estimates.*

When you purchase one of our designs, you'll receive all of the BLUEPRINT components shown here - elevations, foundation plan, floor plans, sections, and/or details. Other helpful building aids are also available to help make your dream home a reality.

INTERIOR ELEVATIONS

Interior elevations provide views of special interior elements such as fireplaces, kitchen cabinets, built-in units and other special features of the home.

FLOOR PLANS

These plans show the placement of walls, doors, closets, plumbing fixtures, electrical outlets, columns, and beams for each level of the home.

COVER SHEET

This sheet is the artist's rendering of the exterior of the home. It will give you an idea of how your home will look when completed and landscaped.

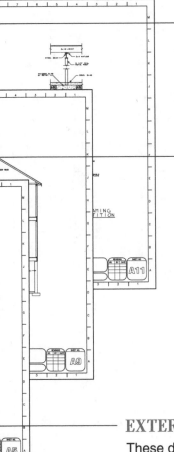

DETAILS

Details show how to construct certain components of your home, such as the roof system, stairs, deck, etc.

SECTIONS

Sections show detail views of the home or portions of the home as if it were sliced from the roof to the foundation. This sheet shows important areas such as load-bearing walls, stairs, joists, trusses and other structural elements, which are critical for proper construction.

EXTERIOR ELEVATIONS

These drawings illustrate the front, rear and both sides of the house, with all details of exterior materials and the required dimensions.

FOUNDATION PLAN

The foundation plan shows the layout of the basement, crawl space, slab, or pier foundation. All necessary notations and dimensions are included. See plan page for the foundation types included. If the home plan you choose does not have your desired foundation type, our Customer Service Representatives can advise you on how to customize your foundation to suit your specific needs or site conditions.

Other Helpful Building Aids...

Your Blueprint Package will contain the necessary construction information to build your home. We also offer the following products and services to save you time and money in the building process.

Express Delivery

Most orders are processed within 24 hours of receipt. Please allow 7 working days for delivery. If you need to place a rush order, please call us by 11:00 a.m. CST and ask for express service (allow 1-2 business days).

Technical Assistance

If you have questions, call our technical support line at 1-314-770-2228 between 8:00 a.m. and 5:00 p.m. CST. Whether it involves design modifications or field assistance, our designers are extremely familiar with all of our designs and will be happy to help you. We want your home to be everything you expect it to be.

Material List

Material lists are available for many of our plans. Each list gives you the quantity, dimensions and description of the building materials necessary to construct your home. You'll get faster and more accurate bids from your contractor while saving money by paying for only the materials you need. Look for the Lowe's Signature Series logo on the plan pages.

 HOME DESIGN ALTERNATIVES, INC.

HOME PLANS INDEX

Plan Number	Sq. Ft.	Price Code	Page	Plan Number	Sq. Ft.	Price Code	Page	Plan Number	Sq. Ft.	Price Code	Page
529-AMD-1219	2,755	E	210	529-HDS-2962	2,962	E	154	529-0152	2,935	E	104
529-AMD-2229	2,287	D	211	529-HDS-3430	3,430	F	239	529-0159	3,368	F	14
529-AP-1914	1,992	C	257	529-HDS-3436	3,436	F	166	529-0169	2,401	D	113
529-AP-2317	2,340	D	157	529-HDS-3556	3,556	F	172	529-0170	2,618	E	48
529-BF-2108	2,194	C	262	529-HP-C316	1,997	C	217	529-0178	2,846	E	45
529-BF-2610	2,684	E	132	529-HP-C619	1,771	B	159	529-0184	2,411	D	30
529-BF-3007	3,012	E	269	529-HP-C662	1,937	C	245	529-0185	2,396	D	83
529-CHD-23-10	2,350	D	174	529-HP-C675	1,673	B	207	529-0187	3,035	E	43
529-CHD-27-35	2,743	E	264	529-HP-C681	1,669	B	179	529-0202	1,958	D	52
529-CHD-29-58	3,369	F	203	529-JA-64396	2,196	C	229	529-0208	2,445	E	47
529-CHP-2032-A-42	2,075	C	192	529-JA-73897	1,794	B	236	529-0215	1,846	C	99
529-CHP-2233-B-21	2,697	E	232	529-JA-74397	2,991	E	148	529-0219	3,222	F	17
529-CHP-2243-A-29	2,246	D	216	529-JFD-10-2178-2	2,178	C	277	529-0220	3,391	F	21
529-CHP-2333-A-29	2,279	D	256	529-JFD-20-1887-1	1,887	C	168	529-0223	2,328	D	69
529-CHP-2443-A-38	2,481	D	238	529-JFD-20-2050-1	2,050	C	228	529-0228	1,996	C	27
529-CHP-2443-A-67	2,450	D	185	529-JFD-20-2211-1	2,211	D	181	529-0232	2,932	F	56
529-CHP-2444-A-2	2,473	D	260	529-JFD-20-2288-1	2,288	D	153	529-0235	2,501	D	101
529-CHP-2543-A-42	2,500	D	176	529-JFD-20-2601-2	2,601	E	131	529-0236	3,357	F	41
529-DBI-2207	2,914	E	284	529-JFD-20-2643-2	2,643	E	281	529-0245	2,260	D	51
529-DBI-2285	2,115	C	163	529-JV-1850-A	1,850	C	202	529-0257	1,862	C	84
529-DBI-2316	2,345	D	171	529-JV-1870-A	1,870	C	140	529-0278	2,847	E	107
529-DBI-2332	3,775	F	144	529-JV-2008-B	2,008	C	285	529-0279	1,993	D	77
529-DBI-2408	2,270	D	209	529-JV-2091-A	2,475	D	186	529-0286	1,856	C	80
529-DBI-2839	3,057	E	165	529-JV-2542-A	2,542	D	218	529-0290	1,700	B	55
529-DBI-4106	2,613	E	267	529-JV-2788-A	2,788	E	173	529-0299	3,013	E	19
529-DBI-5520	2,615	E	215	529-LBD-25-22A	2,586	D	240	529-0302	1,854	D	38
529-DBI-8012	2,266	D	136	529-LBD-26-21A	2,648	E	282	529-0306	2,360	D	53
529-DDI-100-219	2,646	E	252	529-LBD-26-23A	2,678	E	249	529-0307	3,153	E	112
529-DDI-100213	2,202	D	230	529-LBD-26-24A	2,611	E	158	529-0310	2,363	D	76
529-DH-2352	2,352	D	222	529-LBD-27-6A	2,721	E	152	529-0315	2,481	D	79
529-DH-2600	2,669	E	188	529-LBD-27-23A	2,757	E	274	529-0316	1,824	C	33
529-FB-599	2,236	D	206	529-LBD-28-1A	2,838	E	167	529-0320	2,228	D	40
529-FB-698	2,352	D	195	529-LBD-29-28A	2,922	E	279	529-0322	2,135	D	82
529-FB-743	1,978	C	150	529-LBD-31-20A	3,109	E	196	529-0338	2,397	E	98
529-FB-851	2,349	D	147	529-MG-9510	2,379	D	164	529-0339	2,287	E	6
529-FB-902	1,856	C	133	529-MG-9519-B	2,323	D	141	529-0341	3,290	F	109
529-FB-930	2,322	D	237	529-MG-95107	3,029	E	244	529-0342	2,089	C	72
529-FB-969	2,311	D	231	529-MG-96108	2,499	D	155	529-0349	2,204	D	90
529-FB-1224	2,246	D	221	529-MG-96132	2,450	D	225	529-0352	3,144	E	10
529-FDG-8526	2,370	D	265	529-MG-96183	2,737	E	137	529-0354	2,597	D	24
529-FDG-8576-L	3,017	E	226	529-MG-96213	2,751	E	135	529-0355	3,814	F	12
529-FDG-8673	1,604	B	248	529-NDG-134	3,706	F	219	529-0362	1,874	C	102
529-FDG-8729-L	2,529	D	208	529-NDG-147	3,790	F	205	529-0364	2,531	D	57
529-FDG-8753-L	2,674	E	271	529-NDG-204	2,439	D	235	529-0365	2,336	D	106
529-GH-24610	1,785	B	220	529-NDG-275	2,247	D	259	529-0366	2,624	E	28
529-GH-24713	2,269	D	146	529-NDG-300	2,064	C	177	529-0367	2,523	D	18
529-GH-24714	1,771	B	187	529-NDG-307	2,707	E	224	529-0368	2,452	D	87
529-GH-24736	2,044	C	182	529-NDG-321	1,845	C	149	529-0372	1,859	C	44
529-GH-34901	1,763	C	276	529-NDG-322	3,568	F	169	529-0373	2,838	E	37
529-GM-1892	1,892	C	223	529-P-124	2,760	E	184	529-0377	2,459	D	70
529-GM-1966	1,966	C	233	529-RDD-1753-9	1,753	B	258	529-0383	1,813	C	86
529-GM-2010	2,010	C	201	529-RDD-1895-9	1,895	C	272	529-0386	2,186	C	32
529-GM-2158	2,158	C	194	529-SH-SEA-078	2,389	D	241	529-0387	1,958	C	97
529-GM-2235	2,235	D	156	529-SH-SEA-091	1,541	B	190	529-0396	1,880	C	64
529-GSD-1001	3,158	E	213	529-SH-SEA-101	2,750	E	275	529-0400	1,923	C	63
529-GSD-1017	3,671	F	191	529-SH-SEA-212	2,632	E	143	529-0405	3,494	F	58
529-GSD-2107	2,422	D	175	529-SH-SEA-307	2,462	D	189	529-0413	2,182	C	88
529-GSD-2242	2,450	D	160	529-T-109	1,872	C	198	529-0417	2,828	E	67
529-GSD-2424	2,342	D	193	529-0113	1,992	C	108	529-0418	3,850	F	9
529-GSD-2686	3,502	F	183	529-0135	2,529	E	96	529-0420	1,941	C	74
529-HDS-2224	2,224	D	242	529-0137	2,282	E	20	529-0429	3,149	E	42
529-HDS-2244	2,362	D	250	529-0138	2,286	E	75	529-0430	2,869	E	49
529-HDS-2454	2,458	D	273	529-0139	2,773	F	93	529-0434	2,357	D	8
529-HDS-2551	2,551	D	212	529-0141	2,826	E	36	529-0438	2,558	D	85
529-HDS-2597	2,597	D	134	529-0143	2,449	E	25	529-0439	2,665	E	54
529-HDS-2660-2	2,660	E	138	529-0146	3,116	F	39	529-0440	2,365	D	78
529-HDS-2731	2,731	E	142	529-0151	2,874	E	61	529-0443	2,255	D	103

Plan Number	Sq. Ft.	Price Code	Page	Plan Number	Sq. Ft.	Price Code	Page
529-0444	2,500	D	34	529-0751	1,278	A	128
529-0445	3,427	F	7	529-0755	1,787	B	22
529-0449	2,505	D	11	529-0768	1,879	C	127
529-0482	1,619	B	120	529-0772	3,223	F	100
529-0488	2,059	C	122	529-0795	1,399	A	121
529-0491	1,808	C	81	529-0797	2,651	E	118
529-0492	1,829	C	29	529-0801	2,544	D	115
529-0528	2,511	D	95	529-0803	3,366	F	114
529-0598	1,818	C	111	529-0805	2,750	E	119
529-0599	2,511	D	23	529-1079	2,610	E	251
529-0600	3,025	E	105	529-1114	2,851	E	261
529-0677	3,006	E	89	529-1134	2,212	D	278
529-0678	1,567	B	123	529-1207	2,360	D	139
529-0686	1,609	B	124	529-1209	2,304	D	253
529-0691	2,730	E	59	529-1213	2,554	D	283
529-0701	2,308	D	68	529-1217	2,372	D	268
529-0703	2,412	D	62	529-1218	2,751	E	243
529-0705	2,758	E	65	529-1223	3,108	E	263
529-0706	1,791	B	125	529-1236	3,567	F	247
529-0707	2,723	E	13	529-1237	3,417	F	162
529-0708	2,615	E	16	529-1242	3,641	F	170
529-0709	2,521	D	31	529-1245	3,306	F	145
529-0710	2,334	D	50	529-1258	3,013	E	266
529-0713	3,199	E	15	529-1264	2,773	E	270
529-0714	2,808	E	71	529-1266	2,086	C	227
529-0715	4,826	G	60	529-1294	2,645	E	204
529-0716	3,169	F	26	529-1296	2,406	D	180
529-0719	2,483	D	110	529-1300	2,253	D	246
529-0720	3,138	E	126	529-1305	2,009	C	161
529-0721	2,437	D	46	529-1307	2,420	D	254
529-0722	2,266	D	91	529-1308	2,280	D	151
529-0725	1,977	C	35	529-1309	2,562	D	255
529-0728	2,967	E	94	529-1315	3,180	E	199
529-0729	2,218	D	130	529-1340	4,522	G	197
529-0730	2,408	D	129	529-1347	1,948	C	214
529-0735	3,657	F	116	529-1415	2,506	D	178
529-0736	2,900	E	117	529-1425	2,617	E	200
529-0738	4,281	G	66	529-1426	2,602	E	280
529-0747	1,977	C	73	529-1428	2,292	D	234
529-0749	2,727	E	92				

OTHER GREAT PRODUCTS TO HELP YOU BUILD YOUR DREAM HOME

FRAMING, PLUMBING AND ELECTRICAL PLAN PACKAGES

Three separate packages offer homebuilders details for constructing various foundations; numerous floor, wall and roof framing techniques; simple to complex residential wiring; sump and water softener hookups; plumbing connection methods; installation of septic systems, and more. Each package includes three-dimensional illustrations and a glossary of terms. Purchase one or all three. *Cost: $20.00 each or all three for $40.00* Note: These drawings do not pertain to a specific home plan.

THE LEGAL KIT

Avoid many legal pitfalls and build your home with confidence using the forms and contracts featured in this kit. Included are request for proposal documents, various fixed price and cost plus contracts, instructions on how and when to use each form, warranty statements and more. Save time and money before you break ground on your new home or start a remodeling project. All forms are reproducible. The kit is ideal for homebuilders and contractors. *Cost: $35.00*

WHAT KIND OF PLAN PACKAGE DO YOU NEED?

Now that you've found the home plan you've been looking for, here are some suggestions on how to make your Dream Home a reality. To get started, order the type of plans that fit your particular situation.

Your Choices:

The 1-Set Study package - We offer a 1-set plan package so you can study your home in detail. This one set is considered a study set and is marked "not for construction". It is a copyright violation to reproduce blueprints.

The Minimum 5-Set package - If you're ready to start the construction process, this 5-set package is the minimum number of blueprint sets you will need. It will require keeping close track of each set so they can be used by multiple subcontractors and tradespeople.

The Standard 8-set package - For best results in terms of cost, schedule and quality of construction, we recommend you order eight (or more) sets of blueprints. Besides one set for yourself, additional sets of blueprints will be required by your mortgage lender, local building department, general contractor and all subcontractors working on foundation, electrical, plumbing, heating/air conditioning, carpentry work, etc.

Reproducible Masters - If you wish to make some minor design changes, you'll want to order reproducible masters. These drawings contain the same information as the blueprints but are printed on erasable and reproducible paper. This will allow your builder or a local design professional to make the necessary drawing changes without the major expense of redrawing the plans. This package also allows you to print as many copies of the modified plans as you need.

Mirror Reverse Sets - Plans can be printed in mirror reverse. These plans are useful when the house would fit your site better if all the rooms were on the opposite side than shown. They are simply a mirror image of the original drawings causing the lettering and dimensions to read backwards. Therefore, when ordering mirror reverse drawings, you must purchase at least one set of right reading plans.

For fastest service, Call Toll-Free
1-800-DREAM HOME
(1-800-373-2646) day or night

Three Easy Ways To Order

1. CALL toll free 1-800-373-2646 for credit card orders. Lowe's, MasterCard, Visa, Discover and American Express are accepted.

2. FAX your order to 1-314-770-2226.

3. MAIL the Order Form to:

   HDA, Inc.
   4390 Green Ash Drive
   St. Louis, MO 63045

ORDER FORM

Please send me -

PLAN NUMBER 529- _____

PRICE CODE _____ (see Plan Index)

Specify Foundation Type - see plan page for availability
- ☐ Slab   ☐ Crawl space
- ☐ Basement   ☐ Walk-out basement
- ☐ Reproducible Masters $ _____
- ☐ Eight-Set Plan Package $ _____
- ☐ Five-Set Plan Package $ _____
- ☐ One-Set Study Package (no mirror reverse) $ _____
- ☐ Additional Plan Sets
  _____ (Qty.) at $45.00 each $ _____
- ☐ Print in Mirror Reverse
  _____ (Qty.) add $5.00 per set $ _____
- ☐ Material List (see chart at right) $ _____
- ☐ Legal Kit (see page 289) $ _____
- Detail Plan Packages: (see page 289)
  ☐ Framing ☐ Electrical ☐ Plumbing $ _____
  SUBTOTAL $ _____
- SALES TAX (MO residents add 7%) $ _____
- ☐ Shipping / Handling (see chart at right) $ _____
  TOTAL ENCLOSED (US funds only) $ _____
  (Sorry no CODs)

I hereby authorize HDA, Inc. to charge this purchase to my credit card account (check one):

☐ MasterCard   ☐ VISA   ☐ DISCOVER NOVUS   ☐ AMERICAN EXPRESS Cards   ☐ LOWE'S

Credit Card number _____

Expiration date _____

Signature _____

Name _____
(Please print or type)

Street Address _____
(Please **do not** use PO Box)

City _____

State _____ Zip _____

Daytime phone number (_____) - _____

I'm a ☐ Builder/Contractor   I ☐ have
     ☐ Homeowner   ☐ have not
     ☐ Renter   selected my
                            general contractor

290 Thank you for your order!

IMPORTANT INFORMATION TO KNOW BEFORE YOU ORDER

◆ **Exchange Policies -** Since blueprints are printed in response to your order, we cannot honor requests for refunds. However, if for some reason you find that the plan you have purchased does not meet your requirements, you may exchange that plan for another plan in our collection. At the time of the exchange, you will be charged a processing fee of 25% of your original plan package price, plus the difference in price between the plan packages (if applicable) and the cost to ship the new plans to you.

Please note: Reproducible drawings can only be exchanged if the package is unopened, and exchanges are allowed only within 90 days of purchase.

◆ **Building Codes & Requirements -** At the time the construction drawings were prepared, every effort was made to ensure that these plans and specifications meet nationally recognized codes. Our plans conform to most national building codes. Because building codes vary from area to area, some drawing modifications and/or the assistance of a professional designer or architect may be necessary to comply with your local codes or to accommodate specific building site conditions. We advise you to consult with your local building official for information regarding codes governing your area.

Questions? Call Our Customer Service Number
314-770-2228

BLUEPRINT PRICE SCHEDULE — BEST VALUE

Price Code	1-Set	SAVE $110 5-Sets	SAVE $200 8-Sets	Material List*	Reproducible Masters
AAA	$225	$295	$340	$50	$440
AA	$275	$345	$390	$55	$490
A	$325	$395	$440	$60	$540
B	$375	$445	$490	$60	$590
C	$425	$495	$540	$65	$640
D	$475	$545	$590	$65	$690
E	$525	$595	$640	$70	$740
F	$575	$645	$690	$70	$790
G	$650	$720	$765	$75	$865
H	$755	$825	$870	$80	$970

Plan prices guaranteed through June 30, 2004.
Please note that plans are not refundable.

◆ **Additional Sets* -** Additional sets of the plan ordered are available for $45.00 each. Five-set, eight-set, and reproducible packages offer considerable savings.

◆ **Mirror Reverse Plans* -** Available for an additional $5.00 per set, these plans are simply a mirror image of the original drawings causing the dimensions & lettering to read backwards. Therefore, when ordering mirror reverse plans, you must purchase at least one set of right reading plans.

◆ **One-Set Study Package -** We offer a one-set plan package so you can study your home in detail. This one set is considered a study set and is marked "not for construction". It is a copyright violation to reproduce blueprints.

*Available only within 90 days after purchase of plan package or reproducible masters of same plan.

SHIPPING & HANDLING CHARGES

U.S. SHIPPING	1-4 Sets	5-7 Sets	8 Sets or Reproducibles
Regular (allow 7-10 business days)	$15.00	$17.50	$25.00
Priority (allow 3-5 business days)	$25.00	$30.00	$35.00
Express* (allow 1-2 business days)	$35.00	$40.00	$45.00

CANADA SHIPPING (to/from) - Plans with suffix DR & SH	1-4 Sets	5-7 Sets	8 Sets or Reproducibles
Standard (allow 8-12 business days)	$25.00	$30.00	$35.00
Express* (allow 3-5 business days)	$40.00	$40.00	$45.00

Overseas Shipping/International - Call, fax, or e-mail (plans@hdainc.com) for shipping costs.

* For express delivery please call us by 11:00 a.m. CST